TRAVEL SMARTS

Everything You Need to Know

to Go Anywhere

D1196188

TRAVEL SMARTS

Everything You Need to Know

to Go Anywhere

Third Edition

by Herbert Teison & Nancy Dunnan

The Globe Pequot Press

Guilford, Connecticut

Copyright © 1995, 1997, 1999 by Herbert Teison and Nancy Dunnan

All rights reserved. No part of this book may be reproduced or transmitted in any form by any means, electronic or mechanical, including photocopying and recording, or by any information storage and retrieval system, except as may be expressly permitted by the 1976 Copyright Act or by the publisher. Requests for permission should be made in writing to The Globe Pequot Press, P.O. Box 480, Guilford, CT 06437.

Cover design: Lisa Reneson
Cover images: © PhotoDisc and © Art Today
Text design: Lisa C. Ferreira

Library of Congress Cataloging-in-Publication Data
Teison, Herbert.
    Travel smarts : everything you need to know to go anywhere / by Herbert Teison and Nancy Dunnan. — 3rd ed.
        p.   cm.
    Includes bibliographical references and index.
    ISBN 0-7627-0510-8
    1. Travel.   I. Dunnan, Nancy.   II. Title.
G151.T44 2000
910'.2' 02—dc21   99-36951
                                                                      CIP

Manufactured in the United States of America
Third Edition/First Printing

Contents

Introduction xiii

1. MONEY MATTERS 1
Before Leaving Home 1 • Getting Your Passport 2 • Insuring Your Trip 5 •
Taking Along Money 6 • Protecting Your Money 9 • Getting Your Money Back:
VAT Refunds 11 • Sending Money in a Flash 13 • Making Telephone Calls 14

2. CHEAP AIR TRAVEL 19
Smart Air-Travel Tips 20 • Using Consolidators 26 • Frequent Flying 28 • Being
Bumped Pays 31 • Flying as a Courier 35 • Taking Charter Flights 36 • Go
Standby to Europe 37 • Airline Problems 40 • Handling Jet Lag 42 • Being Safe
43 • Eating While Aloft 44 • Airline Clubs 44

3. RIDING THE RAILS: TRAIN TRAVEL, WITH NOTES ON BUS TRAVEL 45
Travel on Amtrak 45 • Great U.S. and Canadian Train Rides 48 • Fall Foliage by
Rail 49 • Riding the Rails to the Slopes 50 • Western Train Tours 52 • European
Train Travel 52 • The *Orient Express* and Other Luxury Trains 53 • A Potpourri
of Train Goodies 54 • Leave the Driving to Us: Bus Travel 57

4. BEHIND THE WHEEL: TRAVELING BY CAR 59
How the Automobile Clubs Stack Up 60 • Renting a Car: How to Avoid the
Potholes 61 • Smart Tips for Car Renters 65 • Protect Yourself and the Car from
Tourist Crime 67 • Cellular-Phone Services 68 • A Potpourri of Smart Driving
Tips 69 • Driving and Renting Abroad 70 • Overseas Motor-Home Tours 72 •
Driving Someone Else's Car 72

5. CRUISES: LUXURY YOU CAN AFFORD 75
Being a Happy Sailor 75 • Using a Cruise Specialist 76 • Determining Your
True Costs 76 • Landing a Bargain 77 • Sleeping and Eating 82 • Taking Shore
Excursions 83 • Cruising Offbeat 83 • Family Cruising 89 • Cruises for the
Physically Handicapped 89 • Picking the Best Insurance 89 • Tipping Just
Right 89

6. GOOD DEALS ON A GOOD NIGHT'S SLEEP 91
Getting the Best Rates 91 • Where to Find Hotel Discounts 94 •

Sleeping Cheaper 96 • Lighthouses 101 • Homestays 101 • Trading Places: Home Exchange 102 • Rentals 103 • Time-Shares 104 • Playing It Safe 106 • Concierges: Getting Just What You Need in Any City 107

7. TRAVELING WITH CHILDREN: GETTING MAXIMUM FUN FOR LESS **111**
On the Road with the Kids 111 • Surviving Disney and Other Theme Parks 113 • Orlando: Beyond Mickey 115 • Family Resorts 116 • Year-Round Family Fun at Ski Resorts 118 • Family Cruises 120 • Train Travel with Kids 122 • Living-History Museums that Kids Like 122 • Plan a Trip to a National Park 124 • Great State Parks 128 • A Potpourri of Other Family Travel Ideas 129 • Where to Take the Grandchildren 133 • When Kids Get Sick Abroad 136

8. GREAT BARGAINS FOR THE FIFTY-PLUS CROWD **139**
How to Pay Less for Being Older 139 • Airline Discounts 140 • Cruise Discounts 141 • Train Discounts 142 • Sightseeing Discounts 143 • Hotel, Motel, and Restaurant Discounts 143 • Learning Vacations 147 • Adventure Tours 148 • Sporting Vacations 149 • Older and Single 150 • Off the Beaten Path 150

9. TRAVELING SOLO **153**
Matchmakers, Clubs, and Singles Tour Operators 154 • Being Paid to Go: The Escort World 156 • Top Trips for Solo Travelers 157 • On the Road 158

10. TRAVEL FOR THE PHYSICALLY HANDICAPPED **159**
The Preliminaries 159 • Organizations That Can Help 160 • Specific Destinations 161

11. SPECIAL-INTEREST VACATIONS **165**
Artistic Retreats 165 • Baseball Camps 166 • Biking Trips 167 • Cooking Schools 167 • Field Research 167 • Fly-Fishing Schools 168 • Foreign-Language Programs 168 • Golf Vacations 169 • Hiking and Trekking Tours 171 • Horseback Riding and Fox Hunting 172 • Ice Fishing 172 • Learning Vacations 172 • Lighthouse Tours 173 • Nature Tours 173 • Parks 174 • Sailing 174 • Spas 175 • Special Events 175 • Tennis Camps 178 • Volunteering 179

12. TRAVELING IN GOOD HEALTH **181**
Medical Coverage Away from Home 181 • Doctors Away From Home 182 • A Compendium of Tips 184

13. SHOPPING—CHIC AND CHEAP **193**
Things to Avoid Buying 193 • Getting through Passport Controls 194 • Duty—to Pay or Not to Pay 195 • If You're in Paris 201 • Where to Find Gems and Precious Stones 202 • A Country-by-Country Guide 203

14. TRAVEL POTPOURRI **205**
Packing Just Right 205 • Pets 206 • Problems with Credit-Card Purchases 207
• Scams 208 • Taxi Tips 209 • Tours 210 • Travel Agent Problems 214

15. USING THE INTERNET **215**
Advantages of Using a Travel Agent 215 • Advantages of Using the Internet for
Airline Seats 216 • Four Steps to Finding the Best Fares On-line 216 • How to
Avoid Getting Ripped Off 217

APPENDICES **221**
Seven Bargain Destinations 221 • The "Top Seven" Charts 225 • Getting
Tickets to Game Shows and Talk Shows 228 • Travel Talk: What the Insiders
Really Mean 230

INDEX **245**

Help Us
KEEP THIS GUIDE UP TO DATE

Every effort has been made by the authors and editors to make this guide as accurate and useful as possible. However, many changes can occur after a guide is published—establishments close, phone numbers change, facilities come under new management, and so forth.

We would love to hear from you concerning your experiences with this guide and how you feel it could be improved and be kept up to date. While we may not be able to respond to all comments and suggestions, we'll take them to heart and we'll make certain to share them with the authors. Please send your comments and suggestions to the following address:

The Globe Pequot Press
Reader Response/Editorial Department
P.O. Box 480
Guilford, CT 06437

Or you may e-mail us at: editorial@globe-pequot.com

Thanks for your input, and happy travels!

Symbols

The following symbols are used throughout this book to draw attention to especially helpful tips and important information. Here's what they stand for:

Helpful hint

Money-saving tip

Cautionary tip

Best bet

Relevant web address

Introduction

Travel, whether to the next town or the next continent, can be a great joy. It introduces you to new and unusual places, to different peoples, cultures, and lifestyles. It is also a wonderful way to renew one's spirit, to spend time with family and friends, to learn a new activity or language—even to appreciate home. Yet the joy of travel can be ruined or at least diminished if you're not properly informed and adequately protected, if you pick the wrong place, become ill, spend too much money, or get "taken."

That's what *Travel Smarts* is all about: information and protection. As the publisher and managing editor of the *Travel Smart Newsletter,* we are devoted to telling you how to travel better for less, how to protect yourself against the unpleasant and often expensive mistakes one can make when leaving home.

One of the most important messages we can give you is that travel products—airline tickets, hotel rooms, rental-car reservations, etc.—are like unrefrigerated food; they're perishable. The unsold plane seat, the empty cruise cabin or hotel room, the unfilled space on a tour, the rental car sitting on the lot all bring in zero revenue, and the airline, cruise line, hotel owner, or tour operator loses money if you're not on board.

Even cities, states, and countries worry when tourism is down. Tourism income from one year can't be recovered the next; you can't store tourism and sell it later. No matter that visits to Chicago were up 3 percent in the past year; if they're down this year, the travel business in the Windy City suffers a loss that can never be recouped.

Because these travel suppliers know their wares are perishable, they do everything possible to sell as much of their capacity as they can, right now. To do so, to get you to book, they offer a variety of incentives, including better prices, free amenities, upgrades, and all kinds of extras.

Understandably, these suppliers don't want their other customers (the one who paid full price) to know that you're getting a better deal. One way they accomplish this is by giving you a discount without calling it one, by using euphemistic terms like "early bird special," "corporate rate," "two-for-one," "frequent-flyer bonus," "senior citizen special," and "upgrade."

Of course, there's much more to traveling smart than getting a good price. When you describe your trip to friends or look at your favorite snapshot, probably the last thing that comes to mind is what you paid for the experience. In fact, a year later, unless it was a truly great bargain, you may not even remember the price. It's unlikely that you'll be saying "Boy, we went to London, Paris, and Rome, and it only cost us $116.37 a day." What you will remember are the experiences, the people, the food, the scenery, the glorious hotel room or fabulous resort.

Although airlines, hotels, cruise lines, and car rental companies at times give the store away, most of the time you must be a good shopper and know where to look, how to speak up, and what the fine print means. To help you, in the following pages we examine each category of travel supplier, telling you about our favorites and giving you hundreds of insider tips that you can put to immediate use.

This book, like our newsletter, *Travel Smart*, will tell you how to travel better for less. We hope that being armed with all this good insider information will help make your next journey and the ones that follow full of joy.

1
Money Matters

*If you will be a traveler, have always ... two bags very full,
that is, one of patience and another of money.*

—*John Florio*

John Florio was right. A key to enjoyable travel is to have enough money and to be careful spending it. You don't need to be paranoid, however, or you may miss all the fun. But ignoring the money issue or spending too much will certainly spoil a good time.

The first step, before going anywhere but around the block, is to figure out the real cost of your trip, whether it's for business or pleasure. If it's for business, your company will determine how much you can spend—whether you fly first class or coach, stay in a luxury suite or a budget hotel. But if you're the one calling the shots, it's tempting to ignore the economics involved until you get home and your credit-card charges start rolling in. So next time, before taking off, get a general idea of your costs by filling in the Vacation/Travel Budget worksheet that follows. You may not change a thing, but at least you'll know whether you're spending several hundred dollars or several thousand. Note the ubiquitous category "other." We've put that in because many travelers dash out to the mall and load up on new clothes, luggage, toiletries, even cameras, just for one trip, often without thinking about it. These purchases become part of a travel budget and, if you're not careful, can run up the total tab. Of course you may indeed need a new bathing suit or a black-tie jacket for a formal cruise, or the kids may require something beyond tattered jeans and sneakers for their trip to visit grandparents. Just keep track.

 To control spending fill out the worksheet on the next page before purchasing tickets or making a deposit on a tour.

BEFORE LEAVING HOME

You also want to protect the things you leave behind you—your house or apartment and the valuables inside. Just as you do, robbers love it when you go on vacation, and an empty house is an inviting target. For a trouble-free trip, follow these twelve tips:

1. *Leave a low-wattage light burning* inside your house and attach timers to several other lights, arranging for them to turn on and off at different times in different areas.

2. *Turn on a radio,* preferably tuned to a talk station.

3. *Arrange for someone to cut your grass,* rake the leaves, and raise and lower your blinds and curtains at random.

4. *Ask the post office* to hold your mail, and put a temporary stop on newspaper delivery. Alternatively, have someone pick up your mail or papers every day.

5. *Have a friend or neighbor house-sit,* or hire someone to check your house regularly. Pipes can freeze, roofs can leak, and furnaces can go on the blink.

6. *Give your itinerary,* with dates and telephone numbers, plus your auto license number and an extra house key, to someone reliable.

7. *Prepare a written record* of your credit-card numbers and the telephone numbers of the credit-card companies; keep them in a separate place from the credit cards themselves.

8. *Arrange in advance for pet care,* as kennels are often booked solid during peak travel seasons.

9. *Have your car thoroughly serviced* prior to your trip and check the condition of your spare tire.

10. *Pack a roadside emergency kit* containing a flashlight, flares, and jumper cables.

11. *Assemble a first-aid kit* and include items for sunburn, bug bites, motion sickness, and diarrhea.

12. *Check the locks on all house windows and doors* before leaving; don't forget the door between the garage and your house.

Finally, don't hide the key under a doormat, in a flowerpot, or on a window ledge. Professional thieves know to look in all these places.

GETTING YOUR PASSPORT

If you don't have a passport or if you need to renew yours, here's the red tape involved and how to cut through some of it. Applications are available at 2,500 courthouses, 900 post offices, and 13 passport agencies in major cities. It can take a month or even six weeks to get a passport, depending on demand.

The State Department has a service that will provide up-to-the-minute details on applying for a new passport or renewing an old one. Call National Passport Information Center, (900) 225-5674. You'll be charged 35 cents per minute.

Work Sheet
VACATION/TRAVEL BUDGET

TOTAL AMOUNT I CAN AFFORD

Packaged tour costs		$ _____
Airline, train, bus tickets		$ _____
Bus/taxi to airport/train station		$ _____
Car rental		$ _____
My car costs (gas, oil, tolls)		$ _____
Lodging cost (per night: $ ____)	Total:	$ _____
Food (per day: $ ____)	Total:	$ _____
Tickets to theater, museums, sites		$ _____
Fees (parking, campsites, etc.)		$ _____
Telephone calls to home/office		$ _____
Souvenirs and gifts		$ _____
Vaccinations/medical supplies		$ _____
Equipment rental/purchase		$ _____
Tips and taxes		$ _____
Kids' allowance		$ _____
Other		$ _____
	Grand Total:	$ _____

Step 1: Determine the total amount you can spend.

Step 2: If you're taking a tour, find out if the price includes meals, all transportation, tips, and taxes, as well as admission fees and airfare to/from the destination.

Step 3: Enter dollar amounts into the appropriate categories.

Step 4: If you're over budget, reduce spending for gifts or souvenirs, get a friend to drive you to and from the airport, and/or cut the length of your vacation.

To obtain your first passport, you must apply in person and provide:

- Proof of U.S. citizenship and a Social Security number

- Two identical 2x2-inch photos taken within the last six months; must be of your head against a plain background

- Proof of identity, such as a driver's license or birth certificate

- The fee

Note: To prove U.S. citizenship, bring a certified copy of your birth certificate if you were born in the United States. If you were born abroad you can use your certificate of naturalization or certificate of citizenship. If you can't get any of these items, call the nearest U.S. Passport Agency for assistance.

To renew a passport you must do so within twelve years of the date of issue. Passports are issued for ten years, but you get a two-year grace period. You can apply by mail, even if your passport has expired. Submit application, your old passport, two identical photos, and your check or money order (made out to Passport Services) to: National Passport Center, Box 371971, Pittsburgh, PA 15250.

 Web site: travel.state.gov/passport_services.html

The U.S. State Department recommends making a photocopy of the page in your passport with your passport number and biographical data. Take it with you and keep it in a safe place, separate from your passport. If your passport is lost, a U.S. embassy or consulate can use this photocopy to expedite replacement of your passport. (The photocopy does not need to be notarized.)

 Many countries require that your passport be valid for six months *after* your intended return. If it's not, you may not be able to take your trip.

If You're in a Hurry

A company called Travisa works with travel agents and the public to get both passports and visas issued quickly, sometimes even in the same day. Its headquarters are in Washington, D.C., with branches in Chicago, Detroit, San Francisco, and Puerto Rico. Call (800) 222-2589.

Or you can pay an extra $30 to the National Passport Information Center's "Expedite Service" and get a passport in three business days—that's three business days after they receive all the necessary papers. Call (900) 225-5674.

 Faster service is also available if you can show plane tickets or confirmed reservations proving you're traveling abroad within ten days.

INSURING YOUR TRIP

Four things are guaranteed to spoil a trip and cost you money: (1) not being able to go due to illness or some other emergency, (2) having the packager or tour operator cancel the trip, (3) losing your luggage, or (4) getting sick while away from home. Various types of travel insurance can provide some degree of protection against such unhappinesses and reduce your potential expenses. Before leaving home, take time to figure out if you need to buy extra protection. Here are the three types of travel insurance you need to know about.

1. *Trip-cancellation coverage:* Many insurance companies, cruise lines, and tour operators sell this type of coverage, with prices that range widely.

    Avoid buying insurance sold by the operator/packager. If the company declares bankruptcy, the coverage won't be valid. Two independent companies that have reasonably priced policies are Travel Guard International, underwritten by CNA Insurance Company and sold by ASTA Marketing Services of Stevens Point, Wisconsin (715-345-0505), and World Access, underwritten by BCS Insurance Company and sold by Access America Service Corp. of Richmond, Virginia (804-285-3300). Call for current rates. CSA Travel Protection (800-348-9505) gives you a full refund for the cost of the insurance if you cancel your trip for any reason within ten days of receiving coverage. If you've been reluctant to purchase travel protection because the cost was nonrefundable, check out details plus type of coverage offered.

2. *Personal-property coverage:* Check your homeowners policy and your credit cards regarding personal-property coverage worldwide. It may protect you against lost or delayed luggage, or if you have a special floater for your camera, jewelry, and other valuables, you may not need additional insurance.

3. *Medical coverage:* See pages 181–82 for a complete discussion of this important topic.

    Airlines accept liability for up to $1,250 per passenger for bags lost or damaged between points within the United States, and up to $9.07 a pound for checked bags and $400 per passenger for unchecked bags on most but not all international flights; however, the airlines cover only the depreciated value of lost possessions, not the replacement cost.

    Report any luggage problem before you leave the airport and insist that a missing-luggage report be filled out, even if the airline officials tell you it will be on the next flight; it may not. Specify that your luggage is to be delivered to your hotel or home free of charge.

TAKING ALONG MONEY

Once you know about how much your trip will cost, you'll need to decide what form of money to take along. We think it's smart to carry a mixture—cash, checks, traveler's checks, and credit cards—because each one has advantages in certain situations. When abroad, for instance, plan to use credit cards for major purchases such as rental cars, hotels, and restaurants, yet have enough foreign currency with you to cover the first day's expenses: transportation from the airport or train station to your hotel, tips, and immediate needs. Then convert traveler's checks to cash on an as-you-need-it basis. Banks almost always give you better exchange rates than do hotels, stores, or private exchange booths.

Two things there's no debate about: Carry small bills and change, and never flash large bills. To do so is asking for trouble.

Empty Your Wallet Take out all items you won't need on your trip. And, take only those credit cards you plan to use.

Cash & Foreign Currency

You'll obviously need enough pocket money to pay for the taxi, bus, or subway from the airport or train station to your hotel or, if you're driving, for tolls and incidentals.

Thomas Cook (800-287-7362 or www.thomascook.com) sells foreign currencies and traveler's checks on-line, twenty-four hours a day. Fees vary depending upon the amount. Currency will be delivered to your home or office, or you can pick it up at a Thomas Cook branch office.

International Currency Express, Inc., will send your foreign currencies within two to four days after payment is received. From the East Coast, call 888-842-0880, and from the West Coast, call 888-278-6628, or log on to www.foreignmoney.com.

Traveler's Checks

Traveler's checks are issued by American Express, First National City Bank, Thomas Cook and Sons, and other companies. If you use American Express, you'll also be able to have your mail held at American Express offices around the world.

Traveler's checks are sold in a variety of denominations. Make two copies of the list of numbers on your checks before leaving home. Leave one copy with a friend or relative and carry one with you, keeping it in a separate place from the checks themselves. You should also keep separate the written directions for replacing lost or stolen checks that accompanied the new checks you purchased. If you're traveling with someone else, divide the checks between you, so if one of you loses them or is robbed you'll still have some left.

Although traveler's checks are safe and replaceable if lost or stolen, you do pay a fee to purchase them and often a service charge when cashing them. Converting checks (or changing money) at hotels can cost 3 to 4 percent over the usual exchange rate in a foreign country. The best place to cash checks is the issuer's service office or a bank. Avoid airport money changers; they usually have the worst exchange rates and highest fees.

Shop Around
More than half the American Express traveler's checks are sold without fees through various travel groups, such as the American Automobile Association, or at local banks. Senior citizens often get them for free at their bank, so shop around and ask.

Thomas Cook does not charge a commission if you cash its checks at any of its U.S. or foreign outlets.

Avoid using traveler's checks to pay for meals in foreign countries without getting details first. Many overseas restaurants have exchange rates that penalize you 5 to 10 percent. If you have difficulty with the language, ask the hotel concierge to call the restaurant for you and ask about its policy.

Be smart and purchase some traveler's checks in foreign currencies to escape currency fluctuations and poor exchange rates; this way you'll avoid a fee when cashing them in that country. American Express, Thomas Cook, VISA, and MasterCard sell traveler's checks denominated in leading currencies, such as the British pound, the German mark, and the French franc. This enables you also to lock in exchange rates before leaving the United States.

Don't go overboard, however, with foreign denomination checks; those that you don't cash will have to be converted back into dollars, running up a needless exchange fee.

To buy foreign-currency traveler's checks without having to leave home, contact Ruesch International at (800) 424–2923 or (800) 292–4685.

Automatic Teller Machine Cards

ATM cards reduce the need to carry a lot of cash, whether you're traveling near home or abroad. CIRRUS and PLUS now have ATMs in many foreign countries, but they are not identical to their U.S. counterparts. You should know the following:

- ATMs outside North America generally do not accept personal identification numbers (PINs) longer than four digits. Check with your bank to see if you need a PIN that machines abroad will accept.

- The keypads on many foreign ATMs do not include letters, so learn the corresponding numerals by checking a telephone keypad.

- Not all foreign ATMs are open twenty-four hours a day.

- ATMs automatically take funds from your account, and daily withdrawal limits do apply, so transfer enough money into your account before leaving the country.

- When you use an ATM bank card abroad, you get the "wholesale" rate, the rate that normally applies to transactions of $1 million or more. This rate is often 5 percent better than the rate tourists get when they cash traveler's checks in a hotel, but ATM transactions usually have a flat fee, from 90 cents to $1.50.

To Find a List of ATMs Abroad

www.mastercard.com/atm

www.visa.com/cgi-bin/vee/main/html

 If you're getting $500 of foreign currency, you'll get as much as $25 more by using an ATM machine outside a foreign bank or American Express office than by cashing traveler's checks at their teller windows inside.

Credit Cards

Another way to travel without carrying large amounts of cash is to take a credit card. When you use a credit card in a foreign country, the rate of exchange that applies is not the prevailing one at the time that you make a purchase or pay for your hotel room or rental car; rather, it is the rate that prevails when the transaction is processed by the credit-card company. The rate could, therefore, be higher or lower than the one at the time you actually use the card. Keep these two points in mind:

- When making a large purchase, use your credit card *if* it carries buyer protection. You will then have some recourse if the product is faulty.

- Credit cards are also best for purchasing packaged tours; airline, bus, and railroad tickets; and car rentals because these vendors may take as much as 8 percent if you use traveler's checks. And if you have a problem with a tour operator or airline that goes out of business, you will have some recourse.

Most hotels will ask you for an imprint of your credit card when you check in. Some, often without telling you, will arbitrarily block (limit) up to $2,000 in charges because they want to make sure they get paid first should you go over your spending limit while on your vacation or trip. To avoid this you can do one of two things: Ask the hotel clerk not to block charges against your credit limit, or give them your Diners Club or American Express card, which does not have limits.

Here are two more ways to use your credit card to get better travel deals:

- If you use MCI or another long-distance telephone service, arrange to have your MCI bills paid by your credit card to get additional miles in an airline frequent-flyer mileage program.

- If you return home from abroad with more than the $400 duty-free allowance on goods, U.S. Customs will let you pay for your extra duty charges with a credit card.

⚠ Insider Tip Some credit-card issuers, especially smaller banks and credit unions, automatically deactivate cards used a lot—more than six times a day—in order to stop use of stolen cards. Reactivation is difficult from foreign countries. **Bottom Line:** Tell your issuer of your travel plans.

PROTECTING YOUR MONEY

Purse-snatching and wallet-swiping can happen to anyone almost anywhere and anytime—at a restaurant, waiting for a train, in line for tickets, etc. You can foil thieves by taking a few preventive measures.

- *Carry only the credit cards you plan to use that day.* It's also a good idea to carry cash, credit cards, driver's license, and keys in separate locations—your purse, wallet, pockets, or briefcase. Then if someone grabs your wallet, for instance, he or she won't get all your valuables.

- *Carry just one or two checks,* not your full checkbook. Replenish as you use them.

- *Memorize the PIN for your bank card.* Don't write it down anywhere, and certainly not in your address book or checkbook.

- *Don't attach your address or telephone number* to your key chain.

- *Keep two up-to-date lists* (one at home, one at the office) of your credit-card account numbers, accompanied by their emergency telephone numbers.

- *Tell your credit card issuer that you'll be using the card more than usual.*

 Wearing a fanny pack or money belt around your waist advertises both your status as a tourist and precisely where you've put your cash or credit cards.

 Fool thieves by keeping only incidentals in these packs or bags (notebook, map, pencil, sunglasses, stamps, mints, Handiwipes, etc.) and hide your money and passport in an underarm or shoulder belt or pack, or around your waist and under your clothing.

If You Are Ripped Off

If your credit cards are stolen, immediately call to cancel them. And remember, you must write to the credit-card company within sixty days of receiving your bill in order to avoid being charged for items over $50 charged by thieves.

Report the theft to the police, keeping a copy of the report. You'll need this information to file an insurance claim or deduct losses on your federal income tax return.

Call your card company as soon as you discover trouble. Photocopy the list of credit-card emergency phone numbers below and carry it with you. (Call collect from abroad.)

- **AMERICAN EXPRESS**
  United States and Canada   (800) 635-5955
  Optima   (336) 393-1111
- **DISCOVER**
  United States   (800) DISCOVER
  Other countries   (801) 902-3100
- **MASTERCARD**
  United States   (800) 826-2181
  Other countries   (314) 275-6690
- **VISA**
  United States   (800) VISA-911
  Other countries   (410) 581-9994

If you lose your checkbook, immediately close your entire account; however, if only one or two checks were stolen, simply arrange for a stop payment on them.

If your ATM card is stolen, ask the bank to issue a new one, even if you didn't write the code number on anything taken by the thieves. Thieves know that many people use their birthday, wedding anniversary, or number sequences (2, 3, 4, 5, 6) for their codes. You will be held liable for $50 of fraudulent use of your ATM card if you report the loss within two days, but as much as $500 if you report it after two days.

To replace long-distance telephone credit cards, call their toll-free numbers:

- **AT&T**   (800) 225-5200
- **SPRINT**   (800) 877-4646
- **MCI**   (800) 444-4444

Safeguarding Your Purchases

Items purchased while traveling and paid for by credit card may be protected. The best way to find out is to call your credit-card issuer before you begin your travels. Issuer coverage seems to change almost every month. Some guidelines:

- *STANDARD CARDS.* Citibank, AT&T, Universal, Chemical, and American Express have purchase protection. Best deal: AmEx, which covers up to $1,000 per incident.

- *GOLD CARDS.* AmEx has a maximum of $50,000 over the life of the account and includes cameras and video equipment in checked baggage. AmEx's per-claim limit is $1,000.

You've Got Mail You can get mail while traveling abroad if it's addressed to you *c/o Poste Restante* and marked "hold," with the name of the city and country.

GETTING YOUR MONEY BACK: VAT REFUNDS

While traveling in Europe, you'll encounter something called VAT, or Value-Added Tax, an indirect sales tax. (Canada has Goods and Services Tax [GST], which is similar to VAT.) VAT is charged or added to the cost of most purchases, hotel rooms, meals, train travel, and rental cars. Most countries allow a refund of the tax to foreigners. However, goods and services used in the country where you buy them, such as hotel rooms and car rentals, are rarely VAT refundable. Purchases taken out of the country, such as clothing, jewelry, and cosmetics, are fully or partially refundable. It's worth taking the time to get the refund. VATs can be as much as 20 percent of your purchases, 28 percent in France on luxury items. The refund turns a pricey item into a bargain, almost.

There are four ways to get refunds:

- *Mail Refunds.* To obtain a refund by mail, make your purchase and pay the amount on the price tag, which includes the VAT. If you show your passport, however, the merchant will fill in (or have you fill in) tax-refund forms and will give you a copy of them, frequently with a self-addressed envelope. Some large department stores, such as Harrods in London and Galeries Lafayette in Paris, have offices to help with the paperwork.

When you leave the country, your form is stamped by a customs official at the airport or frontier as proof of your departure from the country. You then mail the form back to the store. The store will send you a refund, typically in several weeks. In some cases if you paid with a credit card, your refund may be credited to your account.

 Items purchased must be available for inspection by customs officials at the point of departure, so don't pack them at the bottom of your bag.

If you purchased items with a credit card, ask the merchant or shopkeeper to put the purchase price on a charge form and put the VAT charges on a separate form. Ask that they hold the VAT charge until they have received official notification that you've left the country; then they tear up the VAT form.

- *Exit Refunds.* To get an exit refund, go through the same form-filling-out procedure, but when you leave the country, give the papers to a customs person and you'll get cash or a check on the spot. If it's a check, it will be in the local currency, and you can cash it at a bank at the airport and exchange it for dollars (or the currency of the next country on your itinerary).

- *Direct Export.* Some countries allow you to subtract the VAT from the purchase price if you pay the shopkeeper to mail your purchase to you at your U.S. address.

 Shipping can be expensive, and you may have to pay U.S. import duty.

- *Europe Tax-Free Shopping (ETS).* This tax-refund specialist (Europe's largest) operates in about fifteen countries and has signed on about 60,000 individual merchants. Participants display a blue-and-red "Tax Free for Tourists" sticker in English. When you make a purchase at one of these shops, the merchant actually seals your purchase and issues a VAT refund check right on the spot.

ETS has desks at the major airports and terminals, so you can cash your refund check in one of several currencies. If you happen to leave the country from an airport or border crossing where there is no ETS desk, you simply mail the check for a refund. On charge-card purchases, the ETS official can arrange to have the refund credited to your account.

Each country has its own regulations, which are subject to change at any time. As of now, only Austria, Canada, and Israel give refunds on lodging, meals, and car rentals. Most countries have brochures that explain their VAT rates and refunds.

When you receive your VAT refund check, it will probably be in the currency of the country where it was issued. Check with several U.S. banks, as service fees for cashing these checks vary widely, or use a foreign-exchange dealer.

 Ruesch International, which charges $3.00 a check for walk-in or mail transactions. Ruesch has offices in New York, Washington, Chicago, Los Angeles, and Boston. You can also call (800) 292-4685.

 Buy expensive items at stores participating in a tax-refund program, such as ETS. Try to make all your purchases in one large store where employees can do the paperwork. Use your credit card to get a better exchange rate on your purchase and your refund. Before leaving home, get a free brochure explaining VAT from ETS, (312) 382-1001 or (203) 965-5145.

A Freebie For a free copy of *Tax Free Shopping*, which explains how to get cash refunds in twenty-two European countries, Canada, and Singapore, call Global Refund, (800) 566–9828, or log on to www.taxfree.SE/indexO.html.

SENDING MONEY IN A FLASH

If you need to send money to someone in the United States or abroad or if you're caught short, here are your choices:

- FEDERAL GOVERNMENT. The State Department operates a Citizens Emergency Funds Transfer Program for Americans who are stranded in a foreign country. Friends or relatives send the money to the State Department by credit-card charge through Western Union, in the form of a cashier's check or money order, or by overnight mail or bank wire transfer. Personal checks are not accepted. The citizen overseas receives the money in local currency. *How fast:* Usually the same day or the next day. *How much:* Same as Western Union's international service plus a $20 consulate fee. *How to do it:* Call the State Department at (202) 647-5225, or log on to travel.state.gov/money.html.

- BANKS. You can have money wired from your bank account at home to a foreign bank, provided your home bank has a branch office in the country you're visiting. You should set up this procedure before leaving home. *How fast:* Same day, domestically; next business day, internationally. *How much:* Fee varies; average is $25 to $45. *How to do it:* Call your local bank.

- U.S. POSTAL SERVICE. The Postal Service will not send cash through the mail. However, you can send a money order if it's going domestically; for international destinations use a bank draft (a check) in the currency of the country to which it's going. Bank drafts are available from most foreign-exchange brokers, such as Ruesch International, Thomas Cook, Citibank, or American Express. *How fast:* Express Mail has next-day delivery within the United States and to most foreign countries. *How much:* Up to eight ounces, domestically, $11.75; internationally, $15 to $20, depending on the country. There's an $8.25 pickup fee; no fee if you take it to the post office. *How to do it:* Call your local post office, or call (800) 222-1811.

- *AMERICAN EXPRESS.* Money can be transferred from American Express service centers or agents through its "MoneyGram" service. *How fast:* About ten minutes to most places. *How much:* Fees vary, depending on the amount being sent and destination. Up to $100 costs $13; up to $500 is $37, and up to $10,000 is $399. *How to do it:* MoneyGrams are sold at travel-agency offices, American Express travel offices, airports, auto clubs, grocery and convenience stores, packaging/postal outlets, and check cashers. You can pay for the transfer with cash, Visa, MasterCard, or Discover as well as with American Express. Outside the United States, however, you must pay with cash. Call (800) 926-9400 for nearest location and taped information.

- *WESTERN UNION.* Western Union has a similar plan and accepts MasterCard, Discover, and Visa for telephone transfers. If you prefer, you can go in person to any one of many Western Union agencies and pay by cash or certified check. *How fast:* Immediately if paid for with cash; fifteen minutes if using a credit card. *How much:* Fees vary according to amount and destination: $100 sent domestically is $15 if paid for with cash and $25 if with a credit card; internationally, fee varies. *How to do it:* Call (800) 325-4176, or log on to www.westernunion.com.

 Travel Smart Newsletter has an attractive, thin, easy-to-read slide rule that converts foreign currency, wieghts, and measurements. Send $5.00 to Travel Smart, 40 Beechdale Road, Dobbs Ferry, NY 10522.

Worried About Someone Overseas? Contact the

State Department's Overseas Citizen Services Agency (202–647–5225). This agency deals with U.S. citizens who are seriously ill, arrested, or involved in an accident. It is also the best source for information on airline and train crashes, acts of terrorism, and so on.

MAKING TELEPHONE CALLS

Long-Distance Calls from the United States

If you don't have enough change to make a long-distance call from a pay phone, or if you don't want the call to be charged to the phone you're using, you can,

Get Back Your Vat
MINIMUM PURCHASE REQUIRED
FOR VAT REFUND ELIGIBILITY

Use a service. Popular with business travelers, this company will cut through the red tape and do all the work for you. There's no up-front charge, but there is a fee, contingent upon the amount of your VAT rebate. For information contact Meridian VAT Reclaim, 125 West 55th Street, New York, NY 10019; (212) 554–6600, or log onto www. meridianvat.com.

In many countries you need to make a minimum purchase at a particular store to be eligible for a VAT refund. You might want to make as many purchases as possible at one store. Ask before shopping.

Country	VAT	Minimum Purchase Per Store
Austria	20.0%	1001 schillings (about $90)
Belgium	19.5%	5,000 francs (about $150)
Britain	17.5%	None, although some stores require £25–£50 (about $35–$80)
Denmark	20.0%	600 kroner (about $93)
France	18.6%	1,200 francs (about $250)
Germany	5.0%	None, but stores may set minimum
Italy	19.0%	300,000 lire (about $200)
Netherlands	17.5%	350 guilders (about $185)
Spain	6.0%	10,000 pesetas (about $95)
Switzerland	6.5%	500 francs/item (about $340)

of course, call collect. Most of us dial 0 + the area code + the number. But you can save significantly if you dial (800) COLLECT, using MCI. You can call anywhere in the United States and to more than one hundred foreign countries this way; however, the calls must be made from the United States or Puerto Rico. Another alternative: Dial (800) OPERATOR and use AT&T's plan, which is similar. You can also ask how much the call will cost ahead of time.

Long-Distance Dialing within the United States

With the relatively new American Travel Network (ATN) Discount Calling Card, the cost anywhere in the United States, including Hawaii, Alaska, Puerto Rico, and the U.S. Virgin Islands, day or night, is just 14.9 cents per minute. The card is free, and there's no monthly fee or monthly minimum-usage requirements. See the table on page 17 for cost comparisons between ATN calls and those made through other companies.

 Avoid making credit-card calls from pay phones unless you know how much they'll cost. Privately owned pay phones have sprung up around the country, and although they must charge the going local rate for coin calls, they can charge whatever they wish for credit-card calls.

 Pay cash for local calls and ask the operator for the price of long-distance calls made with a credit card.

Long-Distance Calls from Abroad

Getting the right local currency for calls or dealing with a foreign operator who speaks only the local language make long-distance calls in foreign countries somewhat intimidating. One way around this problem: AT&T Direct Service. By dialing a special access code, you're automatically connected to an English-speaking operator. Calls are billed to your AT&T Calling Card, AT&T Universal Card, or a local telephone company card, or they can be placed collect. The service is available in more than 120 countries. It also makes it possible to get 800 numbers in the United States, including those for travel agents, airlines, and hotels, as well as directory assistance for other numbers. For information call AT&T Direct Service at (800) 331-1140 or log on to www.ATT.com/traveler.

Calling Home

Use your credit card when making long-distance calls from a hotel or motel room. Direct-dial calls are assessed at about 40 percent. You can access your particular long-distance carrier by dialing the correct number:

* **AT&T**   (800) 3210-ATT or (800) 225-5288
* **MCI**   (800) 674-7000
* **SPRINT**   (800) 877-4646

When making several credit-card calls from your hotel or motel room, don't hang up in between calls; instead, press the pound (#) key to get a new dial tone and to avoid a fee from the hotel for each separate call.

Three Minute Daytime Call
FROM NEW YORK CITY
TO LOS ANGELES

	Surcharge	Cost/Minute	Total
ATN Card	$0.149	$0.175	$0.53
AT&T	$0	$0.45	$1.96
MCI	$0.99	$0.45	$1.94
Sprint	$0	$0.25	$1.96

Note: ATN is a division of Hospitality Services Group, which has more than 15,000 members, including pilots and business travelers; for information call (800) 477–9692.

Prepaid Telephone Cards

These are often a very good deal for travelers—they're easy to use, available everywhere (convenience stores, gas stations, post offices), and often cheaper for short, long-distance calls than other services. For instance, a card purchased in London provides cheaper U.K. to U.S. rates than one purchased at home.

But don't buy just any prepaid card . . . there are plenty of fly-by-night operators in this business. Stick with known names, such as AT&T, MCI, Sprint, Western Union, PTT Telekom, and FirstClass (sold at U.S. post offices). Follow these protective steps:

1. Know what you're paying for. For international calls, find out how many units it takes to make a one-minute call.

2. Don't accept a card that charges access fees each time you use it.

3. Make sure it has an 800 customer service number (on the back of the card or listed below).

4. If you're on the road a lot, buy only a card that is rechargeable. Otherwise, make sure it won't expire before you get back home.

5. If you have any questions or problems, contact the International Telecard Association, (800) 333–3513 or www.telecard.org.

Sprint's Spree prepaid card has a great advantage when it comes to calling in foreign countries: It automatically lets you know how much value is left—not in foreign currency but in minutes of talk time.

 There are more than 500 companies selling prepaid phone cards; many go out of business every day. That means picking the wrong card can spell disaster. In response to the growing problems and complaints, these two organizations have put together a useful brochure with important tips for purchasing a card. To get a copy contact:

- Better Business Bureau, 257 Park Avenue South, New York, NY 10010; 212-533-7500.

- New York State Attorney General Eliot Spitzer, The Capitol, Albany, NY 12224 (or 120 Broadway, New York, NY 10271); (800) 771-7755.

Customer Service Numbers
FOR PREPAID PHONE CARDS

Card	Number of Countries	Contact Information
AT&T	200	800–462–1818 www.att.com
FirstClass*	31	800–297–2600 www.smartalk.com
MCI	150+	800–830–9444 www.mci.com
PTT TeleKom	n.a.	800–839–9916
Sprint	150+	800–366–0707 www.sprint.com
UniTel	150+	800–242–9856

* Sold at post offices.

INFO: *Consumer Guide to Choosing Your Phone Service*. Free. Send a self-addressed, stamped business-size envelope to: National Consumers League, 1701 K Street, NW, (Suite 1200), Washington, DC 20006.

2
Cheap AirTravel

The most dangerous aspect of flying is driving to the airport.
—Anonymous

Most travelers don't realize (or have never stopped to think about it) that the difference in cost to an airline between an occupied seat and an empty one is minimal. The pilots, ground crew, and cabin attendants get the same pay regardless of whether or not the seats are filled. Fuel cost is almost identical, and so is just about everything else with the exception of meals. If an airline has to feed you, then it must spend another $3.00 to $10.00 per passenger; meals served to first-class passengers cost the airlines slightly more, as do specially ordered meals, but both are included in the cost of your ticket.

Given that the cost to fly a plane from, say, Houston to Chicago is about the same whether it's filled or not, airlines knock themselves out to get the maximum number of people in seats on each flight. Each additional passenger is a profit center. This, of course, is a plus for you because it leads to fare wars, discounts, and seasonally reduced priced tickets.

If you've ever flown late in the afternoon or on a weekend, you'll notice that the plane is likely to be partially empty. On the other hand, early-morning flights and the last flights before the weekend are oversold on popular routes. Why? Business traffic. The airlines love business travelers: They are their bread and butter, paying top dollar for air fare, and they demand a full schedule. Business fliers know when they want to fly, and they want the planes to be available to take them.

The Best Time to Buy Airline Tickets
Don't buy airline tickets on weekends. Many airlines test fare increases by raising prices on Friday nights, Saturdays, and Sundays, when fewer tickets are sold; if other carriers don't follow suit, the prices will come down on Monday.

Pleasure travelers are much more flexible, willing to fly on weekends or holidays and at slack times, if they can get a fair deal. They are what the airlines call "price sensitive." Most airlines look first to business travelers to fill their seats at standard (translate, "high") prices and then fill in the unsold seats with leisure travelers at whatever price gets them to go. It's all done through something called "capacity control."

One thing you can beat: the domino effect. Take flights that leave early in the day. Takeoffs are so tightly scheduled that a single foul-up can lead to a chain of delays. So the earlier your flight, the more likely you won't be a victim of the domino effect.

Tax Deduction A company can deduct the extra cost of extending an employee's business trip over a Saturday night to obtain a lower, excursion airfare. Food and lodging costs incurred during an extra day qualify as a business expense, even if no business is conducted on the extra day, provided that the airfare reduction reduces the overall cost of the trip (IRS Ruling).

SMART AIR-TRAVEL TIPS

Getting the best deal on your next flight takes more than simply calling your agent or the airlines. Here are sixteen ways you can get on board as inexpensively as possible.

1. *Plan in advance.* Regular paper tickets purchased fourteen, twenty-one, or forty-five days in advance are less expensive than tickets purchased closer to departure day, except for on-line specials.

2. *Choose the right airport.* Fares are actually higher at some airports than at others. The highest are at the so-called fortress hubs where just about all the flights are controlled by a single airline. Drive to a nearby airport where there's real competition to save money. Or, make a stop. Flying from New York to St. Louis is at least $100 cheaper if you stop in Detroit. So get out your map and talk with your travel agent about alternative airports.

3. *Buy your ticket as early as possible* after reading about a discount rate in the newspaper. If at any time before you depart the airline announces a lower fare than what you paid, you may be entitled to buy at the lower rate. Ask your travel agent to handle this for you. When buying your ticket, book the best airline seat you can get. Then get to the airport fifty to sixty minutes before flight time and ask at the gate if a better seat is available. Most airlines save some good seats (aisle, window, front cabin) for high-mileage frequent flyers and business travelers paying full fare. One hour before departure these seats are usually freed up.

4. *Pick an inexpensive time to fly.* Night fares (usually after 7:00 P.M.) may be cheaper than daytime fares. Weekend fares can be lower on routes heavily

used by business travelers during the week but not on weekends. Fares to vacation destinations such as Hawaii, Florida, the Caribbean, or ski slopes can be lower if you travel Monday through Thursday because most people want to leave on Friday, Saturday, or Sunday. Lastly, off-season fares tend to be lower than in high season. For example, it's cheaper to fly to Florida in August than in January.

5. *Use a travel agent.* A good agent, through continual computer monitoring, can instantly tell you which carrier has the best fare to your destination. An agent is also ideal if you don't want to spend hours calling various carriers or browsing on-line.

Hub Airports

Major Hubs	Dominant Airline
Atlanta	Delta
Charlotte	USAirways
Chicago O'Hare	United
Dallas/Ft. Worth	American
Denver	United
Detroit	Northwest
Minneapolis	Northwest
Newark	Continental
Phoenix	America West
Pittsburgh	USAirways
St. Louis	TWA

In addition ask your agent if he or she can help you with what we call "ploys," some of which are legal, others, borderline. For example:

- Back-to-back ticketing is a ploy whereby you avoid a required Saturday night stayover on cut-rate tickets by purchasing two or more sets and switching around the dates.

 Some airlines have declared this illegal.

- Hidden-city ticketing occurs when you purchase a ticket to a major city for a price lower than the one to the intermediate city where you actually want to deplane. You have only carry-on luggage because checking it will result in either losing the bags (because they'd be sent to the final destination) or blowing the deal. Airlines don't like this ploy but find it hard to prevent.

6. *Book early-in-the-day flights.* Then if the flight is canceled, you have more options for flying out the same day and avoid getting stuck overnight.

7. *Fly the upstarts.* Fares are lower. Expect only transportation and a bag of peanuts.

🗜 Insider Tip: How to Get an Empty Seat Next to Yours

Request an aisle seat in the center of a wide-bodied plane. Agents typically book middle seats last. If you're traveling with someone else, book one aisle seat and one window seat in a three-seat row. If you're a frequent flyer or a business traveler, ask to be assigned to a "preferred" section where the middle seats are held to the last minute.

8. *Convention fares.* If you are going to a convention, your organization may have made arrangements with one or more airlines for discounts. Check with the people running the show. If the airlines giving the discount do not fly from your local airport, it may pay to drive to one where they do.

9. *Bereavement fares.* If a close relative dies and you need to fly to the funeral, the airlines will give you a lower fare—15 to 50 percent off full price. Some (Continental and TWA as of press time) also offer reduced fares for those visiting an immediate member of the family who is critically ill. The requirements for bereavement fares vary widely from carrier to carrier, so check with your travel agent or directly with the airlines.

10. *Senior coupons.* The older crowd is a prime marketing target for all airlines; presumably, these people have all the time in the world and money to spend. One of the best deals the airlines offers is a coupon book, available to those who are sixty-two and older. Proof of age is required when you purchase the booklets and sometimes upon boarding. The coupons, purchased through your travel agent or directly from the airline, are sold in packets of four and eight coupons, with each coupon good for a one-way ticket from your originating city to your destination. Coupons are valid for domestic and, in some cases, Canadian flights but not for

Basic, No Frills
CARRIERS

If all you want is transportation, you'll save money with these airlines:

AirTran	(800) 825–8538
America West	(800) 235–9292
Kiwi Air	(800) 538–5494
Midway	(800) 446–4392
Midwest Express	(800) 452–2022
Reno Air	(800) 736–6247
Southwest Airlines	(800) 435–9792
Sun Jet	(800) 478–6538
Tower Air	(800) 221–2500

international flights. Coupon deals vary, but a typical one is United's "Silver Pack," which gives passengers over age sixty-two four tickets, good for travel anywhere in the continental United States.

 Coupons expire one year from date of purchase, and reservations must be made two weeks in advance. Book early because only a certain number of seats are available on each flight for coupon holders.

 USAirways lets seniors use coupons for an accompanying child age two to eleven, whereas TWA sells a book of coupons for a companion of any age plus a 20 percent discount on a ticket to Europe. Ask.

11. *Senior discounts.* Most major airlines give 10 percent off rates for those over age sixty-two on excursion fares, so always mention your age to your agent or the airline. One advantage these discounts have over senior coupons is that you can travel with a companion and the companion also gets 10 percent off, regardless of his or her age. (The two of you must travel on the same flight.) There are other variations on the theme, which come and go. For example, Virgin Atlantic gives travelers over age sixty a 20-percent discount. (For more on airline discounts for seniors, see pages 140 and 141.)

 Ask about senior discounts for "off-peak" days (Tuesday, Wednesday, Thursday, and Saturday).

12. *The baby flies free.* Typically there is no charge for a child under age two sitting on the lap of an adult on domestic flights. Lately, however, for safety reasons, airlines have been encouraging passengers to purchase a separate seat for children, into which a child's seat will fit. Most offer baby fares at half price.

13. *Kids' fares.* When traveling with children, check out reduced fares. On American, for example, children traveling domestically in a seat of their own get between 50 and 65 percent off full fare. If the flight is going out of the country, the discount ranges from 10 to 75 percent off the full fare. Periodically airlines have "Kids-Go-Free" promotions—but only if the children are accompanied by a fare-paying adult.

Airlines with the Best On-time Arrivals
(DOT, March 1999)

Southwest	76.7%	America West	68.3%
Continental	72.0%	American	67.1%
Delta	71.4%		

Handy Reference:

Airline	Phone Number	Web Address
Alaska Airlines	(800) 426–0333	www.alaskaair.com
American Airlines	(800) 433–7300 (800) 237–7981	www.aa.com
America West	(800) 235–9292	www.americawest.com
Continental Airlines	(800) 525–0280 (800) 441–1135	www.flycontinental.com
Delta Airlines	(800) 221–1212	www.delta-air.com
Hawaiian Airlines	(800) 367–5320	www.hawaiianair.com
Kiwi International	(800) 538–5494	www.jetkiwi.com
Midwest Express	(800) 452–2022	www.midwestexpress.com
Northwest Airlines	(800) 225–2525	www.nwa.com
Southwest Airlines	(800) 435–9792	www.southwest.com
TWA	(800) 221–2000	www.twa.com
United Airlines	(800) 241–6522	www.ual.com
USAirways	(800) 428–4322	www.usair.com
Virgin Atlantic	(800) 862–8621	www.fly.virgin.com

Handy Reference:

Airline	Phone Number	Web Address
Aerolitoral	(800) 237–6639	www. aeroliteral.com.mx
Aeromexico	(800) 237–6639	www.aeromexico.com
Air Canada	(800) 776–3000	www.aircanada.ca
Air France	(800) 237–2747	www.airfrance.com
Alitalia	(800) 223–5730	www.alitalia.com
British Airways	(800) 247–9297	www.british-airways.com
British West Indies	(800) 327–7401	www.bwee.com/-BWIA
Canadian Airlines	(800) 426–7000	www.cdnair.ca
El Al	(800) 223–6700	www.elal.com
Finnair	(800) 950–5000	www.finnair.com
Iberia	(800) 772–4642	www.iberia.com
KLM Royal Ditch	(800) 347–7747	www.klm.com
Lufthansa	(800) 645–3880	www.lufthansa.com
Mexicana Airlines	(800) 531–7921	www.mexicana.com
Sabena	(800) 950–1000	www.sabena.com
SAS	(800) 221–2350	www.sas.se.com
Swissair	(800) 221–4750	www.swissair.com
TAP Air Portugal	(800) 221–7370	www.tap-airportugal.pt

14. *Military fares.* Personnel on active duty, and often their dependents, get substantial discounts.

15. *Student fares.* These vary all over the place, depending on time of year, place, the student's age, and so on.

16. *Getting on a fully booked flight.* Move to the top of the waiting list by asking for a full-coach or first-class ticket. Discount ticketholders are typically at the bottom of the waiting list, whereas full-fare and standbys tend to get priority.

USING CONSOLIDATORS

About 20 percent of fliers go overseas on consolidator tickets, saving up to 50 percent off regular fares. This business—often called the "gray market" of ticket distribution—is probably the biggest secret of the airline industry. Consolidators are wholesalers who purchase airline tickets in bulk at huge discounts and then sell them at a discount to agents. These discounts range from 25 to 75 percent off retail airline tickets. Consolidators are able to land huge discounts because they buy in volume and they buy seats from airlines fearful of not filling their planes. Initially consolidators handled only discount fares for tour groups. Now some sell to all comers at reduced prices, including your travel agent, who will, in turn, sell the ticket to you, at a slight markup.

Kids Alone in the Air With the proliferation of non-nuclear families, kids are often sent alone to visit one of their parents in another city, or they may be going to visit other relatives. A flight attendant will seat the child in a special section of the plane, talk to him or her from time to time, provide games and special kids' meals, and deliver the child to the right people at the other end. Some airlines require that a child traveling alone be at least five years old for a through flight and eight years old for a connecting flight. Expect to pay a fee (around $30) if the child is on a connecting flight.

 When booking an unaccompanied child on a connecting flight, select a flight that leaves early in the day. Avoid the last one because if the plane fails to take off, the child is left at night in an unfamiliar city.

If you are willing to forgo the niceties and security offered by a travel agent, buy directly from a consolidator. To find the names and phone numbers of consolidators, check the ads in the Sunday travel sections of *The New York Times, The Los Angeles Times,* or your local newspaper, or call those listed on this page. Although the ads are usually very small and seldom use the word consolidator, you will recognize them immediately because they offer tickets at significantly lower prices.

 Use a travel agent you trust who regularly does business with a reliable consolidator.

Some Consolidators

Euro-Asia Express	(800) 782–9625
TFI Tours	(800) 745–8000
	(212) 736–1140
Travac Tours	(800) 872–8800
	(212) 563–3303
"Travel Bargains," part of the Travel Channel TV Network	(800) 872–8385
Travel Discounters	(800) 355–1065
UNI Travel	(800) 325–2222
	(314) 569–0900

If you want to fly from London to Africa or the Middle or Far East, or throughout Europe, try the British version of consolidators, "bucket shops." They're centered around Earls Court Road, and ads appear in the London newspapers.

Is buying a consolidator or bucket-shop ticket safe? Usually, the price is right, and there's no advance purchase, but if you wish to make a change in your reservation or get a refund, it's often difficult. Ask first. Another drawback for some: You rarely know what airline you're flying on until you receive your ticket (airlines don't want it publicized that they are dealing with consolidators or bucket shops), and you may not get your ticket until the last minute.

 To be on the safe side, pay with your credit card when using a consolidator so that you'll have some recourse. If you must pay in cash, first check the consolidator's local Better Business Bureau for complaints. Confirm your flight directly with airlines. Check cancellation and exchange policies.

For a copy of *Advisory on Ticket Consolidators,* with a list of consolidators and their telephone numbers, go to www.newyork.bbb.org.

Discounts for Students

A Student ID Card, in addition to low airfares, gives students discounts on many attractions and sites around the world and in the United States plus basic sickness and accident insurance and a twenty-four-hour traveler's assistance hotline. The card costs $20 and is sponsored by the Council on International Educational Exchange. Current benefits include:

- *Greyhound:* 10 percent off any U.S. destination
- *Emergency evacuation:* up to $25,000 while overseas
- *Miscellaneous travel discounts*

For information call 800–COUNCIL, write to Student Services Council, 205 East 42nd Street, New York, NY 10017, or log on to www.counciltravel.com.

FREQUENT FLYING

The frequent-flyer concept is a marketing gimmick that really took off. Some bright person in the mid-1980s at American Airlines came up with the idea of Frequent-flyer Mileage—a way of rewarding the passenger for flying American to the exclusion of other carriers. Their frequent flyer plan said, "Look Mr. or Ms. Passenger, every time you fly American, we'll give you mileage points, which can be traded in for free trips or cabin upgrades." In effect it was a bribe to create brand loyalty—and it worked.

Within a short time every other airline got into the act. Now, not only does every airline have a frequent-flyer plan, but so do many hotel chains and car rental firms.

One amazing fact is that only about 15 percent of all passengers redeem their frequent-flyer miles. You should be one of them.

Frequent-Flyer Strategies

Even if you don't fly on a regular basis, you can benefit from a frequent-flyer program. Here are eight tips to follow:

1. *Join as many frequent-flyer plans as possible.* There is no charge, and each airline will keep you updated on its specials, discounts, and deals. However . . .

2. *Group your miles.* It's to your advantage to accumulate as many miles as possible in one airline program rather than to have smaller amounts in several programs.

3. *Keep track of your own mileage.* Back your record up with copies of hotel, car-rental, and airline receipts to show you actually deserve the mileage. The chances that the airlines will goof in logging your miles are tremendous.

4. *Try buying points.* If you find you're a little short on bonus miles that you need for a vacation flight, you might be able to buy points from the airline. Ask.

5. *Protect yourself from an airline* that looks as though it won't be around much longer. When you have enough mileage for one or more flights, and there are rumors that the airline might fold, use the mileage immediately, or you can buy Award Guard, a type of insurance that conditionally protects your mileage from being lost; the cost is $119 for one year. Call (800) 487–8893.

6. *Get business frequent-flyer miles.* If you fly on business and your employer feels the company deserves the mileage, describe how onerous business travel really is: canceled flights, long delays, crowded airports, airline food. You undoubtedly merit keeping the mileage.

Insider Tip

Log on to the *Frequent Flyer Magazine* at www.webflyer.com. This site provides information and subscription details.

7. *Don't cash in your miles during the off-season* or when airlines are having fare wars. Wait until fares go back up.

8. *Pass on your frequent-flyer miles* to your heirs through your will, or donate them, through the airline, to charity. (There's no tax deduction, but you'll feel good.) American Airlines supports several charities through its Miles for Kids in Need program; Northwest teams up with a different nonprofit organization every quarter. Other carriers have other arrangements. Ask your travel agent or the airline.

Disadvantage for Frequent Flyers

Frequent flyers traveling on free tickets are not guaranteed the same treatment as passengers who have paid for thier tickets. If the flight is delayed or canceled, the airline is less likely to endorse a frequent-flyer ticket over to another carrier; frequent flyers also are less apt to get hotel and meal vouchers.

 Tell the gate attendant that you fly all the time; airlines don't want to lose good, steady customers.

Get Free Airline Tickets with the Right Credit Card

By selecting one of the airline's credit cards, you can earn free air travel, even if you're not a frequent flyer. For every dollar's worth of goods you charge on an affinity card, you receive credit for mileage in a particular airline's frequent-flyer program.

In addition to American Express and Diners Club—the two big T&E (travel and entertainment) cards—seven big U.S. airlines and British Airways sponsor MasterCard or Visa cards that let you earn frequent-flyer mileage for every dollar you charge. Although these MasterCard and Visa cards are sponsored by the airlines, they are issued by banks. Most give some collision insurance on rental cars.

The T&E cards have more flexibility than the airline-sponsored cards. They don't expire, and you can use them on several airlines. With the airline cards you accrue mileage only with that particular airline and its frequent-flyer partners.

 MONEY TIP: Be aware that "frequent-flyer miles" are not necessarily actual free airline miles on a one-for-one basis. The credit can be used for free tickets, upgrades, and sometimes for vacation packages and goods.

- AMERICAN EXPRESS. AmEx's "Membership Rewards" program lets you bank earned mileage in your AmEx account and transfer credits when needed into a participating frequent-flyer program. You get 1 mile for each dollar charged on your AmEx and they never expire. Members must charge $5,000 to their AmEx card before mileage can be redeemed. Participants: Continental, Delta, Southwest, USAirways, El Al, Sabena, and their frequent-flyer partners. Call (800) 297-3276. There's a $25 fee.

- DINERS CLUB. This is the only card that rewards you with frequent-flyer miles on your choice of any major U.S. airline plus a great many international ones. You earn 1 mile for every dollar you charge to the card, and you don't have to tell them up front to which frequent-flyer program you want your miles applied. When you're ready to fly, you simply call and give the information to them. Your miles do not expire, and there's no limit to the number of miles you can earn. Or you can choose free hotel frequent-guest points or upgrades or travel packages instead of air miles. You save 20 percent on your entire restaurant bill when you eat at any one of the more than 1,700 restaurants that participate in the LeCard program. When you're away on business you have up to sixty days to pay your bill without interest or late fees. And if your card is lost or if you forget it, you can continue charging with a phone call to a representative. Call (800) 234-4034. There's an $80 fee.

- MASTERCARD AND VISA. Airline affinity cards are issued by banks and can be used wherever Visa and MasterCard are accepted. You get frequent-flyer mileage for every dollar charged. Participants: All major U.S. airlines except Delta sponsor one or both cards.

Airline Charge Cards

FINDING THE RIGHT PROGRAM

Airline	Telephone	Credit Card
Alaska	(800) 552–7302	MC, GMC, V, GV
America West	(800) 678–2632	V
American	(800) 359–4444	MC, V
Continental	(800) 245–9850	V, MC (Platinum for both)
Northwest	(800) 360–2900	V, GV
Southwest	(800) SWA–VISA	V, Platinum V
TWA	(800) EAB–TWA1	V, MC
United	(605) 247–3927	V, GV, GMC, MC
USAirways	(800) 282–2273	V, GV, Platinum V

MC = Mastercard   V = Visa   GMC = Gold Mastercard   GV = Gold Visa

Note:Annual fees and interest rates vary with the issuing company or bank.

BEING BUMPED PAYS

It's a fact of life that everyone who makes a reservation doesn't show up for the flight. In airline parlance these are called "no-shows."

To counterbalance the no-shows, the airlines overbook, making reservations for more people than they can get on the flight. Sometimes, however, everyone does show up! Then the airline personnel have to get rid of the excess passenger load, which they do through something called "bumping." The gate attendant will ask passengers with confirmed reservations if they'd like to volunteer to be bumped. If chosen, they get put on the next flight and are given a voucher good for a free flight in the future, usually for anywhere in the United States that the airline flies.

 Even if you have a confirmed reservation, arrive early at the check-in gate if you want to avoid being bumped. On the other hand, if your schedule is not tight, tell the gate attendant that you want to be on the volunteer bumping list.

If your flight is canceled after you arrive at the airport, get to a pay phone and call the airline's toll-free reservation number. If you don't know it, call information, (800) 555-1212. Ask to be rebooked on the next scheduled flight to your destination. By phoning you'll avoid waiting in a long line of passengers who are also trying to rebook.

Work Sheet
PICKING THE BEST CREDIT CARD

To determine which frequent-flyer program and credit card is best for you, complete the worksheet below.

Step 1: Track your travel regularly to note which airline you fly most frequently, by filling in the worksheet below.

DATE	DESTINATION	CARRIER	FARE	HOW PAID

Step 2: Track your T&E charges to note if you meet the minimum-dollar requirements to join the frequent-flyer program by filling in the worksheet on the next page.

Work Sheet
T&E CHARGES

DATE	AMERICAN EXPRESS	DINERS CLUB
_____	$ _____	$ _____
_____	$ _____	$ _____
_____	$ _____	$ _____
_____	$ _____	$ _____
_____	$ _____	$ _____
_____	$ _____	$ _____
_____	$ _____	$ _____
_____	$ _____	$ _____
_____	$ _____	$ _____
_____	$ _____	$ _____
_____	$ _____	$ _____
_____	$ _____	$ _____
_____	$ _____	$ _____
_____	$ _____	$ _____
_____	$ _____	$ _____
_____	$ _____	$ _____
_____	$ _____	$ _____
Annual Total	$ _____	$ _____

Step 3: Check the table on the previous page and select the card that meets your needs.

Tips About Getting Bumped

When a flight is overbooked, the airline must first ask for volunteers willing to give up their seats for one on the next available flight. Only after all volunteers have been accepted can the airline begin bumping ticket holders involuntarily. They start with the last passenger to arrive at the gate.

If you want to get bumped in order to get a free flight in the future:

- *Be flexible.* Decide ahead of time that you're willing to volunteer your seat and arrive later than planned at your final destination.

- *Pack accordingly.* Carry everything you absolutely must have in a carry-on bag—toothbrush, medicine, extra eye glasses or lenses, snacks, change of underwear.

- *Book a flight on a busy travel day.* Best: Thursday, Friday, and Sunday, and during peak travel time (3:00 P.M. to 7:00 P.M.). Call the airline to see if a particular flight is nearly booked; if so, get a ticket but only if there are additional flights later on that day to your destination.

- *Say "no" to a boarding pass or seat assignment* from your travel agent or the airline. Being without these boosts your chances of being bumped.

 To qualify for the airline's compensation, you must have checked in at the gate at least twnety minutes before departure time. If you're not there, the airline has the right to give your seat to someone else, based on your being late. So, arrive on time and . . .

- *Be first in line at the gate check-in.* Ask if the flight is oversold; if it is, offer to give up your seat. If there's any doubt, make sure the agent adds your name to the list of volunteers.

- *Sit near the gate.* You want to hear any announcements. You'll be called to the ticket counter as everyone else is boarding. An airline authority will give you details on compensation, getting booked on another flight, etc.

- *Ask politely for free food and/or lodging.* The airline may give you discount coupons or vouchers if the delay requires your dining out or staying overnight.

 For a copy of *Facts & Advice for Airline Passengers*, which covers your rights if you're bumped, if the airline goes bankrupt, if your ticket is lost, if you're in a crash, send $5.00 to: Aviation Consumer Action Project, Box 19029, Washington, DC 20036; (202) 638-4000.

Get a Hotel Discount If you're bumped and thus forced to stay overnight in a hotel, ask the airline to make the reservation; they often land better rates than individual travelers.

FLYING AS A COURIER

You don't need an attaché case attached to your wrist, a special password, or a trench coat to be a courier, but you do need to be flexible and willing to travel light. If you fulfill these requirements, you can fly to many foreign destinations for about half price by acting as an escort for parcels: financial papers, architectural drawings, manuscripts, etc.

Using ordinary citizens as couriers evolved as a way to solve the problem the air freight companies face. These companies promise to get parcels to foreign countries by next-day or second-day air. If they send them with their regular air-freight shipment, it takes several days to clear customs. Their solution: to use air couriers—you.

In exchange for a reduced fare (about 50 percent off), you agree to fly with only carry-on luggage and give up your checked luggage space to the company, which uses it for its packages. You seldom see the items involved, but it's all legitimate stuff. A representative from the courier company will meet you at the airport and make all the arrangements for handling the parcels. That's it. They get their stuff delivered, and you get cheap airfare.

Air couriers fly from New York, Los Angeles, Miami, Houston, San Francisco, Chicago, Boston, Orlando, Vancouver, Montreal, and Washington, D.C. Some air-courier brokers charge a membership fee ($50–$100) and/or a refundable deposit. To find out about being an air courier, call the International Association of Air Couriers, (561) 582–8320, or log on to www.courier.org. Membership is $45 per year.

 The closer to departure time, the cheaper the ticket. Some couriers have gotten free tickets by being able to leave at the last minute.

Travel Trivia The U.S. Department of Transportation says you're least likely to be put off a flight with American Airlines—it bumps about 0.40 per 10,000 passengers. *Next best:* United, Northwest, Delta. *Worst:* Continental, America West, Southwest.

TAKING CHARTER FLIGHTS

Here's yet another way to get rock-bottom fares—sometimes. Charter operators fly from some forty U.S. and Canadian cities to popular vacation spots and major cities around the world. They tend to be seasonally oriented; that is, in the winter most go from a northern city to a warmer spot, with Mexico and the Caribbean being extremely popular. Most undercut the lowest fares on scheduled airlines, and most sell all seats at the same price. Many run only one trip weekly, and it's tough to get a refund or exchange your ticket. (For a list of leading charter operators, see the table on the next page.)

 Charters are not always your cheapest bet. Before buying a ticket, check Continental and USAirways, which have low-fare flights, as well as any new start-up lines. During fare wars, regularly scheduled lines may actually undercut charters. The difference between a charter flight and a regularly scheduled one has to do with contracts: With a charter your contract is with a tour operator, not an airline. The tour operator actually charters a plane and crew from the airline that then operates the flight. This distinction is not critical unless things go wrong; then it's up to the tour operator to fix it, not the airline. Consequently, travelers have been left stranded because the tour operator went out of business and the airline was never paid for the return flight.

Excess Baggage Charges Airlines charge extra for: antlers, empty scuba tanks, surfboards, and Windsurfing and hang gliding equipment.

Charters usually don't sell seats directly to the public or list fares, schedules, and seat availability in the computerized systems used by travel agencies, although there are some exceptions. Not all travel agents keep up with the charters; in fact, some don't sell them at all.

Charters serve very limited areas, and usually do not make connecting flights. In other words they go from one major city to another or from a major city to a popular vacation spot.

 Don't be misled by the word scheduled. Charters do adhere to a schedule. Scheduled airlines are the majors, such as American, United, etc., but a handful of small airlines operate scheduled service under charter rules. Starting up a charter line involves less red tape than starting a scheduled line.

You should know that airlines are licensed by the government to provide scheduled flights and to sell tickets on them. On the other hand, airlines or charter operators can sell an entire flight to a single club or group. This is called an affinity charter. Or they can sell charter seats to individual travelers, which is called a public charter. Public charters are governed more tightly by the Department of Transportation than are affinity charters. The money paid for a charter ticket must be held in an escrow account and not released until after the trip is over. If you buy directly from the operator, your check should be made out to the escrow bank. If you are using a travel agent, the travel agent deducts his or her commission and also sends a check

Leading Charter Operators

Balair	(800) 322–5247
	(212) 581–3411
Fantasy Holidays	(800) 645–2555
	(516) 935–8500
Homeric Tours	(800) 223–5570
	(212) 753–1100
Martinair Holland	(800) 366–4655
	(561) 391–6165
New Frontiers	(800) 677–0720
	(310) 670–7318
Sun Trips	(800) 786–8747
	(408) 432–1101
Travel Charter	(800) 521–5267
	(810) 641–9677

to the bank. The purpose behind this is to safeguard the money should the operator fail or the trip not be made, and then the money will be refunded.

 These rules apply to cash and checks and do not cover the use of credit cards to pay for public-charter tickets.

GO STANDBY TO EUROPE

One agency, Airhitch, has a standby program for charters to Europe. You give Airhitch a five-day time period in which you wish to leave, with your desired destination and one or two alternative destinations. You must pay in advance, and you'll find out a few days ahead of time when you leave and to which city you'll be flying. Return plans are made in a similar fashion through a European-affiliated office. For information call (212) 864–2000.

European Air Passes

Eurolines. A division of National Express, this company has passes for unlimited travel linking thirty cities, including London, in sixteen countries. Buses have rest rooms and make refreshment stops. Contact DER Travel at (800) 782–2424.

EurAir Pass. A consortium of nine airlines offering passes at $90 one-way to over fifty European cities. You must buy at least three flight coupons. Call (888) 387–2479 for details.

British Midlands Air Pass. Available through travel agents. Flight coupons of $109 for flights under ninety minutes and $149 for long flights, one-way. Call (800) 788–0555 for information.

British Airways Pass Program. This is based on a four-zone system. Coupon prices range from $82 to $166 one-way. You can fly from London to any European city served by British Airways. However, many European destinations require two coupons. For information call (800) 247–9297.

Air France Euroflyer Program. Available only to passengers traveling to Europe on Air France, Sabena, or CSA. You must buy three coupons at $120 each for one-way flights. Covers one hundred European cities. Call (800) 237–2747 for details.

Northwest/KLM's Passport to Europe. Available if you fly on Northwest/KLM from the United States to Europe and then to KLM cities within Europe. Rates start at $300 for three flights during low season. Call (800) 374–7747 for information.

SAS's Visit Europe Pass. Fly to Scandinavia on SAS and then purchase inter-Europe travel, which decreases in price with the number of tickets you buy. Flights available to most Euorpean cities, with most originating in Copenhagen. Call (800) 221–2350.

Austrian Airlines (800–843–0002) and *Malve Hungarian Airlines* (800–223–6884) each offer their transatlantic customers air pass programs that route thorugh their respective hubs—Vienna, Zurich, and Brussels for Austrian Airlines and Budapest for Malev.

Directory of Small Carriers

Carrier	Began Service	Sample Destinations	Hub City
AirTran (800) 825–8538	1993	Atlanta; Washington, D.C.; Memphis; Miami; Boston; Ft. Lauderdale	Atlanta
America Trans Air (800) 225–9919	1981	Las Vegas; Chicago; Indianapolis; Milwaukee; Cancun	Chicago
Frontier (800) 432–1359	1944	Denver; Phoenix; Los Angeles; Atlanta; Dallas	Denver
Kiwi (800) 538–5494	1992	Atlanta; Chicago; Newark; San Juan; Tampa/St. Petersburg; West Palm Beach; Miami	Newark
Midway Airlines (800) 446–4392	1993	New York; Philadelphia; Tampa; Atlanta; West Palm Beach; Washington, D.C.	Raleigh/ Durham
Reno Air (800) 736–6247	1992	Reno; San Jose; Los Angeles; Seattle; and all over the West Coast	Reno
Spirit Airlines (800) 772–7117	1992	East Coast; Florida; Detroit; Atlantic City	Detroit
Sun Jet Int'l (800) 478–6538	1993	Dallas; Long Beach, Calif.; Newark; Tampa/St. Petersburg; West Palm Beach; Orlando	Newark
Tower Air (800) 348–6937	1983	Miami; Los Angeles; San Francisco; Paris; Athens; Tel Aviv	New York

Send Your Luggage Ahead If you have heavy, bulky items,

send them by UPS or post office. You won't have to lug the stuff around and it may be cheaper than the airline's excess luggage charges.

AIRLINE PROBLEMS

Lost Luggage

One out of every 200 bags checked is reported lost. More luggage is lost in December, January, and February than at other times of the year. Airlines that most often lose bags are Continental and USAirways; those that lose the fewest bags are Southwest, American, and America West. To find out how airlines score on baggage handling, call the Department of Transportation at (202) 366-2220.

A Freebie For a free copy of *Tips on Avoiding Baggage Problems*, which

covers packing, check-in, filing claims, etc., call U.S. Department of Transportation, (202) 366-2220.

Airline policies vary, but in general, here's what to do when your luggage doesn't show up.

1. Fill out a complaint form while you're still at the airport. Wait twenty-four hours for results. (Be sure an airline employee signs the form.)

2. If your luggage does not show up, you can get an allowance of $25 to $50. To claim it, you must return to the airport.

3. After forty-eight hours you're entitled to another $25 for emergency supplies; bring receipts from your purchases.

4. Bags never found? The maximum you're entitled to is $1,250 no matter how many bags you had. And that's for depreciated value, not original value, which is why we recommend that you always make a detailed list of what you've packed plus a record of the cost of your bags themselves. And remember, an airline can deny coverage completely for fragile and perishable items that you've packed.

5. Check your homeowner's insurance policy and your credit card coverage to see if you can get more.

6. You may want to purchase extra coverage at the airport—it generally runs 50 cents to $2.00 per $100 extra coverage.

What Your Bag Is Worth

Airlines are liable for provable damages up to $1,250 per passenger. If your luggage and contents are worth more, you're out of luck unless you have extra coverage.

Lost Tickets

Getting a replacement or refund for a lost ticket will be difficult and time consuming—count on it. The airlines are worried about fraudulent claims and so they "encourage" you to be extra careful. That translates into the fact that you may have to pay a fee of up to $50 if you lose your ticket. And, believe it or not, if your ticket is found and used by someone else, your refund request may be denied!

To protect yourself, buy your tickets with a credit card so you have absolute proof of purchase. Then think of your tickets as cash and know where they are at all times. If you do lose them, report the fact at once to the airline or travel agent.

Airline Strikes

If you're booked on an airline that goes on strike, what can you expect? The answer, unfortunately, is very little. Airlines don't care too much that your vacation had to be canceled, that you couldn't get to an important meeting, or that you were stranded with two children for hours at the airport.

If you've made your reservation through a travel agent, he or she will work very hard to get you on the next available flight. That is, if the strike or flight cancelation takes place during regular business hours when you can reach your agent. And, of course, calling your agent means access to information on all airlines—which is a lot easier than dialing a batch of 800 numbers from a pay phone. If you hold a frequent-flyer ticket or have purchased your ticket from a consolidator, other airlines may not accept it.

 Be smart and keep a photocopy of your ticket, ticket number, itinerary, credit card receipt, and photo ID separate from your ticket. Sometimes, if you discover your ticket is lost at the last minute, the airline may let you board without insisting that you purchase another ticket if you have a photocopy of all of the above.

Labor strikes fall into the same category as "Act of God" and "Act of War," which means there's no legal requirement for the airline to help out the consumer. Airlines are not required to compensate passengers when their flights are canceled or delayed. They are only required to provide compensation to passengers bumped from an overbooked flight.

When you hear news of an impending strike at an airline on which you have booked a ticket, call your travel agent. Book refundable tickets on alternative carriers. Then, if your original carrier takes off, the backup ticket can be cashed in.

Registering a Complaint

If you have any complaints about an airline and would like to take action, contact the Aviation Consumer Protection Division, U.S. Department of Transportation (DOT), 400 Seventh Street SW, Room 4107C-75, Washington, DC 20590; (202) 366-2220.

1. Put your complaint in writing. Stick to the point. Keep it short.

2. Enclose copies (not originals) of tickets, receipts, etc.

3. State if you're a member of the airline's frequent-flyer club.

4. State the solution you're seeking.

5. Add something positive about a staff person; you'll be taken more seriously than if you're just a complainer.

6. Send a copy to the airline's customer-service department.

 www.dot.gov/airconsumer/problems.html

HANDLING JET LAG

Left alone, jet lag (extreme drowsiness, insomnia, waking at crazy hours, and other odd feelings that occur when you cross too many time zones in a short period) slowly diminishes, although some effects can last as long as twelve days. It can be a real nuisance and, for the business traveler, a disaster. There have been all kinds of remedies suggested over the years. Some seem to work for some people. These are worth trying:

1. Eat lightly on the plane.

2. Avoid liquor and caffeine.

3. Walk about the cabin every two hours.

4. Wear loose-fitting clothes.

5. Drink water every few hours.

6. A week before departure, if you're traveling east, get up an hour earlier each day and have meals an hour earlier daily until, by the end of the week, you're rising at 2:00 A.M. and having dinner at 2:00 P.M.

7. Get a free copy of "The Argonne Anti-Jet Lag Diet" from: Office of Public Affairs, Argonne National Laboratories, 9700 South Cass Avenue, Argonne, IL 60439; (630) 252-5575.

BEING SAFE

A question we're asked all the time is, "What's the safest part of the plane?" Repeated accident reports indicate that fatalities can occur anywhere, depending on how the accident occurs and the configuration of the aircraft. On the other hand, there is a premium to getting out of a damaged plane at once to avoid ensuing explosions, smoke, fumes, or fire. To exit quickly, sit next to an exit door, or if that's not possible, carefully note where the exits are and be prepared to get to one of them in an emergency. Mentally rehearse what you would do.

Smoke hoods, which you slip over your head in an emergency, protect against smoke and heat and have a clear visor that helps you see in smoky areas. Folded, the hoods are about the size of a man's handkerchief and sell for about $80 from Magellan's. To order call (800) 962-4943.

 The 1999 Airport Transit Guide lists ways to get to the nearest city from more than 400 airports around the world. It also covers wheelchair access, trip times, and rental car companies. It costs $9.95. Contact Magellan's, (800) 962-4943.

The critical times: takeoff and landing. That's why you're asked to keep your seat belt buckled. Don't be macho. Do it.

Another safety measure: Read the safety instructions in the seat-back pocket every single time you fly, no matter how "square" it may seem. Each plane has different instructions.

Sky Safety According to the University of California at Berkeley's "Wellness Letter," if you flew in a commercial airline to random airports in the United States every single day of your life, it would take a mind-boggling average of 26,000 years before you would be killed in a crash.

The Federal Aviation Administration keeps a list of airlines worldwide that do not meet international safety standards. A "conditional" rating means that the airline may fly into the United States, but only under more severe FAA surveillance. The FAA also has a list of carriers that are not allowed to send any planes to the United States. To check up on an airline, call the FAA's hotline at (800) 322-7873.

EATING WHILE ALOFT

Airline food is considered by many to be an oxymoron. In first class or business class, however, the choice and the food itself are usually quite good. In coach, considering that a handful of cabin attendants are trying to feed hundreds within a short period of time, it's surprising when it's not a culinary disaster. At times it is.

 Bring your own large coffee mug. You'll get more, and it will stay warm longer.

Even in coach, you can avoid ordinary airline cuisine and have healthful, appealing food by ordering a special meal, at no extra charge, when you make your reservation. United has the greatest selection of special meals—more than twenty, including seafood and fruit plates, Kosher, Hindu, and Muslim meals, or a chef's salad.

Insider Tip Book your flight and your meal. Order a special meal even if you don't require one for dietary reasons. Special meals are prepared to order.

AIRLINE CLUBS

If you travel often with a particular airline, you might want to consider joining its club. Check first to see if your credit card already provides access to an airport club. For example, American Express Platinum Card lets you into Continental and Northwest lounges when flying those airlines, and Diners Club has sixty-plus airport lounges just for its cardholders.

Airline clubs charge a one-time entrance fee that can range from $25 to $200 plus an annual fee. Some let you pay with frequent-flyer miles; some offer spousal memberships, lifetime membership, longer-term memberships. A couple of clubs have one-day passes. Most let you bring in a guest.

What do you get? Quiet, comfort, fax machines, computers, printers, snacks, TV, magazines, telephones, copiers, maybe even a conference room, clean restrooms, showers. You can also use a club to receive messages or meet someone. In most cases, a ticket agent in the club will handle seat assignments, issue boarding passes, and help you change reservations, so there's no standing in line at the gate or public ticket counter. And, if your flight is either canceled or delayed, you're more apt to get a good seat on the next flight. Club ticket agents are also adept at getting upgrades for members.

The world's best lounge, say many, is Virgin Atlantic's at Heathrow, which comes with virtual ski machines; a music room with CDs; a 5,000-volume library; a salon with free massages, manicures, and hairstyling; a four-hole putting green; and more. If you can, check out the lounge in the airport(s) you use most often before signing on. See if it has what you want.

3
Riding the Rails: Train Travel

To travel by train is to see nature and human beings, towns and churches and rivers, in fact to see life.

—*Agatha Christie*

Agatha Christie knew that speed isn't everything. Along with it come crowded airports, flight delays, cancellations, small seats, and squished legs. Trains, on the other hand, are conveniently located in city centers, so there's none of the hassle and expense involved in going to and from an airport, and there's plenty of legroom to accommodate the tallest basketball player. Riding the rails is also relaxing. You can sit in a wide-windowed coach or in your own compartment and watch the countryside roll by, with no traffic, turbulence, or much thought given to the weather, and anxiety about making connections is pretty much eliminated. Best of all, there's plenty of uninterrupted time in which to work, read, rest, dream.

TRAVEL ON AMTRAK

Amtrak, which took over the nation's passenger rail network in 1971, has been continually upgrading its service, but that, of course, doesn't mean all trains provide equally good service. They don't. The trick to a successful ride is to know which train to take and what type of accommodation to book.

Amtrak Travel Tips

Here are fifteen ways to make riding the rails work for you.

1. *For overnights, go first class,* unless you don't mind sitting up all night; if you don't mind, you'll save a bundle. Meals, but not liquor, are included in the price of all first-class tickets. It's very important to understand the space you're buying. Before booking ask Amtrak to show or send you a diagram of the various sleeping accommodations offered.

 A perk of first-class travel: You can use the special Amtrak "Metropolitan Lounges" in a handful of cities. They are attractive and safe and have comfortable sofas, chairs, writing desks, telephones, faxes, free coffee, tea, cold beverages, reading material, and helpful attendants. You can stow your bags there while waiting, and just before departure a porter will take them from the lounge and deliver them to your train seat.

2. *Bathroom needs must be taken into consideration* when booking a sleeper. If you use the bathroom during the night, you'll need a compartment in which the toilet is not under the bed when the bed is pulled down. On most Amtrak trains the bedrooms have a separate, private bathroom, so you won't need to fold up your bed to use the facilities; in a roomette, however, the toilet is under the folded-down bed. In some smaller roomettes, the toilet is on the side of the folded-down bed. *Ask.* Solution: Take a robe so that you can walk to a car where there is a general bathroom.

3. *Laptop users in sleeping compartments* can get a table that hooks into the wall. Bring your own very long extension cord—in many sleeping compartments, the only electric outlet is in the bathroom, too far away for a computer's standard cord to reach.

 Trains frequently enter blackout periods, so sensitive computers should be run on batteries. Also, pack a three- to two-prong plug and vice versa because outlets are not uniform.

4. *Overnight coach travelers* should bring their own blanket and pillow. Although available (often for a small fee) on most routes, these creature comforts are often in short supply.

5. *Bring your own reading material,* map, playing cards, writing paper, stamps, pen. Headphones are required for Walkmans, Watchmans, and radios.

6. *Ask the conductor for Amtrak route guides* as soon as you board. These useful brochures have detailed maps that highlight key points of interest to look at from both sides of the train. They're available on all long routes.

7. *Get the current issue of Amtrak's* America, a magazine that describes the major trains, their routes (with maps), and equipment, as well as details on vacation packages, escorted rail tours, and a list of hotels where Amtrak passengers get reduced rates. Call (800) USA–RAIL for a free copy.

8. *Check out discounts.* In conjunction with United Express, Amtrak now serves eighty-six U.S. cities with a rail trip one way and an airline flight the other—at one price. There are also discounts for kids ages two to fifteen, and for seniors over age sixty-two. United Airlines Mileage Plus members get credit for the air portion of the trip. For information call Amtrak's Great American Vacations at (800) 321–8684. Periodically Amtrak gives 55 percent off one-way fares if the fare costs $75 or more, so ask if there's an "Amtrak

Meets You More Than Half Way" fare when booking (not available on Metroliner or auto trains).

9. *Go coach.* Check out the "All Aboard America" rates. Amtrak has divided the United States into three major geographical areas. With this plan you can stop off three times with each pass. The plan costs $140 for travel within one region, $180 for two regions, and $225 for all three regions. For example, you can go from New York to Los Angeles, stop off in three cities in three different areas, and then ride back to New York for just $225. The passes are not good in peak seasons and are nonrefundable. Children ages two to fifteen go half price, and seniors age sixty-two and older get a 15 percent discount. Call (800) USA–RAIL.

10. *Save more money.* Stay at hotels within walking distance (or a short bus or taxi ride) of train stations, and make the longest train trips during the night, when fares are lower.

11. *Tell your age.* If you're sixty-two or over, you can get a 15 percent discount off the lowest available rail fare every day of the week, but not during Christmas/New Year's or on Metroliners or auto trains at any time. The lowest round-trip rail fares usually sell out quickly, so book well in advance.

12. *Use the club car on Metroliner service* between major East Coast cities, especially if you're traveling during mealtime. You won't save money; in fact, you'll need a first-class ticket, but you will get more privacy and legroom, and meals (delivered to your seat) are included in the price. There are single seats on one side of the aisle and two seats on the opposite side.

13. *Ask about special fares*—weekend fares, one-week fares, one-month fares, tours, seasonal discounts, and round-trip savings—not only in the United States but also abroad. For example, a one-way Metroliner ticket between New York and Philadelphia is $58 on weekdays, but a round-trip excursion is only $39 and takes just fifteen minutes longer.

14. *Buy on-line.* Rail Sale reserved, one-way tickets on selected routes are 40 percent to 90 percent less at www.amtrak.com. Tickets will be mailed to you.

15. *Get a sleeper* in a "sold-out" car by calling (800) 872–7245 after 3:00 A.M., when Amtrak clears out those spaces not paid for.

Insider Tip: Maintaining Your Privacy If you're not in the mood for a conversation with your seatmate on a train, plane, or bus, wear headphones, even if you're not listening to music. You'll be less likely to be disturbed by a talkative fellow traveler.

GREAT U.S. & CANADIAN TRAIN RIDES

Amtrak Journeys

There are a number of spectacular Amtrak routes that showcase the great diversity and grandeur of the United States. Book well in advance for these six popular trains. For reservations call (800) USA-RAIL.

- *ADIRONDACK* (New York to Montreal). A lovely trip up the Hudson River, through the Adirondacks, with a view of Lake Champlain and the St. Lawrence River and Seaway as you pull into Montreal.

 Sit on the left side (the river side) when leaving Manhattan. At Albany switch to the right, or east side.

- *CALIFORNIA ZEPHYR* (Chicago to Oakland via Denver and Salt Lake City). See the Rocky Mountains and the Colorado River, and pass through the sheer-walled Glenwood Canyon. The train goes through the 6-mile Moffat Tunnel beneath the Continental Divide (rivers on the east side flow to the Atlantic Ocean and on the west side to the Pacific Ocean). You'll also go through the Sierra Nevada Mountains and Donner Pass.

 Take the trip heading west because the most interesting stretch is crossing the Rockies out of Denver, which you'll do in the daylight.

- *CAPITOL LIMITED* (Washington, D.C., to Chicago). Winds up the Potomac River and through the Appalachians. Between Pittsburgh and Washington, D.C., the train follows the old Baltimore & Ohio line through some of the prettiest scenery in the East.

- *CARDINAL* (Chicago to Washington, D.C.). Goes along the Ohio River, twisting through the Blue Ridge Moutains and the Appalachians, cutting through the dramatic New River Gorge.

- *COAST STARLIGHT* (Seattle to Los Angeles). Speeds along the West Coast, known for its sheer cliffs and dazzling drops to the ocean. You'll see the Pacific Palisades, the Cascade Mountains, and Puget Sound.

 Head north to capture the most daylight.

- *PIONEER* (Chicago to Seattle). This is part of the *California Zephyr* train until Salt Lake City, where it branches off and then climbs through the Blue

Mountains, on to the Columbia River and to Portland. The last lap is along the Cascade Range to Seattle.

Excursion Railroads

The following railroad companies offer short, scenic trips and run primarily in the spring/summer/fall, with some special Thanksgiving and holiday-time excursions.

In the East:

- Strasburg Rail Co., Box 96, Strasburg, PA 17597; (717) 687–7522
- East Broad Top Railroad, Rockhill Furnace, PA 17249; (814) 447–3011
- Valley Railroad Co., Box 452, Essex, CT 06426; (203) 767–0103

In the West:

- Durango & Silverton Narrow-Gauge Railroad, 479 Main Avenue, Durango, CO 81301; (970) 247–2733

In the South:

- Cass Scenic Railroad State Park, Box 107, Cass, WV 24927; (304) 456–4300

Canadian Train Trip

Rail Canada runs a special train called the *Chaleur,* which consists of recently restored 1950s vintage cars. There are two sleepers, a coach car, and a domed lounge/diner.

It leaves Montreal's Central Station at 7:00 P.M. several times a week. After it crosses the St. Lawrence River, you're served cocktails and dinner (linen tablecloths, fresh flowers, great food, china). By the time the train pulls into Quebec, you'll probably be in bed. Around sunrise the train stops at Matapedia, where it splits into two sections: the Halifax-bound *Ocean* and the Gaspe-bound *Chaleur.* From there you'll wind through countryside, along beaches, and through forests. Breakfast is served starting at 6:30 A.M. At 11:10 you arrive in Gaspe. Departure back to Montreal is at 3:50 P.M. with arrival the next morning.

For information call Via Rail Canada, (800) 561-3949.

FALL FOLIAGE BY RAIL

Most of us see autumn's blaze of color from a car or bus window, yet leaf-peeping by train completely eliminates all the hassle of highway and back-road traffic jams. For more information contact Amtrak in summer, long before the leaves begin to turn.

- *NORTHEAST.* The best color is on the route between New Haven and Boston, which parallels the Atlantic shoreline, and on Empire Service trains, which leave New York City for Albany, Montreal, or Niagara Falls. The tracks run right alongside the Hudson River.

 The best rides are on the *Adirondack* (see above) and the *Maple Leaf*—the latter continues west to Buffalo, Niagara Falls, and Toronto.

- *MID-ATLANTIC.* The trains between Philadelphia and Harrisburg go through Pennsylvania Dutch country.

 The *Pennsylvanian* and the eastbound *Broadway Limited* have great views of the Allegheny Mountains. (Book on the Keystone Classic Club, a luxurious lounge car attached to the *Pennsylvanian*.) Amtrak's triweekly *Cardinal* has spectacular views of the Skyline Drive in the Blue Ridge Mountains.

- *SOUTHEAST.* Take Amtrak's *Crescent* through the Virginia foothills and Piedmont area of Georgia. The *Carolinian* has superb views on the northbound run.

- *MIDWEST.* Any train from Chicago to Michigan is worth riding. In Michigan Amtrak offers a hotel package at Dearborn's Best Western/Greenfield Inn. There are good views also on the route between St. Louis and Kansas City, Missouri, with a special stop at Hermann, Missouri, during its five "Oktoberfest" weekends.

- *WEST.* Heading west from Chicago, the *Empire Builder* travels through brilliant colors in Wisconsin and Minnesota and along the Mississippi River. The *California Zephyr* (see above) passes through Aspen's yellow foliage and the flaming reds in the Rocky Mountains.

RIDING THE RAILS TO THE SLOPES

Toss out the ice scrapers and tire chains; instead, ride the rails to the trails. Amtrak lets you check your skis when boarding and retrieve them at your destination, or you can bring them aboard as carry-on luggage when checked baggage service is not available. Amtrak not only has trains that stop at the country's leading ski resorts, but it also has a number of well-priced packaged tours. (See Amtrak Ski Packages on next page.)

* *NORTHEAST.* The *Vermonter,* which travels between Washington, D.C., and Montreal, stops at White River Junction for Woodstock and Killington; at Essex Junction for Bolton Valley and Smugglers' Notch; at Waterbury-Stowe for Sugarbush and Stowe; and at St. Albans for Jay Peak.

* *MID-ATLANTIC.* The Chicago–New York *Broadway Limited* and the Chicago–Washington, D.C., *Capitol Limited* make stops in Pittsburgh near Seven Springs and Hidden Valley resorts. The *Capitol Limited* also stops in Cumberland, Maryland, near Wisp.

* *WEST.* The *Southwest Chief* from Los Angeles has a stop in Flagstaff for the Fairfield Snowbowl and in Lamy, New Mexico, for Taos and Santa Fe ski resorts. The *Pioneer* stops at Rock Springs for Jackson Hole skiing. On the *Empire Builder* you can train it to Big Mountain in Whitefish, Montana; Schweitzer in Sandpoint, Idaho; and other ski areas in Washington state.

The *California Zephyr,* which runs between Chicago and San Francisco, stops in Denver for shuttle service to Breckenridge, Copper Mountain, Arapahoe Basin, Keystone, Vail, and Beaver Creek. Then, west of Denver, the *Zephyr* stops at Winter Park. From the Salt Lake City stop, skiers can reach Park City, Alta/Snowbird, and Brighton/Solitude.

Amtrak Ski Packages

Amtrak ski packages include round-trip coach fare, lodging, resort amenities, lift tickets, and free transfers from the Amtrak train station to the front door of the resort. Accomodations range from well-known luxury resorts to family-style condos, with per person rates going from about $295 to $465 for three nights up to $600 for five nights.

* For Ski Amtrak packages in New Mexico and Colorado, call: RMA Travel & Tours at (800) 841–9800.

* For packages in Utah, call Sports America Tours at (800) 876–8551.

* With Amtrak's AirRail Travel Plan, in conjunction with United Airlines, you can travel by rail with stopovers and return by air. For information call (800) 321–8684.

WESTERN TRAIN TOURS

There are three interesting rides—a Rockies Tour, a Yellowstone Tour, and a Continental Divide Tour—ranging in price from about $400 to $1,500 per person, double occupancy. These trains depart from Spokane, Washington, and Billings, Montana, and range from three to five nights, staying overnight in hotels. Pre- and post-tour hotel nights are available at reasonable rates. For information call Montana Rockies Rail Tours, (800) 519-RAIL.

The Skunk Train, departing from Fort Bragg, California, traverses the famous Redwood Route originally laid out in 1855—in fact, it's a 40-mile trip back into American history, along the scenic Noyo River north to its final destination of Willits. For information call (707) 964-6371.

EUROPEAN TRAIN TRAVEL

It's easy to speed through Europe riding the rails—in style, safety, and comfort. Trains on some of the new high-tech tracks now average 130 to 170 miles per hour. Depending on how many places you'll be visiting, it may pay to buy a rail pass and get unlimited travel over a certain number of days rather than individual train tickets.

The most comprehensive of the passes is the Eurailpass, which lets you ride on the major national rails of seventeen Western European countries (but not Great Britain) and Hungary. With a full-time Eurailpass, you can travel on any day during the time period. With a flexible pass you can travel on only a certain number of days within the overall time period. For example, with a five-day/two-month pass, you can travel on any five days during a two-month period. The Eurailpass also lets you travel either free or at a discount on some suburban trains (but not on city transit systems), private railways, national buses, ferries, and excursion boats.

Here are some general recommendations:

1. *A Eurailpass is best* for extended, multicountry travel. If you're just going to one country, then a national or regional pass is a better bet.

2. *A flexible pass is cheaper* than a full-time pass, but you must keep your train travel within a limited number of days.

3. *If you're staying in only one city* or perhaps just two, buy a separate ticket for any intercity trip(s).

4. *A rail/car pass* is a good deal if you're combining a long train trip with just one-day auto trips. On the other hand, if you're going to do a lot of driving, you'll be better off going with a weekly car rental. A car is also more economical for two or more people traveling together.

5. *Fly if you're going to only a few cities* that are far apart.

Following are various passes that are now available. A number of these passes give discounts to senior citizens, who can buy individual tickets at discounted rates in many countries, often at 50 percent off.

- Regional passes, available for Benelux (Belgium, Luxem-bourg, and the Netherlands) and Scandinavia (Denmark, Finland, Norway, and Sweden), are cheaper than the Eurailpass, especially in second class.

- The European East pass is good for Austria, the Czech Republic, Hungary, Poland, and Slovakia. The Central Europe pass covers the Czech Republic, Germany, Poland, and Slovakia.

- Other regional passes: BritRail and Ireland (Britain, the Republic, Ulster, and the Irish Sea ferry), BritFrance, and BritGermany.

Is first class worth it? It's generally sold at a premium of 50 percent (versus as much as 500 percent on airlines) and gives you much more spacious seating areas as well as meal service. On long trips during the high season, when second class is invariably jammed, it's worth it.

THE *ORIENT EXPRESS* AND OTHER LUXURY TRAINS

If you like to travel in the manner favored by royalty, Isadora Duncan, and Mata Hari, the *Orient Express* is the ideal trip. After indulging the whims and fancies of the wealthy for nearly one hundred years, the *Orient Express* ground to a halt in 1977. In 1982, the born-again train resumed service from London to Venice. The train runs once a week, with a morning departure from Victoria Station. After a two-hour ride to Folkstone, passengers board the Sea Link British Ferry for a ninety-minute trip to Boulogne, France. In Boulogne sleeping cars are assigned. The train goes through France and the Swiss Alps before arriving in Venice. The trip takes thirty-two hours, with the nighttime portion occurring between Paris and Zurich; you'll have more than twenty daylight hours in which to enjoy spectacular scenery. Passengers may stop over in Paris, Zurich, St. Anton, Innsbruck, or Verona for an additional fee of $240 per stopover on the southbound journey. Return-trip arrangements must be scheduled in advance. At the

(§) Insider Tip If you want to sample the trip but not pay the full price, you can purchase day seats on these segments: London to Paris, $745; Zurich to Venice, $860; Zurich to Innsbruck, $690; Innsbruck to Venice, $530.

present time northbound stopovers are free. The current fare from London to Venice, including cabin and dinner, is $1,910 per person, double occupancy. If you book round-trip, the discounted fare is $2,770. Singles pay an additional $321 one way and $465 round-trip.

Most of the London-to-Venice trains have seventeen carriages—ten are sleeping cars, three are for dining, and one is for drinking and listening to a piano player. Cabins have been restored to their original elegance; you'll have a washstand but no private toilet—those are at the end of the carriage, so take a robe and slippers. There are no showers.

 Try to book an air-conditioned car (not all are) and one of the first or last cars. These are quieter and more private because fewer passengers walk through them on their way to the dining and drinking cars.

Men will need a dark suit and necktie; in fact, nearly half the men on board wear black tie. Women can dress to the nines; many wear long dresses from the 1920s and 1930s.

There's also a new sister train from Singapore to Bangkok. The *Eastern Orient Express* leaves Sunday afternoon and arrives in Bangkok on Tuesday, a journey of two nights. One way is currently $1,300 per person, double occupancy.

For information on both trains, call (800) 524-2420, or log on to www.orient-expresstrains.com.

For Further Information

If you yearn for the days when train travel was the transportation of choice, check with Maupintour, (800) 255-4266, (785) 331-1000. This company has assembled a number of vacations on restored and modern trains throughout Europe, Britain, Mexico, the United States, and Canada.

For information on the *Orient Express* and other refurbished train trips in Britain, Europe, and the United States, contact Abercrombie & Kent, 1520 Kensington Road, Oak Brook, IL 60523; (800) 323-7308 or (630) 954-2944.

A POTPOURRI OF TRAIN GOODIES

Here's a sampling of ways you can enjoy train travel.

- GREAT BRITAIN. An economical way to tour both Ireland and Britain is with a BritRail and Ireland pass, whereby you'll get unlimited train travel in the Republic of Ireland, Scotland, Wales, and Northern Ireland *plus* a round-trip cruise-style ferry crossing of the Irish Sea. The 30-day pass, recently priced at $408 for second class and $530 for first class, is good for five days of travel. A one-month pass provides ten days of travel for $570 for second class and $770 for first class.

If you're over age sixty, ask for a senior discount (you must prepurchase the pass in the United States).

There are also passes for Scotland only. They include ferries to the Hebridean Islands and some local buses as well as a pass for Britain and France and for England and Wales.

For information contact BritRail, (888) BRIT-RAIL

- *THE CHUNNEL.* Rail Europe's new high-speed Eurostar service through the Chunnel links Paris to London in three hours, and Brussels to London in three hours fifteen minutes. Lowest fare, "Discovery Special," a fourteen-day second-class advance purchase, is $75, nonrefundable and nonexchangeable. Bernard Frelat, president of Rail Europe Group, told us that "this compares favorably with the best current London–Paris airfare, which runs above $100." If you don't want to risk the nonrefundable advance purchase ticket, regular Paris/London tickets in second class are $149 and $219 in first class. First class includes a breakfast, lunch, or dinner served at your seat, free newspapers, and access to a special lounge in London's Waterloo Station. Service through the Channel Tunnel takes about twenty minutes with trains traveling at 100 miles per hour. There are frequent departures and reservations are compulsory. Obtain tickets from Rail Europe, (800) EUROSTAR, or from BritRail Travel, (888) BRIT-RAIL.

- *IRELAND.* Get unlimited bus *or* train travel at reduced rates by using the Rambler Pass throughout Ireland, priced at $108 for eight days or $162 for twelve days. A "combination pass" lets you use both trains and buses and costs $150 for eight days or $207 for twelve days. The eight-day passes are good for a fifteen-day period, whereas the 12-day tickets are valid for thirty days.

 Children under twelve pay 50 percent less. For information call CIE Tours at (800) CIE-TOUR.

- *GRAND CANYON RAILWAY.* For detailed information call (800) 843-8724.

- *VIA RAIL CANADA.* This government-owned passenger railroad can be reached by calling (800) 561-3949.

Where to Buy Rail Passes

Although most rail passes can be purchased in Europe, the Eurailpass generally cannot. For passes and more information, contact the following:

- BritRail Travel International, (888) BRIT-RAIL. *Handles:* BritFrance, BritGermany, BritRail and Ireland, BritRail, Chunnel tickets.

- CIE Tours International, (800) 243-8687 or (201) 292-3899. *Handles:* Ireland.

- CIT Rail, 342 Madison Avenue, Suite 207, New York, NY 10173; (800) 223-7987 or (212) 697-2100. *Handles:* Eurail, Germany, Italy.

- DER Tours/German Rail, 9501 West Devon Avenue, Suite 400, Rosemont, IL 60018; (800) 421-2929. *Handles:* Eurail, Benelux, Austria, Britain, Germany, Italy.

- Orbis Polish Travel Bureau, (800) 223-6037 or (212) 867-5011. *Handles:* Poland.

- Rail Europe, (800) 438-7245. *Handles:* Eurail, Benelux, BritFrance, European East, Scandinavia, Czech Republic, France, Greece, Hungary, Poland, Portugal, Russia, Spain, Switzerland, and Euro Star.

- Scandinavian American World Tours, (800) 545-2204. *Handles:* Eurail, Scandinavia.

- Scantours, 3439 Wade Street, Los Angeles, CA 90066; (800) 223-7226. *Handles:* Eurail, Scandinavia, Finland.

Books on Train Travel in Europe

- *Europe by Eurail* by LaVerne Ferguson, Globe Pequot, updated annually; $15.95.

- *Eurail Guide* by Kathryn M. Turpin and Marvin L. Saltzman, Eurail Guide Annual; $14.95.

- *Europe by Train* by Katie Wood and George McDonald, Harper Perennial; $14.00.

Insider Tip The Society of International Railroad Travelers, (800) IRT–4881 or (502) 454–0277, runs unique exotic train trips each year. Call for current list.

LEAVE THE DRIVING TO US: BUS TRAVEL

There's nothing mysterious about bus travel in the United States. Bear in mind, nevertheless, that long trips can wind up being as expensive (or almost) as train or plane travel if you pay for your meals and/or hotel or motel rooms. On short routes, however, the bus is very economical, and since travel is from center city to center city, very convenient as well.

Greyhound, (800) 231-2222 or www.greyhound.com, from time to time has advance-purchase, rock-bottom rates. (See the table below for sample rates.)

For a free copy of *The Motorcoach Travel Directory*, which lists 700 members and types of service, arranged by state, call American Bus Association, (800) 283-2877.

 Whether in the United States or abroad, always ask about discounts for seniors, children, and families. Excursion, weekend, and special promotional rates will also cut your cost.

Sample Advance-Purchase Rates
ON GREYHOUND BUS

Route	Standard	7-Day Advance	14-Day Advance	21-Day Advance
New York City–Dallas	$192.00	$158.00	$118.00	$99.00
Los Angeles–San Francisco	$69.00	$55.00	n/a	n/a
Los Angeles–Phoenix	$62.00	$45.00	n/a	n/a
New York City–Boston	$60.00	n/a	n/a	n/a
New York City–Washington	$60.00	n/a	n/a	n/a

Rail and Bus Passes

The wide array of rail and bus passes can be confusing. Here's a thumbnail sketch of what's currently available.

IN EUROPE

Eurailpass. The basic Eurailpass gives you unlimited travel for fifteen days in seventeen countries. There are occasional discounts for seniors, children, and families. Call (800) 722–7151 for information.

Eurobus. This pass gives you one month of unlimited bus travel. The bus picks up and drops off passengers at hotels, youth hostels, and campgrounds in major cities and resorts in eleven countries. Call 800–EUROBUS.

IN THE UNITED STATES

Greyhound. The AmeriPass gives you unrestricted travel, day and night, for seven days or up to sixty days throughout the United States. It's also valid for nonstop rides between Seattle and Vancouver, New York and Boston, Montreal and Buffalo, Detroit and Toronto. Call (800) 231–2222 for information.

The U.S. Bus. A group of minibuses and coaches link some fifty cities and places of interest across the country. Pickups and drop-offs are at hostels, not bus stations. Travel is only during the daytime. The Travel America Pass, available for two to forty-five days includes thirty-minute phone card and voice mailbox. Call (617) 773–8287 for information.

4
Behind the Wheel: Traveling by Car

The automobile—a walking stick; and one of the finest
things in life is going on a journey with it.

—*Robert Holliday*

I t's true; driving a car—your own or a rented one—certainly comes with a lot
of advantages, especially for trips that aren't too long. It's convenient, you can
take along as much baggage as you want, and you can go exactly where you
want, door to door.

It seems terribly logical, doesn't it? After all, your car is there, parked in front
of your house or in the garage, so why not use it? You should, especially for short
trips, but before pulling out of the driveway for a longer journey, think twice. Will
you be bored? Are there too many of you crammed into the back seat? Can your
back take it? Are the kids likely to get car sick? Will you push to cover too many
miles in too short a time? Before packing the overhead rack with your tent,
canoe, and bikes, read Chapter 7, Traveling with Children, on how to make
family travel a happy occasion.

If, on the other hand, you decide to drive, take time to do all those obvious
yet important things your dad told you about that help prevent disasters. One of
the perpetual pretrip nightmares vacationers have is that the car will break
down on the road in the middle of a storm or heat wave, with the whole family
fussing and fuming as hundreds of stalled motorists behind you honk loudly. To
prevent this nightmare from turning into stark reality, do the following.

- Get a tune-up.

- Check the level of all fluids: gas, oil, coolant, windshield cleaner.

- Test the air pressure in the tires.

- Find the spare tire.

- Replace the windshield wipers.

- Locate your license and car registration.

- Know where you're going and mark the route on a map.

- Put your auto club materials in the glove compartment, along with the map.

Insider Tip Sam's Club (800–955–7267) and Costco Wholesale (800–800–8505), the two discount warehouse chains, have some travel discounts.

HOW THE AUTOMOBILE CLUBS STACK UP

If after taking all these precautions, trouble comes honking, you'll be glad you joined an auto club. The average car on the road is now almost seven and a half years old, so it makes good sense to belong to a club. There are seventeen national clubs around the country competing with the oldest—the 36-million-member American Automobile Association (AAA). For an annual fee they all offer similar roadside services: fixing flats, delivering gasoline, jump-starting engines, towing your vehicle. In some cases for an extra few dollars you get additional goodies, such as extra trip-interruption insurance. Some clubs provide 10- to 50-percent discounts on hotel rooms and other travel expenses.

According to a recent survey of the eight largest clubs, the Exxon Travel Club was found to be the best deal for most drivers, simply because it has the greatest number of contracted emergency-service providers as well as family coverage. Second place went to AAA. Here's what you need to consider:

1. *If you have an older car,* pick a club that has excellent road service for free. (A *Money* magazine survey warns against Chevron, which has no contracted service providers.)

2. *If you have lots of drivers in your family,* pick a club that covers all of them. (Most clubs simply cover spouses and charge $12 to $20 more per year for each extra person.) Exxon's basic membership covers spouses, children up to age nineteen, and unmarried domestic partners.

3. *If you take long vacations by car,* pick a club with good trip-routing service. Allstate and AAA are particularly good.

4. *If you tend to lose your keys or lock yourself out of your car,* pick a club with a good lock-out plan, such as Amoco, Exxon, or Cross Country.

5. *If you're looking for discounts,* AAA gives 10 to 40 percent off at 45,000 retail establishments throughout the country. AAA and Exxon give up to 50 percent off at major hotel chains.

6. *If you drive abroad,* sign up with AAA. It is the only club that provides contracted free road service in most countries.

7. *If you have a luxury car,* you may automatically be enrolled in the Cross Country Motor Club.

To determine which club is best for you, call each for answers to these questions:

- Will I be towed? How far? How much will it cost?

- What if my spouse has trouble in another car?

- What if I don't have cash with me?

- What if I lock my keys in my car?

- What if I need road help while I'm driving a friend's car?

- What travel insurance comes with my membership?

- Is there trip continuation money if I have an accident away from home?

- Do you pay for ambulance service?

- Do you have credit-card protection?

- Do you plan trips? Provide maps?

- Do you give senior citizens a discount?

- Do you have cellular-phone service?

- Do you cover vans, trucks, antique cars, luxury models?

Two phrases you will encounter as you shop the clubs are these: *trip continuation allowance,* which reimburses you for lodging, meals, and other expenses incurred after an accident; and *lockout plan,* which pays for a locksmith to get into your car and possibly into your home if you've lost your house or apartment keys as well.

To compare the advantages of various automobile clubs, fill out the worksheet on the following page.

RENTING A CAR: HOW TO AVOID THE POTHOLES

The world of car renting has become increasingly complex; simply having a valid driver's license and a credit card is no longer enough. Today there are a myriad of rental companies, rules, regulations, and deals. Chances are you're like most people and won't take the time to read all the fine print in the rental contract before you pull out of the lot, so here are the questions you should ask and the facts you should know about car rentals.

Some research and advance planning will increase your chances of renting the car you want at the best possible price.

Insider Tip Check Hertz on-line for periodic discounts of 20 percent. Go to www.hertz.com.

Work Sheet
COMPARING THE AUTO CLUBS

CLUB INFORMATION	ANNUAL FEE	YOUR NOTES
AAA local office or (800) 222–4357; www.aaa.com	$50.oo average, but varies within 130 individual clubs	_____
Allstate (800) 255–2582; www.allstate.com	$59.95 and $69.95	_____
Amoco Motor Club (800) 334–3300; www.amocomotorclub.com	$59.95 and $84.95	_____
Chevron (800) 255–2273; www.chevron.com	$72.00	_____
Exxon (800) 833–9966	$51.00 and $72.00	_____
Montgomery Ward (800) 621–5151	$95.00	_____
Shell Motorist Club (800) 621–8663 www.shellus.com/ shellmotoristclub	$54.00	_____
Texaco Travel Club (800) 526–6786	$52.00, including spouse	_____

Before You Get to the Counter

- *How's your driving record?* Many rental firms can now look at your driving record by tapping into computerized data supplied by state departments of motor vehicles. You will be rejected if the company considers you a bad risk. What's a bad risk? If you have a drunk-driving conviction or several moving violations within the past twenty-four to forty-eight months. Self-defense: Call the company first and ask about their policy. Turn to the smaller companies, which have not yet begun to check.

- *Special equipment needs.* Many companies need at least twenty-four hours advance notice if you want a station wagon, luggage rack, child's seat, smoke-free car, or one designed for the disabled.

- *Shop around.* A phone call or two will pay off. For example, summer 1999 rates in the Orlando International Airport for one week for a mid-sized sedan ranged from $145 with Thrifty to $250 for Avis and Hertz.

- *Tally up the extras.* Many airports and cities have extra fees and taxes. Surcharges for additional drivers and special equipment are also common. If you're under age twenty-five, the big companies won't rent to you, but Alamo and Thrifty will—for $10 to $20 extra a day.

Collision Damage Waiver

Within the rental world collision-damage waiver is the most common area of confusion, full of changing regulations and misinformation. CDW, as it is called, pays for damage you do to the rental car, and this premium can run anywhere from $4.50 to $16.00 per day, depending on the amount of coverage. New York and Illinois do not permit CDW discounts, and California, Indiana, Nevada, and Texas have dollar limits on CDW charges.

You may not need to pay for the additional collision-damage insurance offered by the rental company if you already have coverage through your personal automobile insurance or your credit-card company. Check both in advance of renting. (Most U.S. automobile-insurance policies do not apply when you're driving outside the United States or Canada; some credit-card coverage does.) Among the things you need to check on are these:

- Does my personal automobile insurance policy limit the amount of damage it will pay to the value of my personal car? If so, and if you rent a more valuable car than your own, you'll need additional coverage.

- Does my credit-card or personal insurance collision-damage insurance cover additional drivers listed on the rental contract?

- How long is my rental insurance good for? American Express covers thirty-one days; MasterCard and Visa, fifteen days.

- Does my insurance cover unusual cars (such as a Mercedes), minivans, trailers, recreational vehicles, campers, and trucks? What about antique and exotic cars?

- Does my insurance cover damage to the other car?

- What is my deductible? (If you have a $500 deductible for collision damage to your personal car, then you will be responsible for the first $500 damage to a rental car. *Note:* Your credit card may pick up your deductible.)

- What personal-effect coverage do I have?

- What coverage do I have for personal injury? Car companies offer an umbrella liability policy for up to $1 million of coverage. It costs $8.00 to $9.00 per day but is unnecessary if you already have personal-liability coverage with your own auto insurance or if you carry a separate liability policy.

 If you are in an accident caused because you were under the influence of drugs or alcohol, most credit-card collision-damage policies will not pay any claims.

Another point to keep in mind: When signing the rental agreement, put in the name of every additional family member driver, unless the form reads that "immediate family members may drive the car." If not, any collision-damage or liability insurance will be null and void in the event of an accident caused by a driver not listed on the form.

If the Car Breaks Down

You'll find that generally the larger rental car companies are more helpful than the smaller ones if your car breaks down. Regardless of who rented you the car, however, you're not financially responsible. Most rental companies pay for towing and mechanical repairs. An exception: breakdown due to off-the-road or illegal use of the car.

Before leaving the car-rental office, always ask for the phone number to call in case of trouble. Also jot down the license number and color of the car so that you can find it in a big parking lot or report it if it's stolen.

If you do break down, check the agreement (given to you when you rented the car or in the glove compartment) and follow the directions. In all cases notify the rental agency as soon as possible. Never make repairs until you've received authorization from the company. Self-defense: If you're in a remote spot or foreign country and you simply must make repairs, keep all receipts for reimbursement.

Paying for Gas

Rental companies continually change the rules on who pays for the gas. Ask if it is to your advantage to return the car with a full tank of gas.

SMART TIPS FOR CAR RENTERS

Here are sixteen smart tips to keep in mind when you rent a car.

1. *Don't rent* if you're simply going to go to one place, such as a hotel. Instead take the hotel shuttle, a cab, a limo, or public transportation.

2. *Start with your travel agent.* Your travel agent can scan computerized reservation systems for low rental prices and short-term deals. Some larger firms give travel agents discount coupons good for up to 20 percent off at hotels, free car upgrades, and, occasionally, 10 percent off rental rates. Ask your agent, too, about fly-drive packages.

3. *Reserve small.* Rental companies tend to have more large-sized models on hand than smaller ones. That means there's a good chance that if you reserve a compact at the cheaper rate, it will not be available when you arrive. Then you'll be upgraded to a larger car at no extra cost.

4. *Ask the rental company for the car with the least mileage.* This information is in their computer but rarely volunteered.

5. *Don't rent a car at the airport.* "Off-airport" car-rental companies don't have to pay airport taxes and high fees for being on the site, so they charge you less. Doing this, however, requires patience, as they're often difficult to find. Self-defense: Take the shuttle or bus to your hotel; check the yellow pages for alternative car-rental firms.

6. *Look for the little guys.* The feisty companies, such as Alamo, Thrifty, National, Agency, Enterprise, and Snappy, are often 10 to 20 percent cheaper than Hertz, Avis, and National. There are also companies not affiliated with the chains that may have even lower rates in major cities. Check with the local convention and visitors bureau in the city you plan to visit.

7. *Skip beauty.* You'll pay less for cars from Rent-a-Wreck (800–535–1391), Ugly Duckling (800–843–3825), and U Save (800–272–8728). Be prepared for a car that's older and has some dents or scratches but is in good mechanical condition.

8. *Use the right credit card.* Use a credit card that has a high or an unlimited credit line, such as American Express. Some rental companies put a hold of up to $2,500 on cards while you're driving their car around. Check the fine print in the contract where such restrictions are spelled out. This can put you at or over your limit, making it difficult or impossible to charge meals, hotel rooms, or purchases.

9. *Quote rates.* If you read about a low rate in the newspaper, move quickly, as these are often short-lived. When reserving, mention the ad and the discount code, which is listed in small print beneath the rate, or in the description of the terms and conditions of rental. Better yet, bring a copy of the ad with you to the rental counter.

10. *Drop names.* Always mention clubs or associations to which you belong, such as a professional trade or travel group, including Amoco Motor Club, AAA, AARP, American Small Business Association, American Bar Association, National Association of Retired Federal Employees, National Association for the Self-Employed, or any travel club, as well as the name of your employer or corporation. You may be entitled to at least a 10-percent discount. (Also keep the association or club's toll-free number with you in case you need assistance.)

11. *Check out the car before driving away.* You are not obligated to take the car you're given if, for some reason, it doesn't suit you. Have major dents and scratches noted on your contract, and make certain there is a spare tire, jack, and window scraper.

12. *Join a frequent-renter program if you rent often.* Hertz #1 Gold, Budget Frequent-Renter Reward Plan, or National's Emerald Aisle offer upgrades, quicker check-in and check-out, and sometimes discounts.

13. *Understand your insurance.* Don't fall for the rental firm's hard-sell tactics about collision-damage waivers that relieve you from financial responsibility if you damage the car. In most cases your personal insurance or your credit card will automatically cover collision damage, so avoid being sucked into buying the $7–$15/day CDW. Each time you rent a car check with your insurance company and your credit-card issuer, as they may have withdrawn this protection without your knowledge since the last time.

 Credit card companies provide only collision coverage, not liability coverage.

14. *Plan the hour.* If you're renting at or near the airport, book flight arrival and departure times for the same time of day to avoid hourly overtime charges that, if you're not careful, can mount up and be as high as the daily rate.

15. *Avoid late-return penalties.* Ask the car-rental company exactly what time you *must* return the car. Some companies give at least a one-hour grace period and then charge an hourly late-return rate. Some companies charge an additional half or full day for being just one hour over the deadline.

16. *Know the one-way drop-off fee.* If you return the car to a city other than the one you rented it in, know the price for doing so. It can be hefty.

Roads in Foreign Countries The most dangerous countries
for driving are Egypt, Kenya, Latvia, Morocco, and Turkey. The safest:
Canada, Denmark, Great Britain, Ireland. For information on specific countries, call the Association for Safe International Road Travel, (301) 983–5252.

PROTECT YOURSELF AND THE CAR
FROM TOURIST CRIME

Unfortunately, we've all been forced to come to grips with the surge in auto
thefts, highway crimes, and tourist attacks in and around our nation's cities and
even in some rural areas. Those driving out-of-state and rental cars are natural victims because they are apt to be carrying more luggage and valuables than the
natives. *Self defense:* Make your car look as much like a resident's as possible,
and use common sense:

• *Don't accept a car that has markings designating it as a rented car,* such
as the name of the rental company on a sticker on the license plate.

• *Ask for specific directions to your destination* before you leave the rental
counter. If you do become lost, do not pull over on the side of the road to
study your map. Instead, find a well-lighted, populated public place, such as a
service station.

• *Don't park an obvious rental car in an unprotected lot* or on a dark street.
Thieves target these cars for luggage and cameras.

• *Keep luggage and valuables in the trunk* and lock it.

• *Place your purse, wallet, briefcase, tote bag, and maps on the floor,* and not
on the front passenger seat.

• *Never ask directions from strangers.*

Small Is Smarter Reserve the smallest model available at the low-
est rate. More than half the time, the rental company won't have it available
and will upgrade you to a larger car at the same rate.

- *Never stop if a driver flashes his headlights at you.* Instead, drive to the first well-lighted and busy gas station or a police station.

- *Don't pick up hitchhikers.*

- *Don't stop to inspect damage* if you are bumped in the rear on a lonely road or even on a major highway. Instead, drive to the nearest police station or simply forget it.

- *Don't stop for a car with flashing red or yellow lights* unless you're certain it's a police car.

- *Don't drive home if you think you're being followed.* Instead, make a series of left turns. If after four such turns the vehicle in question is still following you, drive immediately to the nearest police station or busy gas station.

- *Keep windows and doors locked* when stopping at a red light or stop sign. Carjackers and others up to no good often prey on legitimately stopped cars.

Amazing Annual Car Rental Deal
Every year car rental agencies must move part of their fleets to the south or to ski areas during winter to meet seasonal demand. Look for ads in the newspaper. Our picks:

- Avis and Preferred Holidays' "See America" program. For around $300, you get a rental car, hotel vouchers for a week, plus one-way fare. You must pick up the car in Florida or Arizona and then drive to the Northeast or California, or vice versa. Your airfare home will be paid by Avis. For information call (800) 990–1919. (Preferred Holidays is Avis' tour subsidiary. Call 800–508–5454.)

- National Car Rental has a similar deal. Call (800) CAR–RENT and ask for rate code FLDR.

CELLULAR-PHONE SERVICES

A good way to protect yourself on the highway is to have a car cellular service. In fact, it may already be part of your telephone package. If not, it easily can be added for a nominal monthly fee.

The cellular-phone companies' emergency roadside assistance programs will send a locksmith, bring gas, jump-start dead batteries, change flats, and tow disabled cars—all for a monthly fee.

A similar service comes with most new-car warranties. Almost all auto manufacturers offer roadside assistance as part of their basic warranty. With this service you simply dial a special number and within minutes a tow truck rescues you. Exceptions are Chrysler, Toyota, and Honda.

Rescue service is also provided by the automobile clubs, discussed on page 60. For example, AAA sells cellular telephones with a "safety button" that automatically connects you to AAA Emergency Road Service. For information call (800) 222-4357.

A POTPOURRI OF SMART DRIVING TIPS

1. *Pump your own gas.* You'll save about 14 cents per gallon on all octane levels. If you're disabled, you still get the discount, although the attendant does the pumping.

2. *Drive under the speed limit.* You'll conserve gas and avoid expensive speeding tickets.

3. *Don't overload the carrier* on the top of the car. It can lower your gas mileage and be hazardous in a high wind.

4. *Carry a picnic basket, an ice chest, or a thermos* to cut food costs.

5. *Use a reliable gas station.* Premium gas isn't always premium. AAA estimates that as much as half the time, octane is lower than claimed on premium pumps. Very few states conduct gasoline quality tests on a regular basis.

6. *Remember:* The majority of accidents take place in good weather when people are not exercising the same degree of caution as they do during fog, rain, snow, or storms.

An International License Watch out for Internet sites that charge up to $300 for an international license. From an authorized site it's only $10. Web sites are catering to motorists with bad driving records. The State Department authorizes only two sources of international licenses:

- *AAA:* (800) 222–4357
- *American Touring Alliance:* (650) 294–7000

DRIVING AND RENTING ABROAD

You'll find that driving in a foreign country is not quite the same as it is at home, but then, that's why you're going there—to experience something different. For example, air conditioning and automatic transmissions are not standard in European rental cars except on expensive luxury models. You can get them but they cost extra. Gasoline is much more expensive, often $5.00 a gallon.

Travel Trivia: Enlightened Auto Travel A study by Avis discovered that motorists who drive with headlights on during the day have fewer severe accidents than those with no lights on. Damage severity in the non-light group was 69 percent greater than in the group with cars with lights on.

Most European countries recognize a U.S. driver's license, but in Greece, Hungary, Russia, and Spain you'll need an International Driving Permit, which is valid for one year. Start the paperwork about a month in advance by calling your local AAA office or (800) AAA–HELP for the necessary forms. You'll need your license, two passport-type photographs, and $10.

Note: You cannot drive a rental car in China, Egypt, or Nepal; they come with chauffeurs.

Here's what you need to know.

- *Rent in the United States.* You'll save up to 50 percent over renting in a foreign country. You might save even more if you prepay here in dollars. You can rent foreign cars from U.S. rental companies—such as Alamo, Avis, Budget, Hertz, Payless, Kemwel, and Thrifty—as well as from tour operators—such as Auto Europe, Europe by Car, and DER Tours.

- *Ask about the following;* regardless whom you rent from: air conditioning, shift or automatic, size, payment up front or at end, return fees, VAT rate, country-to-country, driver age requirement, U.S. or international driver's license.

- *Let the agent know* how many people there will be as well as how much luggage. Some European models are very small, especially by American standards.

Know Left from Right Drive on the left side of the road in England, Australia, Japan, and Jamaica.

- *Know if you're insured.* Your auto insurance and credit-card coverage may not extend overseas.

Handy Reference:
THE LEADING CAR RENTAL FIRMS

AIRLINE	PHONE NUMBER	WEB ADDRESS
Alamo	(800) 522–9696	www.goalamo.com
Auto Europe	(800) 223–5555	www.autoeurope.com
Avis	(800) 331–1084	www.avis.com
Budget	(800) 472–3325	www.budgetrentacar.com
DER Tours	(800) 782–2424	www.dertravel.com
European Car	(800) 535–3303	
Europe by Car	(800) 223–1516	www.europebycar.com
Hertz	(800) 654–3001	www.hertz.com
ITS	(800) 521–0643	www.its-cars-hotels.com
Kemwel/Holiday	(800) 678–0678	www.kemwel.com
Payless	(800) 237 2804	www.paylesscar.com
Thrifty	(800) 331–9111	www.thrifty.com

Our favorites for low rates: Kemwel and Auto Europe. Auto Europe, with more than 4,000 locations throughout Europe, guarantees the best rates; in fact, if you find a lower one, the company will beat it. It has car-rental counters inside airport terminals, but hotel delivery is also available. There's no cancellation charge, and rates are guaranteed in dollars. The company is also in the hotel business and has many excellent discounts.

A Freebie For a free copy of *Twelve Car Rental Tips*, which explains exactly what you need to know *before* renting, send a self-addressed, stamped, business-size envelope to American Society of Travel Agents, 101 King Street, Alexandria, VA 22314.

OVERSEAS MOTOR-HOME TOURS

If you want to see the world in an RV, contact Overseas Motorhome Tours in Redondo Beach, California, at (800) 322–2127. They have organized tours in Europe, with reasonably priced round-trip airfare from the East Coast. Most are planned so that you do your own driving and simply wind up at the same place with others by evening. The company will also design and conduct tours for groups of twenty-four or more people.

Recently, a one-month trip with round-trip airfare from East Coast cities, with everything included, was $4,000.

Rent an RV or Motorhome before buying one. Take a weekend trip or spend a few days at a campsite. Free information is available from Recreation Vehicle Industry Association, Box 2999, Reston, VA 20195.

DRIVING SOMEONE ELSE'S CAR

Driving another person's car is definitely a cheap way to see the country, but first you have to find someone who needs to have his or her car driven from point A to point B. Of course this person could have the car transported by truck or train, but that's expensive. The inexpensive alternative is *you*.

There are three basic systems.

1. The first, known as the *direct* method, involves placing a classified ad in a newspaper under the heading "Driver Available," offering to drive to, say, the West Coast or to Memphis; or alternatively, reading the ads run by those who are looking for a driver, which are usually found under the heading "Car Transport" or "Auto Transport." The two of you then make the deal directly. Usually no money changes hands. You pay for the gas, and the two of you will determine who pays for repairs and tolls. Have your agreement in writing.

2. A variation on this theme is called *exchange transportation*. This occurs when the owner of the car goes with you to share expenses and driving. You can find out about exchange deals by reading notices on office, school, and college bulletin boards and by checking the classified ads in the newspapers.

3. The third method, *drive-away*, is somewhat more complicated and is run by agencies that transport cars for owners. These agencies are listed in the yellow pages under "Automobile Transport," or "Drive-Away Companies." Contact the agency, tell them where and when you'd like to go, and they'll let you know if they have a car going your way. You must have a valid license, several other forms of identification, and references. You will be required to leave a deposit, which will be returned at the end of the trip. You pay for your own gas and lodging, and while you can route your own trip, you cannot exceed a certain odometer mileage for the given distance.

Buying a Car Abroad

You can save about 10 percent off the cost of a Volvo, BMW, Mercedes, or Saab if you purchase the car in Europe and have it shipped back to the United States. You must make arrangements, however, with a U.S. dealer at least one month, preferabley two, in advance, to make sure that you get the model you want. The car must be built to meet U.S. safety standards and pass all U.S. environmental tests prior to shipment.

Save even more by purchasing the car at the very beginning of your vacation and pocketing what you would have shelled out for a rental vehicle.

Contact the following companies about buying a car abroad.

- BMW: 800–932–0831; www.bmwusa.com
- Mercedes Benz: 800–243–3876; www.mbusa.com
- Volvo: 800–631–1667; www.volvocars.com
- Saab: 800–955–9007; www.saabusa.com

Getting Someone Else to Drive Your Car

The Auto Driveaway Company, headquartered in Chicago, will drive your car from your home or business to your next out-of-town destination. Great if you're moving, or if you want your car on a long vacation. The company uses only professional drivers and/or very experienced, prescreened members of the public. Drivers pay for their own gas, tolls, motels, food.

Auto Driveaway has eighty offices in the United States and Canada. Check your phone book for the one nearest you or call (800) 346-2277.

5

Cruises: Luxury You Can Afford

The sea: a highway between the doorways of the nations.

—Francis K. Lane

You should not miss the opportunity to sail upon this highway. In fact, for many of us, taking a cruise is a lifelong dream. It's also a smart dream, for cruising is an incredibly easy way to vacation. You can visit different ports of call, have a carefree few days or weeks at sea, alone or with family and friends, and, best of all, you unpack just once!

Cruise lines have innovative itineraries and creative on-board programs tailored to families, lovers, gourmands, sports enthusiasts, naturalists, historians, gamblers, and party people. On some ships kids can go to day camp, babies to the nursery, parents to lectures, and everyone to the pool.

Hundreds of cruise ships are waiting for you to climb the gangplank. They range in size from several thousand passengers down to small sailing yachts, barges, and houseboats. You can ply the Mississippi River, the Caribbean, or the Baltic Sea. You can sign up for a three-day escape, a five-day crossing of the Atlantic, or a three-month 'round-the-world voyage.

Whichever or whatever you decide on, your ticket includes your cabin, all meals, entertainment, and activities. The ship lines are anxious to have you on board, and they offer all kinds of amenities to get you there: discounts, free airfare to and from the points of departure and return, upgrades to a better cabin, free precruise or postcruise hotel rooms, tours, and even credits you can use on board. After all, their costs are just about the same whether you go or not.

Nevertheless, beware. There are extra expenses, such as tips, shore excursions, and alcoholic drinks. (Check the fill-in worksheet on page 79.)

BEING A HAPPY SAILOR

To make certain that your cruise matches your dream, follow this strategy: Do some up-front homework and be clear about your personal preferences. If you need plenty of space around you or if you plan to spend time in your cabin, you must pick a cabin that is large enough. Many cabins are not; in fact, many are barely large enough to turn around in, let alone accommodate two people and all their luggage.

On the other hand, if you plan to spend most of your time on the deck, in the pool, or working out in the fitness center, you can save money by booking a smaller cabin.

If you're prone to seasickness, pick a large ship with good stabilization and a cabin in the middle-deck area. By all means avoid small ships designed for shallower waters and routes that cross open, choppy seas. Always ask your travel agent or the cruise line about this. Even whale-watching off the coast of California can be rough. Pick instead calmer waters: most of the Caribbean, the protected archipelagos in the South Pacific, Alaska's Inland Passage, the Pacific Coast, and, in the United States, voyages on the Columbia, Snake, Sacramento, Hudson, and Mississippi Rivers.

USING A CRUISE SPECIALIST

Ships also vary widely in terms of amenities, service, and itineraries, as well as the age and the socioeconomic profile of the passengers. If you read the brochure, you obviously can get a clear fix on the itinerary, the layout of the ship, a list of activities, and the size of the cabins, but the brochures never tell you about your fellow passengers. It's extremely difficult to ascertain the passenger profile, although quite obviously expensive cruises are paid for by people who can afford them. But is the cruise geared toward singles? Families? People from certain parts of the country? An international clientele? A party crowd?

 A good rule of thumb: Longer, more expensive cruises tend to attract an older, more affluent crowd, whereas shorter, less pricey cruises appeal to younger people, singles, and families. But the best ways to find out are to work with a cruise specialist, who can guide you in the right direction, and to ask friends who have taken cruises (see page 77).

Another good reason to use a cruise specialist is that you'll save money. Because there is no regulation of rates, different travel agents may quote you different rates for the very same ship, cabin, and itinerary. An agent who specializes in cruises not only will have the best deals but will also be familiar with individual ships and their character. These agents can often get you added amenities, cabin upgrades, and other goodies because they have extra clout with the cruise lines.

DETERMINING YOUR TRUE COSTS

Understanding Your Expenses

Although cruises are promoted as all-inclusive, meaning that food, on-board activities, drinks (nonalcoholic and sometimes alcoholic), and your cabin are paid for, there are optional extras that you may want to include in your budget. You'll enjoy your trip much more if you plan for them in advance. To avoid unpleasant hidden surprises, estimate what you're likely to spend on your cruise by filling in the budget worksheet My Cruise Dollars (see page 79) before purchasing your ticket and traveler's checks.

Handy Reference:
THE SEVEN TOP CRUISE SPECIALISTS

Cruise lines almost always offer discounts if you buy early or at the last minute. Even so you should shop around to find the best prices. In addition to asking your own travel agent, consult with one or more of these specialists:

CRUISE LINE	PHONE NUMBER	WEB ADDRESS
All Cruise Travel	(800) 227–8473	www.allcruise.com
Cruise Pro	(800) 222–7447	
Cruises, Inc.	(800) 854–0500	www.cruisesinc.com
Cruises Only	(800) 777–0707	www.cruiseline.com
Cruises of Distinction	(800) 634–3445	
World Wide Cruises	(800) 882–9000	www.cruises.com
Cruiseworld	(800) 321–2784	www.cruiseworld.com

LANDING A BARGAIN

All cruise lines offer promotional discounts. However, you may not be aware of some. Here are eleven ways to save money on your next cruise.

1. *Early Booking.* Most lines have an early-bird discount. Early-bird may mean six months in advance in some cases. Call the cruise line or your travel agent and ask.

2. *Alumni Rates.* Known in the business as "past passenger rates," these are given to those who have sailed previously with the cruise compnay. Discount: typically 35 percent.

3. *Regional Discounts.* These are determined by the city you live in. Given by the cruise line only to travel agents. Discount: 45 percent.

4. *Credit Card Specials.* Offered if you pay using your AmEx, Visa, or MasterCard. Discount: varies widely.

5. *Unadvertised Discounts.* The country's top producing travel agents receive piles of faxes every day from cruise lines offering deep discounts on unsold cabins. Discount: 50 percent, or two for the price of one.

6. *Airfare.* Cruise lines with air/sea rates do not always offer the lowest possible airfares. Have your agent check out discounted air first. If you book separate airfare, however, you give up the free transfers to and from the ship, but it may be worth it.

7. *AARP.* Open to people fifty and older. Discount: negotiated on a ship-by-ship basis.

8. *AAA.* Open to members of the American Automobile Association. Discount: negotiated on a ship-by-ship basis.

9. *Off-peak.* Cruising during the offseason . . . in the Caribbean rates are lowest during the spring and summer; in Alaska, very late fall. Discount: varies.

10. *Last-minute.* If you're flexible about the departure date and cabin location, get a last-minute discount—anywhere from a month to a week before sailing. Discount: 25 percent or more.

 To get a bargain on a cruise, look for a ship that's "repositioning," the industry term for when a ship goes from service in one area to service in another, say from the Caribbean to the Mediterranean. Call your travel agent or the specialists listed on page 77 to learn of repositioning.

Ways to Cut Costs

Here are ten surefire ways to cut the cost of a cruise:

1. *Be flexible about your dates.*

2. *Ask about a discount* for second person or children.

3. *Find out if there's free airfare* to the departure city. If so, ask what the fare is. You may be able to get a cheaper rate on your own, or use your frequent-flyer award to get to the pier. Then you can pocket the flight allowance.

4. *Get a price quote* from several cruise specialists (see page 77) and see if your travel agent can match the rate or better it.

5. *Tell about yourself.* Discounts are often given to newlyweds and couples celebrating big-number wedding anniversaries, as well as senior citizens.

6. *Look for new ships,* new routes, third- or fourth-person-in-cabin discounts, twofers, and rates for children and seniors.

Work Sheet
MY CRUISE DOLLARS

EXPENSES BEFORE BOARDING

Price of ticket $ _____

Toiletries, miscellaneous $ _____

Cruise clothes $ _____

Pet care (dog to kennel, etc.) $ _____

New luggage $ _____

Books and games $ _____

Hotel overnight before/after the cruise $ _____

Transportation to/from ship $ _____

Other $ _____

Subtotal $ _____

EXPENSES AFTER BOARDING

Hairdresser/barber $ _____

Spa/fitness fees $ _____

Telephone calls and faxes $ _____

Laundry/dry cleaning $ _____

Gambling/bingo $ _____

Alcoholic drinks and wine $ _____

On-board shopping $ _____

Excess-baggage fee $ _____

Postage and postcards $ _____

Photos $ _____

Souvenirs $ _____

Shore excursions and purchases $ _____

Tips $ _____

Other $ _____

Subtotal $ _____

TOTAL $ _____

7. *Book a fly/cruise or air/sea ticket.* These packages include much-reduced, or even free, airfare from most major North American cities. Sometimes the package includes a program with one-way free airfare when the ship starts its voyage in one port and ends up in another. Other times it includes free round-trip airfare to the point of embarkation and disembarkation. It typically includes transfers between airport and ship.

8. *Get free trip insurance,* if offered, to protect against sudden cancellation, lost luggage, or other problems. Most cruise lines sell such insurance at about $50 a ticket, but ask to have it included in the price.

9. *Travel in a group.* Put together a dozen friends or colleagues and ask for a group discount. Policies vary, depending on time of year and space availability. A group cruise is a great idea for family reunions.

Insider Tip Put off making purchases in the on-board gift shops. The closer it is to the end of your cruise, the lower the prices on clothing, jewelry, gifts, trinkets.

10. *Upgrade.* Large ships have some leeway in offering upgrades. If you think you can qualify, pay for the lowest-cost cabin. Nicer cabins and suites often go for the asking. You might be upgraded one or more levels. Upgrades typically go to business travelers, anniversary/wedding couples, seniors, frequent travelers, and members of travel clubs and organizations. Speak up.

Seasick or Bored Sick Carnival (800–227–6482 or www.carnival.com) will let you off at the first non-U.S. port if you're unhappy, but you must tell the purser's office before arrival. You'll get your money back—the prorated, unused amount plus airfare to the departure port.

Even the venerable old lady the *QE II* has reduced fares. For example, it offers a standby fare on its six-day voyage across the Atlantic from New York City to Southampton, England. At various times, when bookings are slow, Cunard runs a special deal in which you can bring a companion on this crossing for the price of full fare. Fares include all meals plus one-way economy airfare on British Airways between London and a number of U.S. cities. Depending on the grade of cabin you book, a special fare for a one-way flight on the *Concorde* from London to New York or to Washington, D.C., is also part of the package.

Who Has the Best
DISCOUNTS AND DEALS?

These major cruise lines, among many others, offer particularly good discounts and packages at various times during the year. Call directly, then check with a cruise specialist.

CRUISE LINE	PHONE NUMBER	WEB ADDRESS
Cunard	(800) 221–4770	www.cunardline.com
Holland America	(800) 426–0327	www.hollandamerica.com
Norwegian Cruise Line	(800) 327–7030	www.ncl.com-norwegian
Radisson Seven seas	(800) 285–1835	www.rssc.com
Renaissance Cruises	(800) 525–5350	www.renaissancecruises.com
Royal Viking	(800) 634–8000	www.royalviking.com
World Explorer	(800) 854–3835	www.lcruise.com/ worldexplorer.com

Getting Free Passage

Cruise lines are always looking for talent to keep passengers happy. If you fit into any of the categories they are looking for, you might get free passage and, possibly, a fee. Ships need experts in teaching and lecturing in foreign languages, finance and investing, botany, archaeology, gardening, gambling, history, golf, tennis, and bridge. At times they also need doctors and nurses. If you're a celebrity singer, a storyteller, an entertainer, a dancer, or a movie or TV personality, you may find a free berth.

A new category that might get you free passage is that of older, presentable, unattached men who are good dancers and willing to do the tango with unaccompanied women on board. It helps if you also play bridge. (For more on this type of free passage, see pp. 150 and 156.)

Cruises that specialize in family vacations need counselors—people with experience in taking care of and entertaining children from nursery-school age up through the teen years.

To apply, call any of the cruise lines and ask for the personnel department.

SLEEPING AND EATING

Choosing a Cabin

After you've selected an itinerary and a ship, your next important decision is the choice of a cabin. Go over the deck plan in the brochure very carefully, ideally with a cruise agent who is familiar with the ship. Don't be dumb and pick a cabin next to the restaurant or disco. Decide, too, if you want an inside or outside cabin. An inside cabin has no porthole and is dark twenty-four hours a day, but it is significantly cheaper than an outside cabin, which has a porthole or, on some ships, sliding glass doors onto a minideck.

 Study the cabin diagram carefully, noting the size; compare the amount of square feet with, say, your bedroom at home, to have a realistic sense of the space you're buying.

Another viewpoint: Book the least expensive cabin on the best ship that you can afford, rather than the most expensive cabin on the least expensive ship. Why? On all ships except the *QE II*, passengers have equal access to all the public facilities, and, if you don't spend much time in your cabin, except to sleep, why not?

Travel Trivia Skip the Eggs: A study by the Centers for Disease Control & Prevention found that eggs, served in a "pooled" fashion in large serving dishes, and undercooked shellfish accounted for one-third of the diarrhea outbreaks aboard cruise ships.

Dining Arrangements

All your meals will be on board (except for shore excursions), so you certainly want to be happy with your dining situation. If you want to dine only with your spouse or friend, make certain that the ship actually has tables for two before booking passage. Some have none, others only a very few.

If you are traveling with friends, request a table for your group; otherwise you will find yourself seated with strangers.

You will also be given a choice of early or late seating and whether you want to dine in a smoking or nonsmoking area. Generally, older people opt for the early seating and night owls pick the late one.

Your agent will relay your dining preferences and any special dietary requests to the ship when you pay for your ticket. In most cases you receive your dining-room assignment with your ticket and other documents, or a card with your table number and seating time will be in your cabin.

Note: If you find you don't care for your dining companions, ask the maitre d' to reassign you as soon as possible. It's a good idea to give him a $10 tip as an incentive for juggling things around. Don't be shy about seeking a change—you don't want to be "stuck" at every meal with people who are not your type—and, you never know, your tablemates may wish to dine with someone else, too.

TAKING SHORE EXCURSIONS

Shore excursions are, of course, not mandatory, but if you go, be prepared to pay anywhere from $10 to $150 per person, depending on the activity. The fee covers the cost of getting you ashore if it's in a smaller vessel. It may also cover guided tours of local sites, lunch or tea and snacks, and overnight shore accommodations, including drinks and dinner. If there's no planned on-shore program, you might want to join several other passengers and share the cost of a taxi ride to town or a guided tour of the area (this may in fact save you money over the cost of the standard shore excursion bought on board).

CRUISING OFFBEAT

Got a hankering to do something unusual? Read on. You'll discover that offbeat cruises are frequently less expensive than the traditional Caribbean cruise and even if not, they're always fascinating.

Theme Cruises

If you think that the standard cruise itinerary will leave you bored, try a theme cruise. It will add to your life, be it knowledge about art, wine, gardening, music, theater, or investing. You may even improve a skill such as cooking, golf, baseball, dancing, or speaking a foreign language. (See the table for a list of cruise lines that add purpose to pleasure; call and ask them what theme cruises they have coming up.)

Leading Theme
CRUISE LINES

Cunard	(800) 221–4770
Norwegian	(800) 634–8000
Royal Caribbean	(800) 327–6700
Clipper Cruises	(800) 325–0010
Delta Queen	(800) 543–1949
World Explorer	(800) 854–3835

Cruising without Leaving the United States

You don't have to fly to a faraway port to start your cruise, nor do you have to leave North America once you're on board. Here are some ways to keep your cruise simple and inexpensive:

- THE GREAT LAKES. During summer, the ninety-passenger *Mayan Prince* cruises the four Great Lakes as well as along the New England coast. Call American Canadian Caribbean Line at (800) 556-7450.

- MORE GREAT LAKES. Three ten-day cruises aboard the new 420-passenger *Columbus* sail between Montreal and Chicago on Lakes Erie, Huron, Ontario, Superior, and Michigan. All itineraries include historic sites and a stop at Mackinaw Island. Call Hapag-Lloyd, (519) 624-5513.

- THE HUDSON RIVER. The lovely yacht *Teal* cruises from New York City to Troy, stopping at famous historic landmarks along the way, including West Point and President Franklin Delano Roosevelt's Hyde Park. Sleep at The Beekman Arms, America's oldest inn, and at a peaceful monastery. There are six fall trips, each one week long. Call River Valley Tours at (800) 836-2128.

Insider Tip Houseboating is an inexpensive family-and-friends type vacation and no special license is required. For a list of houseboat rentals, send $3.00 to Houseboat Association of America, 4940 North Rhett Avenue, Charleston, SC 29405.

- THE MISSISSIPPI RIVER. The quintessential river cruise is on the paddle wheeler that goes from New Orleans to St. Paul. Today you can take the *Delta Queen,* an elegant ship (designated a National Historic Landmark), which does not have air conditioning, and the *Mississippi Queen,* which does. The food on both ships is quite good, the accommodations rather small and basic, and the entertainment not terribly sophisticated. Shore excursions to river towns, Civil War sites, and southern mansions cost extra but are excellent and really worth the price. The whole cruise takes twelve days, but you can take shorter segments. Call Delta Queen Steamboat Co. at (800) 543-1949.

- FLORIDA'S WATERWAYS. The seventy-two-passenger *New Shoreham II* departs from West Palm Beach, crosses Lake Okeechobee to Sanibel, Sarasota, Panama City, Biloxi, and, lastly, New Orleans. It has similar cruises on the Mississippi and through the bayou as well as a cruise that leaves West Palm Beach and sails to Rhode Island on the Atlantic Intracoastal Waterway. For information call American Odyssey Voyages at (800) 556-7450 or (401) 247-0955.

- *East Coast.* American Canadian Caribbean Line has three ships carrying eighty-four to one hundred passengers each that go on fifteen-day cruises from Warren, Rhode Island, to Port of Palm, Florida, and vice versa, stopping in Baltimore, Maryland; Norfolk, Virginia; Belhaven, Beaufort, and Southport, North Carolina; Georgetown and Charleston, South Carolina; Savannah and St. Simons Island, Georgia; and in Florida—St. Augustine, Titusville, and Hobe Sound. Call 800-556-7450 or log on to www.acclsmallships.com.

- *Alaska Drive/Cruise Package.* If you'd like to drive your camper or RV up the 1,000-mile Alaska Highway but can't stand the thought of getting behind the wheel for the long trip back, here's a solution. This nine-day cruise along the Gulf of Alaska and through the Inside Passage includes transport for your RV. You check your vehicle in at Anchorage for shipment on an enclosed ocean-going ship to Tacoma, Washington, where you pick it up after your cruise. For information call Gray Line of Alaska at (800) 628-3843.

- *More Alaska.* The Alaska Sightseeing Cruise West Company specializes in small-ship cruises that take you very close to sites on two dramatic rivers, the Columbia and the Snake, through Glacier Bay, and into other places where the big ships simply can't go. For information call (800) 426-7702.

- *Puget Sound.* The 59-foot M/V *Sacajawea* cruises Puget Sound on the Inside Passage of British Columbia. An informal atmosphere pervades, with family-style meals. You'll sail only during the day, so you won't miss any great scenery while sleeping.

 If you book a group of six, you can get a 10-percent discount. For information call Catalyst Cruise Line at (206) 537-7678.

Cruises Abroad

After you've exhausted local cruises you may want to test foreign waters. Here are some of our favorites:

- *River Barging.* River-barging trips are extremely popular in Europe and the United Kingdom. Although most of them end in late autumn, this company has two centrally heated luxury hotel barges that cruise in the south of France until mid-December and in Scotland all year round. The price of a six-night trip is considerably less in off-peak times than in the peak summer season. For information call European Waterways, c/o Le Boat, Inc., at (800) 217-4447 or (201) 342-1838. Other leading river-barging/cruise operators are KD River Cruises (800-346-6525), and Kemwell (800-234-4000).

- *Exotic Nature Cruises.* Take an elegant small ship and sail into very remote areas of the Arctic, the Aleutian Islands, and the Russian Far East. If you prefer to stay closer to home, sign up for a cruise along either coast of the United States or through the U.S. Intracoastal Highway. Naturalists and lecturers are on board. For information call Clipper Cruises at (800) 325-0010.

Similar first-rate nature-oriented cruises are run by Special Expeditions. For information call them at (800) 762-0003.

 Avoid the five claustrophobic cabins on the lower deck of the Sea Bird and Sea Lion; their portholes are almost useless for viewing.

- *DELIVER THE MAIL.* Every day one of the Bergen Line's eleven coastal steamers leaves Bergen, on the southern coast of Norway, and heads north, through a series of dramatic fjords, for ports within the Arctic Circle, and back again— a round-trip of 1,250 miles. Each ship carries cargo, mail, and a handful of passengers. You can go part of the way or all the way, and in between you can take interesting, inexpensive shore excursions. For information call Bergen Line at (800) 323-7436.

- *CRUISE ON A YACHT.* With Moorings Preferred Yacht Holidays you can cruise the Caribbean or South Pacific without chartering the entire ship. Book just a stateroom with a private bath and get access to the rest of the yacht, including the dining area. For more information call (800) 437-7880.

Windjammer and Tall Ship Cruises

Windjammers are sailing ships with auxiliary power, and passengers are allowed to help with the sailing. Sometimes they're called tall ships, schooners, or sloops, but whatever name they go by, they are much loved by those who prefer to cruise by wind rather than by motor, who opt for the unfurling of the canvas sail over the purr (some say churn) of the engine. These ships are found around the globe but are primarily centered in the Caribbean and off the coast of Maine. For the most part these cruises are less expensive and more informal and they attract a lively young crowd.

 Dirigo Cruises in Clinton, Connecticut (860-669-7068) represents a number of windjammer cruises that sail out of ports around the globe.

Before booking:

1. *Make certain you're not susceptible to seasickness*—after all, you won't be sailing on the stable *QE II.* Or take along appropriate medication.

2. *Talk to someone* who has been on this type of sailing trip to get an idea of what to expect.

3. *Gather as much literature as you can;* it will help you make a decision about whether or not this is your cup of tea, what the ship is like, and where you'll be sailing.

4. *Call one of the cruise specialists* (see page 77) or your travel agent, if he or she is knowledgeable in this area, and ask what the accommodations are *really like.* You may have to share a cabin or a shower; space may be very tight. If you need privacy, make certain you can indeed have it ... and at what price.

Tall Ship Companies

Here are the leading companies to contact for further information. Do so six months in advance of your vacation, if possible; otherwise add your name to the waiting list.

CRUISE LINE	PHONE NUMBER	WEB ADDRESS
Ocean Voyages, Sausalito, CA	(415) 332–4681	www.oceanvoyages.com
Windjammer Barefoot Cruises, Miami, FL	(800) 327–2601	www.windjammer.com
Maine Windjammer Association, Blue Hill, ME	(800) 807–WIND	www.sailmainecoast.com
Tall Ship Adventures, Aurora, CO	(800) 662–0090	www.tallshipadventures.com
Star Clippers, Coral Gables, FL	(800) 442–0551	www.starclippers.com
Yankee Schooner Cruises, Camden, ME	(800) 255–4449	www.roseway.com

Freighter Travel

Sailing by tramp steamer, as freighters were once called, is somewhat less romantic than the term implies. Neither Humphrey Bogart nor Sydney Greenstreet will be on the voyage, nor is it any longer a really cheap means of transportation. On the other hand, freighter travel holds special appeal for those who love an adventure into the unknown and who are willing to forgo luxury and nightlife to accompany a cargo of bananas or diamonds bound for distant ports with exotic-sounding names.

Keep in mind that freighter lines are essentially in the freight business; transporting passengers is secondary. Their itineraries, although firm, are not engraved in stone. They can and do change their schedules, but you won't be charged more for extra days at sea. You simply need to be flexible in terms of time.

Be prepared: Cabins vary considerably, from small to outside full-facility singles and doubles, but none are in the four-star category. You may dine with officers or at separate tables for passengers only. The food will be plentiful but not gourmet quality. Entertainment is pretty much limited to reading, board and card games, videos, and sing-alongs, although some freighters have swimming pools and exercise equipment. An exception is Ivaran's *Americana,* which has gambling, a bar, and a pianist.

The number of passengers is usually twelve or fewer, because the presence of a physician is required on board when there are more than twelve passengers. Many have an upper age limit that varies from seventy-five to eighty-two.

Because freighters rarely advertise, you'll need to book through one of these two specialized agencies:

1. Freighter World Cruises, 180 South Lake Avenue, Pasadena, CA 91101; (818) 449-3106. This company acts as the exclusive passenger agent in North America for fourteen freighter lines.

2. TravLtips, Box 188, Flushing, NY 11358; (800) 872-8584, (718) 939-2400. This travel agency publishes a bimonthly listing of services, discounted trips, and general freighter travel information, $25/year.

 The firm also handles unusual cruises as well as inexpensive repositioning voyages. Ask, too, for copies of their free pamphlets.

You can also get ideas from the standard reference book *Ford's Freighter Travel Guide and Waterways of the World,* at your library, or for $15.95 from Ford's Travel Guides, 19448 Londelius Street, Northridge, CA 91324; (818) 701-7414.

Note: If you're single, you might like to know that Ivaran Line's *Americana* is the first and, as far as we know, the only passenger freighter with gentlemen hosts on board. These unpaid, unattached men (age fifty and over) will dance with, play cards with, and escort women who are traveling alone on shore excursions. If you're interested in being a gentleman host on a cruise, call (800) 451-1639.

FAMILY CRUISING

Cruises are ideal for family reunions. They let everyone do what they like. Because you can all go your own way during the day, too much "togetherness" is not a problem, when you gather together for meals. Among the lines that specialize in family cruises are Premier, Regency, and Carnival.

For telephone numbers and more information about family cruises, see page 120 in Chapter 7, Traveling with Children.

CRUISES FOR THE PHYSICALLY HANDICAPPED

Le Boat, Inc., operates vessels that provide facilities for people in wheelchairs and for other disabled travelers. You can go barging in France and yachting in the Caribbean. For more information call (800) 922-0291 or (201) 342-1838.

Insider Tip ADA Vactions (800–778–7953; www.vacations-plus.com) runs forty-plus cruises a year for people on dialysis, who need oxygen tanks, are diabetic, or have spinal cord injuries.

PICKING THE BEST INSURANCE

In view of the fact that you must pay in advance for your entire cruise, trip insurance is important. Should you have to cancel at the last minute, you could lose the whole amount if you don't have coverage. Cruise lines and travel agents usually sell insurance, or you can buy a policy on your own.

Before purchasing the cruise line's protection, study it carefully with your cruise specialist or insurance agent. Many are simply waivers and do not take care of all the likely reasons why you might not make the trip. Some, for example, cease coverage the minute you leave home, so if you become ill on the flight or the night before in the debarkation city, you'll get no money back. Others will not cover you if you cancel less than seventy-two hours before sailing. Find out, too, if there are any preexisting conditions that exclude coverage and which relatives are covered under "due to illness in the family" clause.

Two policies that have good track records are Cruise and Tour from Mutual of Omaha (800-228-9792) and Travel Guard from CNA (800-826-1300). The Mutual of Omaha policy, with $5,000 of trip-cancellation coverage, costs about $265 for one person. Travel Guard provides $5,000 in trip-cancellation coverage for $310.

TIPPING JUST RIGHT

Unless tipping is included in the price of your cruise (in which case it's called an all-inclusive cruise, and you'll be told), you are expected to tip all those who helped you during the voyage, with the exception of the ship's captain and its officers.

Traditional thinking is to tip everyone the last night on board. We disagree. You're much more likely to obtain good service if you tip as you go along (remember: the word *tip* stands for "to insure promptness").

Cruise lines have printed guidelines suggesting how much to tip. This information is usually left in your cabin. If not, request a copy from the purser's office. Do so on the first, not the last, day. Then make it a point to give a portion of the total amount recommended to each person as they initially help you: the maître d' the first evening, the cabin steward when he or she does something useful, and the wine steward and your waiter at the end of the first dinner. Depending on the length of the cruise, tip everyone yet again halfway through the voyage and on the final day.

The recommended amounts on most cruise lines are $3.50 a day each for your waiter and your cabin steward and $1.50 a day for the busboy. This is absolute minimum; if they are particularly good, be more generous. They depend heavily on tips. If you order wine on a regular basis, tip the sommelier, or wine steward (usually $1.00 per bottle), and do the same for the bartender, hairdresser or barber, and staff in the spa and fitness center—and don't forget, upon arriving and leaving the ship, to give the baggage handler at least $1.00 to $2.00 per bag.

 Because it is improper to tip the captain and officers, we recommend writing a thank-you note, telling them what you liked in particular about their ship. Be extra nice and mention any outstanding staff members by name.

6
Good Deals on a
Good Night's Sleep

Hotel: A refuge from home life.

—George Bernard Shaw

M ost travelers would probably agree with this definition, as long as they can find the right ones at the right price—something that's not always easy to do. An inside look at the hospitality industry will help you see things the same way as old George.

Obviously hotels and resorts in prime areas charge the highest rates, and their facilities—swimming pools, spas, fitness clubs, marinas, and the like—raise the price per room. Exceptions to this rule of thumb are hotels with successful casinos on the premises. Their gaming take helps pay the mortgage and salaries, so rates are often somewhat lower. Regardless of whether or not hotels or motels have casinos, or where they're located or how gorgeous or shabby they are, every single one of them has something in common: perishability. This means that any night a room is empty, the revenue is lost and gone forever. This factor accounts for why lodgings of all types turn themselves inside out not to have vacant rooms, and knowing this can make you a shrewder, more confident consumer and negotiator.

GETTING THE BEST RATES

Here's the inside scoop on getting the best rates at hotels, motels, and resorts.

- *Never accept the first rate offered.* Always ask about specials. Do it with a smile and when the front-desk person is not busy with another guest.

- *Don't drag huge pieces of heavy luggage into the lobby* and then try to bargain. A smart hotel clerk knows you're a prisoner of your bags and that it's highly unlikely you will go elsewhere, regardless of the room rates.

- *Call early.* As your arrival date nears, the demand for that room typically increases, and any discounted rate is closed out, leaving only the rack rate (hotel jargon for full rate). It always pays to book your room well in advance.

- *Call direct.* If you call the 800 toll-free chain reservation number, you will be quoted only rates authorized by the chain. The operator simply reads them off a screen and has no authority to negotiate and may not even know about special discounts. So call the hotel directly and deal directly with the manager. *Note:* At times the 800-number operator may tell you the hotel has no vacancies when in reality it may not be full at all. This is because many of the huge chains allot a limited number of rooms to the central reservation system. If you're told there's no room at the inn, call the inn directly.

- *Avoid rate add-ons.* Special requests, such as a pool or beach view, are usually more expensive than an ordinary room. If a special view doesn't matter to you, ask for the lowest rate possible.

- *Confirm.* Always get a reservation number and/or the name of the person who took your reservation. This information can be very useful should there be an error or if, when you arrive, you're told the hotel is sold out.

- *Super-saver rates.* Hotels often have what are known as "fall-back rates," which they will quote if they sense you're resisting the regular rate. They don't want you to "walk." Ask for super-saver rates, specials, discounts, convention deals, or weekend rates.

- *The AAA rate.* Many hotels and motels give at least 10-percent discounts to members of the American Automobile Association and other travel clubs. It's best to arrange this when booking.

- *Senior rate.* If you're fifty or over, ask if a senior discount is available. It varies with each hotel or motel but is often worth 10 to 15 percent off the rack rate.

- *Hotel membership rate.* Special rates are often available to members of the hotel's club. You may have to join before your arrival date. These are frequently the best discounted rates a hotel provides.

- *Government discounts.* If you're in the military or if you work for a government agency or as a government contractor, you possibly can get up to 50 percent off.

- *Corporate rates.* Business travelers should always ask for the corporate rate. Be prepared to show your business card or letterhead.

- *Frequent flyer.* Many hotels and motels have teamed up with airlines to provide discounts for frequent-flyer members. If you are a frequent-flyer member, mention it when booking.

- *Convention rates.* When large sporting groups or conventioneers come to a city, the local convention and visitor's bureau usually organizes discounts at the major hotels. Always tell the reservationist if you are attending a function in order to qualify for the reduced rate.

- *Shareholder rate.* If you are a stockholder in a publicly held company in the travel business, such as Marriott or Disney, ask for a discount.

- *Package rates.* Packages are used to boost overall revenue. They range from an overnight room with breakfast to deluxe golf, tennis, scuba diving, and family packages. They tend to be offered seasonally or on the weekends.

- *Long-term-stay rates.* If you are planning an extended vacation or are relocating to a new area, ask for a long-term stay rate. These typically require a stay of at least five to seven consecutive nights.

- *Good Samaritan rates.* Many independent hotel operators and some major chains give special rates for those who are experiencing hardship—such as visiting a family member in a hospital or going to a funeral—as well as for storm or fire victims or for persons who are stranded on the road.

- *Travel agent or travel industry.* If you or an immediate member of your family is a travel agent or works in the travel industry, you may get a reduced rate.

Sold Out? Maybe, but Probably Not

Here are some other points to keep in mind. Virtually every hotel has restricted periods. Business hotels, for example, are filled during the week but look for tourists on the weekends; just the opposite tends to be true for resort hotels. Also, check at the last minute for accommodations that were previously "sold out." The convention may have been canceled or the expected crowd didn't show up or maybe the home team didn't make it to the finals. Many "sold out" hotels actually have space available in a "suite connector," which is the living-room portion of the suite. If you're willing to sleep on a sofa bed, ask if you can rent the connector portion of a suite that's rented to someone else. Ask if there are any "out of service" rooms—the problem may only be a faulty TV set.

Finally, don't forget to look into small hotels. They may be more or less expensive but because they are less well known and not always a part of a chain, they are less apt to be sold out. They also tend to be more personal, often more charming and intimate than the huge business hotels. *The Small Hotel Directory* lists one hundred carefully selected hotels in the medium and expensive price range in the United States and abroad. To obtain a copy ($9.95), call (800) 327-3633.

WHERE TO FIND HOTEL DISCOUNTS

As we've stated, hotels want your head on their pillows. And just as airlines sell empty seats to consolidators, hotels make deals with discounters and publishers of discount coupon books. Take advantage of them.

Hotel Brokers

The following hotel brokers (also known as consolidators) give anywhere from 20 to 70 percent off rack or corporate rates. Always ask what the cancellation policy is prior to booking rooms through a consolidator.

Hotel brokers are to the hotel business what consolidators are to the airlines—they buy blocks of rooms and sell them to the public at a discount. You wind up getting up to 40 percent off the rack rate in most major cities. Some guidelines:

- *Some simply book the room for you.* Others require prepayment and then send you a voucher. Ask.

- *The higher the rack rate,* generally the better the discount. In other words, you save more by booking a Four Seasons than a Quality Inn.

- *Ask what the cancellation policy is.*

- *Check with several brokers* before making a final decision. And then, always call the hotel directly; sometimes you can get an even better rate—a special weekend package, an AARP or AAA discount, etc.

- *If you book directly,* you may get extras, such as breakfast, free parking, shuttle service to the airport or downtown.

- *If you belong to a hotel's frequent guest program,* you may get a better rate and a room upgrade.

Hotel-ese

Deluxe hotels have personalized, European-style service; fewer than 350 rooms.

Luxury hotels have mostly executive clientele; 400 or more rooms.

First-class hotels have primarily business and private clientele; up to 1,200 rooms

Convention hotels have large meeting spaces; 1,500 rooms or more.

Tourist hotels are chain affiliated or independent economy hotels without luxury and amenities; 500 to 1,000 rooms.

(Source: Lodging Index)

The Brokers

Accommodations Express. Books nationwide. (800) 444–7666;
www.accommodationsexpress.com

Branson Nights Reservations. Books only Branson, Missouri. (800) 329–9999;
www.branson-nights.com

California Reservation. Books only California. (800) 576–0003.
www.cal-res.com

Capitol Reservations. Books nationwide but particularly knowledgeable
about Washington, D.C. (800) 847–4832; www.hotelsdc.com

Express Reservations. New York and Los Angeles. (800) 548–3311;
www.reservation-services.com

Hotel Reservations Network. Books nationwide, London and Paris. (800)
964–6835; www.hoteldiscount.com

Hot Rooms. Chicago only. (800) 468–3500; www.hotrooms.com

Quikbook. Major U.S. cities. (800) 789–9887; www.quikbook.com

San Francisco Reservations. Bay area only. (800) 677–1550;
www.hotelres.com

Washington, D.C. Accommodations. District of Columbia area only. (800)
554–2220; www.dcaccomodations.com

Half-Price Hotels Abroad

The dollar doesn't always buy as nice a hotel room in foreign countries as it does
here at home. One way to keep the cost down when sleeping abroad is to use a
half-price hotel room program. You can do this by purchasing a directory of participating hotels or by joining a club that then issues a directory to members.
The major ones have more than 2,000 hotels. In order to get the discount, you
call or fax the hotel directly, usually about thirty days in advance, and give them
your membership number. If the hotel is not too full at the time you plan to
arrive, you'll get a discount. (Don't ask your travel agent to arrange this type of
discount as half-price hotels are not commissionable.)

Not all discounts are really 50 percent off. Sometimes you get 20 to 40
percent off, occasionally only 5 to 10 percent off. A small discount, however, is better than no discount at all.

Some discount programs are better suited to certain geographical areas than others. (Check the table on page 97.) Call and ask about the geographical areas you're likely to visit before signing up with any program.

SLEEPING CHEAPER

There are also places that offer really basic accommodations for only a few dollars a night that are not part of the organized hospitality industry. For example, an ashram run by Sydda Yoga in picturesque South Fallsburg, New York, has very low rates, but you have to get up at 4:00 A.M. to do an assigned task. Here are some other places with low rates and later wakeup times:

- *COLLEGES AND UNIVERSITIES.* Colleges and universities often rent out dormitory rooms and suites to tourists at low prices. As a bonus you get to enjoy the school's facilities—tennis courts, pool, library, gym, even an occasional lecture. Campus accommodations range in price from $15 to $30 a night. For a copy of *Campus Lodging Guide,* specializing in campus lodging, call (800) 525-6633 or log on to www.campus-lodging.com. The book is $16.95 plus $2.00 shipping. This annual directory lists 600 U.S., Canadian, and foreign colleges and universities as well as B&Bs, YMCAs, YWCAs, foreign study programs, farms and cottages, and home-exchange programs.

  For information on universities throughout the United Kingdom, contact British Universities Accommodation Consortium, Box 966-ATW, University Park, Nottingham NG7 2RD, England; 011-44-115-950-45-71.

Travel Trivia: Men vs. Women According to a survey done by the Novotel New York, a hotel at Broadway and West Fifty-second Street in Manhattan, men and women are indeed different:

- Of the people who locked themselves out of their rooms: 70 percent were women; 30 percent were men.

- Of the 30 percent who were in various stages of undress in the corridor: 65 percent were women; 35 percent were men.

- Men average two towels per day; women, four towels.

- Items men leave behind: aftershave and shoes.

- Items women leave behind: nightgowns.

- Who leaves a cleaner room? Men.

Half-Price
DISCOUNT PROGRAMS

PROGRAM/PHONE	COST	AREAS
America At 50% Discount (800) 248–2783	$14.95	United States
Encore Preferred (800) 638–0930	$49.00	United States, Canada, United Kingdom
Entertainment Publications (800) 445–4137	varies	Europe, United States, Canada
Access Development (800) 331–8867	varies	Austria, Germany, France
ITC (800) 342–0558	$49.00	Asia, South Pacific
Privilege Card International (800) 236–9732	$74.95	Caribbean, Bermuda, United Kingdom, Mexico

- *HOSTELS.* The American Youth Hostels at 733 Fifteenth Street, NW, Suite 840, Washington, DC 20005 (202- 783-6161), publishes a directory that's free if you're a member; otherwise, it costs $8.00. This organization publishes two other publications: *Hostelling International's Guide to Budget Accommodations,* one for Europe and the Mediterranean and one for Africa, America, Asia, and Australia, at $13.95 each. Historic Hostels, which describes architecturally interesting hostels, has a directory for $3.00.

- *BED & BREAKFAST ESTABLISHMENTS.* Bookstores and libraries are filled with B&B directories, but to get you started from home, send a SASE to Bed & Breakfast Reservation Services Worldwide, Inc., Box 14841, Baton Rouge, LA 70898; (504) 336-4035.

  If you want to book a B&B in the United Kingdom, France, or Italy, before leaving the United States, get in touch with Hometours International, P.O. Box 11503, Knoxville, TN 37939; (800) 367-4668. This agency will also book air and rail travel and car rentals. Prices, if booked in the United States, start at $26 per person and go up to $66 for the best rooms, including VAT, service, and a hearty English breakfast. Children under age eight are usually free if they stay in their parents' room.

 If more than three people book at the same time, there's a 7-percent discount.

- *RETREATS.* If you're looking for peace and quiet, you'll find that retreat centers and guest houses are oases of calm where anyone can recharge body and soul, whether single, a couple, or a family. For example, you can stay at the California Mission San Luis Rey Retreat Center, complete with swimming pool and spa, for about $35 a night. For an average price of $30 to $40 per person per night, including three meals a day, you can stay at retreats in forty-nine states and fourteen countries. Many retreat centers simply ask for a donation or gift. They all are church- or religious-affiliated, safe, serene, and often in extraordinarily beautiful settings. You do not have to be religious, however, to stay at one. Guest houses range from elegant English manor houses to cabins in Colorado.

  Check out 450 other inexpensive retreat centers in *U.S. & Worldwide Guide to Retreat Center Guest Houses* by John and Ma&ry Jensen. Contact CTS Publications, Box 8355, Newport Beach, CA 92660, and send $15.95 (add $2.00 for first-class postage) or call (714) 720–3729. This is the only such guide we know of published in North America or Europe.

- *MONASTERIES, ABBEYS, AND CONVENTS.* Spain's General Office of Tourism, 50 Maria de Molina, 28071 Madrid, publishes a free list of seventy-five monasteries, abbeys, and convents that take guests.

- *MOTELS.* There are many cheap motels around the United States. They are often individually owned even though they have well-known franchise names such as Comfort, Holiday Inn Express, or Rodeway. When booking in person, particularly if the motel is the non-chain, mom-and-pop variety, look behind the clerk at the keys hanging on their hooks. If there are a lot of keys, there are probably a lot of unoccupied rooms, and you can get a good rate. Before you decide to stay, however, check the room: Is it clean? Does it have a phone that connects directly to the office? Is there a dead-bolt lock, a peephole in the door? Are the corridors interior ones, or can they be accessed directly from the street or parking lot? The answers to these questions should determine your decision.

Insider Tip Hotel Conxions (800–522–9991) can get you up to 40 percent off on budget to luxury hotels in Manhattan, even during conventions.

- *ALL-SUITE HOTELS.* These accommodations give you more room, privacy, and cooking facilities, often at the same price as a standard hotel room. They're particularly great for longer stays or if you're traveling with kids. They have, at the very least, a microwave, mini-refrigerator, and coffeemaker.

  The four largest, with 100 plus locations:

  - *Best Western,* (800) 528-1234; www.bestwestern.com/best.html

  - *Comfort Suites,* (800) 228-5150; www.comfortinn.com

  - *Embassy Suites,* (800) 362-2779; www.embassy-suites.com

  - *Residence Inn by Marriott,* (800) 331-3131; www.marriott.com/residenceinn

  Others:

  - *Aston Hotels & Resorts (Hawaii),* (800) 922-7866; www.aston-hotels.com

  - *Clarion Suites,* (800) 252-7466; www.hotelchoice.com

  - *Country Inns & Suites by Carlson,* (800) 456-4000; www.countryinns.com

  - *DoubleTree Guest Suites,* (800) 222-8733; www.doubletreehotels.com

  - *Hampton Inn & Suites,* (800) 426-7866; www.hampton-inn.com

  - *Homewood Suites,* (800) 225-5466; www.homewood-suites.com

  - *Manhattan East Suite Hotels,* (800) 637-8483; www.mesuite.com

Sleeping Cheaper in New York City

Here are four ways to save money when staying in Manhattan:

1. Every year the New York Convention & Visitors Bureau updates its list of more than one hundred promotional hotel packages. They include Broadway shows, sightseeing excursions, shopping discounts, complimentary meals, and parking. Rates start at $100-$135 a night. Call (212) 397-8222 for a free copy.

2. These New York hotels are clean but not fancy:

   - *Best Western,* 17 West 32nd Street, (800) 551-2303; (212) 736-1600

   - *Carlton Arms Hotel,* 160 East 25th Street, (212) 679-0680

   - *Excelsior Hotel,* 45 West 81st Street, (212) 362-9200

   - *Gramercy Park,* 2 Lexington Avenue, (212) 475-4320

   - *Herald Square,* 19 West 31st Street, (212) 279-4017

   - *Hotel Edison,* 228 West 47th Street, (212) 840-5000

- *Madison Towers,* Madison Avenue at 38th Street, (212) 802-0600

- *Malibu Hotel,* Broadway and 103rd Street, (212) 222-2954

- *The Milburn,* 242 West 76th Street, (800) 833-0622; (212) 362-1006

- *Milford Plaza,* Eighth Avenue, theater district, (212) 869-3600

- *Olcott Hotel,* 27 West 72nd Street, (212) 877-4200

- *Quality Hotel East Side,* 161 Lexington Avenue, (800) 567-7720; (212) 545-1800

- *Washington Square Hotel,* 103 Waverly Place, (800) 222-0418; (212) 777-9515

- *Wellington Hotel,* 57th Street (across from Carnegie Hall), (212) 247-3900

- *Wolcott Hotel,* 31st Street (west of Fifth Avenue), (212) 268-2900

3. Get a free copy of the helpful brochure *Nine to Five:The Insider's Business Guide to Getting Around, Getting Things Done in Manhattan,* which covers a myriad of things such as clean public rest rooms, small public parks, an address finder, emergency help numbers, what's open twenty-four hours a day, etc. Write to Manhattan East Suite Hotels, 500 West 37th Street, New York, NY 10018; or call (212) 465-3600.

4. Stay in a B&B in Manhattan. City Lights has rooms with bath that start around $70 per person; more glamorous digs begin at $100. Contact City Lights, Box 20355, Cherokee Station, New York, NY 10028; (212) 737-7049.

Late Check-outs at Chains

A handful of hotel chains realize that checking in at 4:00 P.M. and out by noon the next day is not much of a stay. These have addressed the issues:

- *Sheraton.* Expanded its 9:00 A.M. check-in and 5:00 P.M. check-out program to include any business traveler on a corporate rate who makes a reservation and is a member of Sheraton's frequent-guest program. Details: (800) 325-3535.

- *Crowne Plaza.* Guests can check in at 7:00 A.M. and leave as late as 3:00 P.M., if they're members of the frequent-guest program, Priority Club Worldwide. Membership is free. Details: (800) 277-6963.

- *Ritz-Carlton.* Has a twenty-four-hour check-in/check-out policy for its Asian hotels. Will expand to other locations. Details: (800) 241-3333.

- *Radisson SAS.* Will let you check out at 3:00 P.M. if you ask ahead of time. Details: (800) 333-3333.

LIGHTHOUSES

If you have an urge to sleep in a lighthouse, you can. Here are nine that will welcome you. Ask if there are kitchen facilities, linens, electricity, telephones, and showers, and get the specific location. They vary from very basic with no facilities to quite luxurious—you'll want to know in advance. Some are on paved, marked roads, while others are on off-the-beaten path dirt roads.

Point Montara Lighthouse
Box 7370
Montara, CA 94037
(415) 728-7177

Tibbetts Point Lighthouse
RR1
Cape Vincent, NY 13618
(315) 654-3450

Big Bay Point Lighthouse
3 Lighthouse Road
Big Bay, MI 49808
(906) 345-9957

Selkirk Lighthouse
Box 228
Pulaski, NY 13142
(315) 298-6688

East Brother Island Light Station
117 Park Place
Point Richmond, CA 94801
(510) 233-2385

Pigeon Point Lighthouse
Pigeon Point Road
Pescadero, CA 94060
(415) 879-0633

Point Arena Lighthouse
Box 11
Point Arena, CA 95468
(707) 882-2777

Rose Island Lighthouse
Box 1419
Newport, RI 02840
(401) 847-4242

Isle au Haut Lighthouse
Box 26
Isle au Haut, ME 04645
(207) 367-2261

HOMESTAYS

Here's an interesting and homey approach to sleeping around the world. A homestay is an all-inclusive travel program that includes round-trip airfare (usually from either U.S. coast), and lodging in someone's house, often with meals with the family or kitchen privileges or both. The typical homestay runs two weeks, living with English-speaking hosts in two or three different cities. The hosts are often selected according to your interests or occupation. They may actually be on vacation, too, so they can spend time guiding you around their locale. You generally have your own bedroom and bathroom. With some homestays, two travelers are placed in each home, although single and family placements can be arranged, too. Smoking and nonsmoking preferences are also taken into consideration.

One of our favorites is American-International Homestays, which has programs in Berlin, Budapest, Prague, Crakow, Tashkent, Riga and Vilnius, St. Petersburg, Moscow, Kiev, Bishkek, Beijing, Shanghai, Ulan Bator, and Irkutsk/Lake Baikal.

For a list of homestay organizations, see the table below.

Homestay Organizations

NAME/PHONE	COUNTRIES
American-International Homestays (800) 876–2048	Eastern Europe, Russia, China
Elderhostel (877) 426–8056	Europe, Asia, New Zealand, Mexico
Friendship Force, Inc. (404) 522–9490	Europe
Intervac International (800) 756–HOME	Europe
Servas (212) 267–0252	United States and eighty other countries
Visiting Friends, Inc. (409) 297–7367	United States

TRADING PLACES: HOME EXCHANGE

A great way to have a vacation and avoid hotel/motel costs is to trade your house or apartment for someone else's. In this way, you get to really "live in" and not just "visit" the city or country. The people you exchange with also may give you the use of their boat, country club, domestic service, and other nice things.

Begin by contacting the agents listed in the sidebar on page 104. For a membership fee in the neighborhood of $50 to $85, these agents will list your property, often accompanied by a picture. Here are some hints for first-time traders:

- Start planning about a year in advance.

- Write or talk on the phone to potential swappers in order to get to know them.

- If possible, have a friend who lives nearby take a look at the house. What's described as a castle could be something slightly less. Don't trust the photo.

- Be wary of swapping with someone very young or with groups. They may not be as careful with your possessions as you would wish.

- Ask about the location. Is it near a bus stop or subway stop, or will you need a car?

- Check your homeowners insurance policy. Are you covered for any damage they might incur? For any accidents they might have while on your property? Should you get a floater? Extra liability?

- Put any valuables and priceless mementos in a locked "off-limits" room or closet or in your safe-deposit box.

- Ask about feeding pets, watering plants, and what items you can and cannot use (and vice versa).

- Agree upon cleanliness standards and who pays the utilities—you don't want a lot of long-distance calls on your phone bill.

- Get in writing that your swapper will pay the replacement value of anything damaged; always get an up-front security deposit as well.

- Use the contract available from the home-swap network.

RENTALS

A logical alternative to trading places if you want to stay awhile is to rent. You can rent anything from a studio apartment to a country estate or a houseboat. Most agents specialize in a few countries, but the ones listed below generally cover wide geographical areas. Remember to book several months in advance. Europeans often reserve their vacation houses a full year ahead of time, and, to some extent, you are competing with them. Be careful about the nuances of language: A "ranch" may be a down-at-the-heels farm. Make certain you know if linens will be supplied and get the name of someone to contact if you need a plumber or some other repair. Be prepared to pay the full rent in advance, even if it's for a month, and possibly a refundable security deposit. Finally, find out what the firm's cancellation policy is.

If you don't want to deal with a broker, you can take a different approach and try to make arrangements on your own. Magazines and newspapers, such as the *International Herald Tribune, the New York Times,* and big-city newspapers, have classified ads. If you're a free spirit and don't mind waiting until you arrive in the country or city where you want to be, check local tourist offices for listings or book a hotel room for a day or two and shop around with a local real-estate agent.

For a country cottage in France, known as a *gite,* get a copy of *Gites Guide,* published annually by FHG Publications of Paisley, Scotland; $19.95 in U.S. bookstores. It lists more than 1,200 gites in English, with a picture of each and directions about how to reserve them.

Note: Two travel clubs that arrange luxury rentals for members are Hideaways International in Portsmouth, New Hampshire

Home-Exchange Agents	
Intervac U.S	(800) 756–HOME
Teacher Swap	(516) 244–2845
The Invented City	(800) 788–CITY
Trading Homes International	(800) 877–8723
Vacation Exchange Club	(800) 638–3841

(800-843-4433), and the Preferred Travelers Club in Lanham, Maryland (800-638-0930), which also arranges yachts, cruises, and hotels.

TIME-SHARES

If you've discovered an area you like, you may be able to buy a week or month's stay for once a year for the next ten to twenty-five years in a time-share program. These programs are available around the world for villas, resorts, and apartments. You pay a purchase price for the week or month plus an annual maintenance fee.

Before buying a time-share, check the classifieds in the local newspapers; you may be able to purchase the same or similar property in the secondary market for a lot less. Buy the best time you can afford—Christmas, Easter, presidents' birthdays—even if you have to pay a little more because it will make it easier in the future to trade or sell. Before writing out a check, talk with other time-share owners, the local chamber of commerce, and Better Business Bureau. Scam artists have found this to be fertile territory with naive, uninformed consumers.

One day your spouse or your children may ask, "Do we have to go back *there* again?" Then the bloom is off the rose and it's time to either trade your time-share or sell it.

To try a new area, contact Interval International (800-843-8843) or Resort Condominiums International (800-446-1700); for a fee these organizations will try to find someone with whom you can trade your time-share.

You can also try to sell your time-share. You may not get what you paid for it if the economy is weak or if you don't have many years left. To sell, place ads in real-estate or travel sections of newspapers, both at home and in the area where the time-share is located. The developer or manager may be willing to buy it back or to contact other time-share owners on the property. Local real-estate brokers may want to handle it for you on a commission basis.

Whether you are purchasing, trading, or selling, always consult an experienced real-estate lawyer and proceed cautiously, bearing in mind that this is not really an investment; it's an arrangement that guarantees you a vacation spot every year for a limited time, in a given place. That's all.

Read *Consumer's Guide to Resort and Urban Timesharing,* available for $3.00 from American Resort Development Association, 1220 L Street, NW, Washington, DC 20005; (202) 371-6700.

Major International
BUDGET HOTEL/MOTEL CHAINS

HOTEL/MOTEL	PHONE NUMBER	WED ADDRESS
Baymont Inns	(800) 301–0200	www.baymontinn.com
Clubhouse Inns	(800) CLUB–INN	www.clubhouseinn.com
Comfort Inns	(800) 4–CHOICE	
Country Inns	(800) 456–4000	www.countryinns.com
Courtyard Marriott	(800) 321–2211	www.marriott.com
Days Inns	(800) 325–2525	www.daysinns.com
Econo Lodge	(800) 4–CHOICE	
Fairfield Inn	(800) 228–2800	www.fairfieldinn.com
Friendship Inns	(800) 4–CHOICE	
Hampton Inn	(800) HAMPTON	www.hamptoninn.com
HoJo Inn	(800) 654–2000	www.hojo.com
Holiday Inn Express	(800) HOLIDAY	www.basshotels.com/holiday-inn
La Quinta	(800) 531–5900	www.travelweb.com/travelweb/lq/ common/laquinta.html
Motel 6	(800) 466–8356	www.motel6.com/
Ramada	(800) 2–RAMADA	www.ramada.com
Red Roof Inns	(800) THE–ROOF	www.redroof.com
Super 8	(800) 800–8000	www.super8.com
Travelodge	(800) 255–3050	www.travelodge.com

PLAYING IT SAFE

Nothing ruins a trip faster than being robbed, but by exercising common sense you can reduce your chances of being a victim. If you insist on traveling with valuables, be aware that a hotel's liability for items you place in a room safe or the hotel's safe is really very limited. Laws vary by state, but they are essentially written to protect the innkeepers from huge liability claims. Call the hotel in advance to discuss its policy. Make sure that the policy adequately covers your items. Also check your homeowners policy regarding coverage.

 Leave precious things at home, or in your safe-deposit box.

Anyone traveling alone, but particularly a woman, needs to take special precautions. Ask for a room that is in a well-lighted area of the corridor and, if you get in late, have the bellman accompany you to your room. When picking up or leaving your key, be extremely circumspect about revealing your room number.
Here are six safety tips:

1. *Don't flash cash, jewelry, car keys, or hotel-room keys.* Use hidden money belts rather than fanny packs for valuables. Fanny packs not only advertise just where your valuables are located, they also scream out: *Tourist!* So do guidebooks and maps.

2. *When leaving your hotel key at the front desk,* make certain that the hotel personnel puts it away at once. Better yet, unless it has a humongous attachment, keep it with you.

3. *When you leave your hotel room,* leave on one light and a radio or TV playing softly.

4. *Hanging out the* MAID SERVICE *sign* advertises the fact that you've left the room.

5. *Travel with a mini flashlight.*

6. *If a fire breaks out in your hotel, leave immediately* (provided the door handle is cool), taking your room key with you. If there's smoke in the hall, wet two towels and put them around your head and proceed to the fire exit. If the door handle in your room is hot, that means there's a fire in the corridor; call the front desk and let them know where you are. Hang a sheet out the window and then close the window. If smoke is coming in, close the space under the door with damp towels, cover your nose and mouth with a wet washcloth or towel, and stay close to the floor until help arrives.

International Rental Agents

At Home Abroad	(212) 421–9165
Barclay International Group	(800) 854–6636
Caribbean Destinations	(800) 888–0897
Castles, Cottages, & Flats	(800) 742–6030
Chez Vous	(415) 331–2535
Country Cottages	(800) 674–8883
Europa Let	(800) 462–4486
The French Experience	(212) 986–3800
Home At First	(800) 5–CELTIC
Hometours International	(800) 367–4668
Interhome	(800) 882–6864
Keith Prowse	(800) 669–8687
Landmark Trust UK	011–44–628–825–925
Rent a Home International	(800) 488–7368
Rentals in Italy	(800) 726–6702
Vacanze Italia & France	(800) 533–5405
Vacation Home Rentals Worldwide	(800) 633–3284
Villas International	(800) 221–2260

CONCIERGES: GETTING JUST WHAT YOU NEED IN ANY CITY

Travel writer C. Paul Luongo has the inside scoop on how a hotel concierge can get you what you want—and in a hurry. Luongo, who's dealt with a number of concierges over the years, has even come up with some things you probably never knew you wanted, but now you will.

Here's an alphabetical potpourri of what a concierge can arrange, obtain, or find out for you.

Appraisals—of jewelry, art work, antiques, etc.

Babysitting—for an hour or a day

Bagels—the best in town

Boats—rent everything from a canoe to a yacht

Business cards—printed in any language

Clothing—for any occasion, including costume parties, plus pressing, mending, and tailoring

Couriers—to deliver anything anywhere

Dinner parties—in the hotel, on a yacht, in a park

Discos and dancing—where to go depending upon your age and sexual inclinations

Emergency medical service—doctors, dentists, psychiatrists, podiatrists, acupuncturists, etc.

Escorts—to accompany you to parties or about town

Flowers and plants—bouquets, bushes, potted palms

Games—a tennis partner, bridge foursome, jogging pal, chess mate

Gifts—for any occasion, for anyone

Haircare—cuts, color, sets, perms, wigs

Information—on just about anything

Jacks—for an automobile, van, or truck

Jeeves—where to find your own butler

Jewelry—where to find it; how to get it appraised

Jogging—location of a safe track or route

Kennels—where to put Fido

Kosher—restaurants and food

Lessons—dancing, language, acting, etiquette, bridge

Limo service—to anywhere, if you're willing to pay

Makeup and/or massage—in your room or elsewhere

Newspapers—out-of-town, out-of-the-country

Notary service—in an instant

Off-site betting—with tips

Packages—pickup, delivery, wrapping, mailing

Pet services—sitting, walking, patting, feeding, boarding

Photographers—for passports or portrait

Quilts—and blankets and pillows (soft, hard, square, round)

Restaurants—selection and hard-to-get reservations

Religious services—time, place, and proper attire

Secretarial services—from typing to transcription

Soap—or perfume or cologne or oil—your favorite

Tickets—to the hottest shows or sports events in town or for a plane or train—even the *QE II*

Tours—around the city, behind the scenes, etc.

Translation—A to Z

Unisex—clothes, haircuts, etc.

U-haul—and storage sources, if you shopped until you dropped

Videos—VCR movies of your party, wedding, trip

Water fun—swimming pools and dinner cruises

Xeroxing—and printing services—twenty-four hours

Youth—playgrounds, trips, outings, activities

Zoos—from large to small

Following are five ways to ensure the best service at your hotel.

1. Stop by the concierge's desk and introduce yourself.

2. Tell him or her how long you'll be staying and what you might need.

3. Smile and be polite.

4. Give the concierge a little advance notice of your request.

5. *Don't forget to tip:* Although tipping is not required, you'll long be remembered favorably if you do; it can be anywhere from $5 to $20, or 8 percent to 15 percent of the cost of the service rendered. It's also smart and nice to call or write the hotel manager, complimenting the concierge by name.

As Jim Roberts, concierge at the Jefferson Hotel in our nation's capital, said, "As long as it's legal, we will do, locate, and go anywhere, anytime, for anything. No request is too odd."

So keep that in mind the next time you check into a hotel.

 Even if you're not staying at a hotel, you can use the services of the concierge, but make it clear up front that you'll tip.

7
Traveling with Children

There are two classes of travel: first class, and with children.

—Robert Benchley

Maybe so, but even if traveling with your family means forgoing deluxe accommodations, it can be a great experience. In fact, with most parents working, time off with the children has become a top priority. To meet this "quality time" demand, many hotels, the chains in particular, have geared up to cater to parents traveling with infants, youngsters, teens, and even older offspring, with most offering family packages and discounts, spacious rooms, and children's activities. For example, at Ramada Hotels, kids under eighteen stay free in their parents' rooms. Marriott Resorts sometimes have weekend family discounts and special programs for children ages five to twelve. The Washington, D.C., Hilton's "Bounce Back Weekend" package, which has been popular for years, includes many freebies and no charge for kids who share their parents' room. The two Holiday Inns in the Disney World area have free child care, activity programs, and kids-only restaurants. The Radisson Suite Beach Resort on Marco Island, Florida, often runs a "family" package with low rates for one-bedroom suites that sleep up to six and includes a supervised kids' program.

You can now even book child-proofed rooms with night-lights, diaper-changing rooms, cribs, strollers, etc. Many hotels also run on-site camps with adult-supervised, age-appropriate activities. Some even offer free food: More than 1,000 Holiday Inns give free meals to children twelve and under at certain times of the year and when the children pick from the children's menu and eat with their parents. Many Club Med properties have camps for kids, which are free at certain times of the year. Call and ask.

The message: Always ask about special deals for kids when booking a room or planning a family vacation.

ON THE ROAD WITH THE KIDS

Every summer thousands of parents pack up their kids and hit the road in search of the perfect family vacation. They delight in watching Old Faithful, climbing to the top of the Statue of Liberty, dodging waves at the beach, or riding a horse along a wooded trail. But to make your family outing really work, to cut down on bickering, and to boost the fun quotient, do some careful planning first.

Before Leaving Home

Here are seven ways to avoid snags before you even leave home.

1. *THINK ABOUT WHAT VACATIONS ARE FOR.* They give us a chance to rest and perhaps, more important, to move out of our usual patterns so that children see parents in nonworking roles and when they are relaxed and free from pressure. Vacations also provide a time to break away from bad habits, to improve oneself, perhaps by exercising regularly, eating healthfully, and even studying together as a family about plants, animals, birds, and wildlife. Or you may decide to take sailing or tennis lessons or learn how to scuba dive, cook, or ski.

2. *HOLD A FAMILY CONFERENCE.* Discuss previous trips and what worked and didn't work and incorporate that information into this year's vacation. Then go over the itinerary with everyone so that there won't be any surprises or false expectations. Discuss how you'll travel, where you'll stay, and what the family budget can accommodate. Let each child list two or three things he or she really wants to do while on the family vacation. Give teenagers special attention, making certain that they have time to be on their own, without your watching them every minute. They not only need time with other teens, they need time alone as well, even if it's just to sleep late one or two mornings.

3. *DRAW UP A BUDGET.* In addition to doing a family budget, decide with your children how much money they can spend. Will you give them a lump sum? Are they expected to use their allowance? Who will buy the T-shirts, souvenirs, and snacks? What will you do if a child runs through his or her money before the vacation is half over?

4. *READ Miles of Smiles: 101 Great Car Games & Activities* by Carole Meyers. To obtain a copy ($8.95 plus $3.50 shipping), write to Carousel Press, Box 6038, Berkeley, CA 94706 or call (510) 527-5849.

5. *BRING JUST ONE SUITCASE PER PERSON.* Leave behind the family pet, expensive or important jewelry, huge hats, duplicates (one tube of toothpaste and one bottle of shampoo ought to keep the family in style for a week), and elegant dress clothes (unless you're going to a fancy place).

6. *TAKE ALONG* a night-light for strange bathrooms, a small child's security blanket, a Swiss army knife, batteries for Walkmans, plastic bags for wet swimsuits and leftover food, paper towels, children's aspirin and medications, sunscreen, foldable hats, sunglasses, insect repellent, calamine lotion, Band-Aids, iodine, a thermometer, Handiwipes, instant coffee, teabags, iced-tea mix, a

thermos, an ice chest, books, games, notepads, pencils or pens, stamps, addresses, and maps and guidebooks that kids can read.

7. *PACK JUST RIGHT.* When filling suitcases for a family vacation, mix clothes for all family members in each suitcase. If one bag is lost, everyone will have at least one change of clothing.

Once you leave home, smell the roses. Set aside time each evening to talk about what you did during the day. Let each family member describe his or her favorite event or experience. Designate at least one person to be the family recorder and keep a diary of the vacation and one to be the official photographer.

SURVIVING DISNEY AND OTHER THEME PARKS

It's pretty difficult to skip what seemingly has become a child's right of passage: at least one visit to a theme park. Thanks to the children's underground network in this country, by the age of four or five they know the names of the key players in the field, from Disney to Sea World. It's hard to fall back on that old response, "I don't care if everyone else is doing it, you're not." So once you bite the bullet and say yes, here's how to make your visit with Mickey or Shamu less daunting.

Step 1: Begin with a promise that you'll pace yourself. It's too grueling for little kids and older parents to take in absolutely everything. Investigate three- and five-day passes to the park and spend at least one non-theme-park day lolligagging next to the hotel pool or going to the beach or lake. Because it's pricey to stay at hotels inside the parks, look into one of the many bargain hotels that have sprouted up outside the gates—they can cost as much as 50 percent less. Pick one with a pool and minikitchen and then call the park for literature and maps.

Step 2: Check with the theme park, your travel agent, and friends who have been there regarding the least-crowded times of the year, of the week, and of the day. Generally, from opening to 11:00 A.M. on Sundays and from 5:00 to 7:00 P.M. any day are your best bets. School-vacation weeks are obviously jammed and are to be avoided if at all possible.

Step 3: Prepare an itinerary before you go. List the sites you must see (no more than two or three per day) and those you'd like to see, time permitting. Involve your children in the decision, explaining that you simply cannot see everything. This is a good opportunity to teach them about making choices. Look at the park map and organize each day so that you'll do things one day at one end of the park, etc. If you'll be there in hot weather, arrange to do cool, indoor, or water activities in the afternoon.

Step 4: Call to find opening hours the night before and then be at the gate a good thirty minutes ahead of time.

Orlando Hotel for Families

If you're thinking of visiting Mickey or the Universal Studios with kids in tow and you don't want to pay top dollar, check out the Delta Orlando Resort, located on twenty-five acres across from Universal Studios and ten minutes from Walt Disney World and downtown Orlando. It offers a lot:

- Free shuttle to the Studios, Wet 'n' Wild, Sea World, and shopping areas.

- Wally's Kids Club, with supervised activities for ages four through twelve, with day and evening events

- Free use of the nearby Bally's Health Club.

- Free swimming lessons, tennis, volleyball, saunas, basketball

- Kids ages twelve and under get a free meal with any adult meal purchased in the restaurant.

- Kids eighteen and under sleep free in parents' room

Rates for a double room are usually under $99 per night—about what an ordinary motel charges. For information call Delta Orlando Resort, (800) 634–4763 or (407) 351–3340.

Step 5: Eating can be time consuming and expensive. Have a good breakfast; carry snack food and in-between-meal nibbles such as popcorn, trail mix, fresh fruit, and juice in boxes. Eat lunch before noon or after 1:30, when restaurants are less crowded.

Step 6: Go over each child's clothing selections; dress in layers, especially if you won't be returning to your hotel or motel room during the day. No brand-new, flimsy, or high-heeled shoes. Take sunglasses, sunscreen, lip balm, hats, a folding umbrella if you think it might rain, and sweaters and bathing suits for swim days, plus a plastic bag for wet suits.

Step 7: Upon arrival at the theme park, show kids where the lost-and-found area and bathrooms are. Point out what the guards and police look like. Each child should carry an ID card, with his or her name and the hotel name and phone number, pinned inside a pocket. You should note what each child is wearing and carry a photograph of the child.

ORLANDO: BEYOND MICKEY

Thousands of tourists pour into Orlando and central Florida every day, primarily flocking to the famous theme parks located there. Long lines, high hotel prices, and hot weather can make these trips less than 100 percent joyful. Our insider's tip: Look for fun beyond Mickey. Here are some suggestions.

Disney Institute

Located on the Disney "campus" in Lake Buena Vista outside Orlando, the Disney Institute gives you a chance to participate in more than eighty hands-on learning programs, from cooking to basketball. Kids are divided into two age groups—seven to ten and eleven to fifteen—and get to participate in such activities as day trips to Epcot and other theme parks, art labs, learning to be a radio DJ, and rock climbing.

There's also an artist-in-residence program that gives you the opportunity to learn from well-known movie directors, composers, authors, and scientists. Figure around $1,100 for two people for three nights. The fee includes hotel room, tuition, taxes; a meal plan is available.

For accommodations call (800) 282-9282; for classes call (800) 496-6337.

Dinner Theaters

Orlando has a number of these, each with a different theme. The prices range from $35 to $40 per person, including four-course dinners, unlimited drinks, and entertainment. You can check the phone book or get a list from the Convention & Visitor's Bureau, but to give you some idea, here are several.

- Arabian Nights, (407) 239-9223

- Capone's Dinner, (407) 397-2378

- King Henry's Feast, (407) 351-5151

- Medieval Times, (800) 229-8300

- Murder Watch Mystery, (407) 828-4444

- Wild Bill's West, (407) 351-5151

On the Water

Although Orlando is not on the ocean or gulf, there are some little-known, delightful cruises on nearby lakes and canals. Call for details about lunch, dinner, and specials:

- *Dead River & Canal,* Heritage Lake Cruises; (352) 343-4337

- *Winter Park Lake & Canal Cruise,* Scenic Boat Tours; (407) 644-4056
- LA REINA ON LAKE HARRIS, Mission Inn Marina; (352) 324-3101

Museums and Zoos

Several museums are nearby and well worth a visit.

- FLYING TIGERS WARBIRD MUSEUM. Specializes in World War II aircraft. At the Kissimmee Airport; (407) 933-1942.

- HOLOCAUST MEMORIAL MUSEUM. Library, research center, artifacts, films. Located in Maitland; (407) 628-0555.

- SPLENDID CHINA. Replicas of China's Forbidden City, Great Wall, and other sites; (800) 244-6226.

- ORLANDO SCIENCE CENTER. Hands-on displays, planetarium, activities. Located in Loch Haven Park, Orlando; (407) 896-7151.

- CENTRAL FLORIDA ZOOLOGICAL PARK. Native and exotic animals. Located in Sanford, north of Orlando; (407) 323-4450.

Six Free Attractions in/around Orlando

- DOWNTOWN DISNEY. Marketplace with paddle boats, playground, Lego. Lake Buena Vista; (407) 939-7727.

- EATONVILLE. America's oldest African-American incorporated community; churches, museums, exhibits. Ten minutes north of Orlando; (407) 647-3307.

- FARMERS MARKET. On Saturday mornings in downtown Orlando at Church Street; (407) 623-3200.

- FORT CHRISTMAS PARK. Replica of pioneer homes, a fort, picnic areas, softball, tennis, volleyball. About thirty-five minutes west of Orlando; (407) 568-4149.

- HISTORIC WATERHOUSE RESIDENCE AND CARPENTRY MUSEUMS. Vintage buildings reflecting late Victorian life. In Lake Lily Park, Maitland; (407) 644-2451.

- LAKE EOLA PARK. Swan boats, playground, picnic areas, cafe. Free family comedy program on the second Tuesday of the month; (407) 246-2827.

Family Resorts

You'll find that many resorts run family-vacation packages at various times of the year. All include a potpourri of goodies for parents, grandparents, and kids: free or half-price room for the kids, fitness classes, a children's program or camp, tennis and sailing lessons, hiking, cooking, nature walks, hayrides, bonfires, cook-outs, square dancing, and parties. Following are our top picks.

- *WINTERGREEN RESORT,* Wintergreen, Virginia; (800) 325-2200. Our most sophis-ticated selection is on 11,000 acres in the Blue Ridge Mountains, about three hours from Washington, D.C. Stay in houses, condos, or lodge rooms and enjoy two golf courses, a myriad of activities, plus a nature camp and a teen camp. The best views are from the condos along Blue Ridge Drive.

- *BISHOP'S LODGE,* Santa Fe, New Mexico; (800) 732-2240. This 1,000-acre ranch/resort at the foothills of the Sangre de Cristo Mountains has seventy-four rooms in several adobe buildings. The supervised day camp runs from 8:00 A.M. to 4:00 P.M. and 6:00 P.M. to 9:00 P.M. every day.

- *FAIR HILLS RESORT,* Detroit Lakes, Minnesota; (800) 323-2849. On 4,300-acre Pelican Lake. Noted for tennis, sailing, overnight canoe trips; lessons for all ages. Live in cottages or main lodge.

- *HOBSON'S BLUFFDALE,* Eldred, Illinois; (217) 983-2854. Run by the Hobson fam-ily, this 320-acre working farm, 70 miles north of St. Louis, accommodates eight families in three two-bedroom suites or in family rooms with bunk beds. Everyone is invited to feed the pigs and gather the eggs. Among the supervised children's activities are fishing, hiking, canoeing, and swimming. In the evening for everyone are ball games, bonfires, hayrides, and square dancing. (Has B&B guests year-round.)

- *MONTECITO-SEQUOIA FAMILY VACATION CAMP,* Sequoia National Forest, Los Altos, California; (800) 227-9900). On a private lake 65 miles north of Fresno, this camp accommodates up to 130 people. There's plenty to do: horseback rid-ing, an arts and crafts program, tennis, swimming, and kids' activities for dif-ferent age groups. You'll sleep in a cabin or lodge room with private bath.

- *ROCKING HORSE RANCH,* Highland, New York; (800) 647-2624. Just 75 miles north of New York City on 500 acres with its own lake, this ranch has some thirty activities plus a supervised day camp and kids' playground. Not only are there tennis, miniature golf, basketball, fishing, water skiing, hayrides, and pony rides, in the evening there's special entertainment for parents along with swing and square dancing.

- *LAKE UPSATA GUEST RANCH,* Ovando, Montana; (406) 793-5890. In the moun-tains of western Montana, overlooking a picturesque lake, this ranch runs a unique wildlife program in which your family can learn about wolves, elk, owls, and Native American customs. Enjoy canoeing, fishing, horseback trips, and white-water rafting. You'll stay in a lakeside cabin and dine in the main lodge. The ranch offers free airport pickup at the Missoula and Helena airports and discounts for groups, which makes it ideal for a family reunion. Plan a float trip on the Big Blackfoot River, inspiration for the movie *A River Runs through It.*

- *LUDLOW'S ISLAND LODGE,* Lake Vermilion Island, Cook, Minnesota; (800) 877–LUDLOWS. This rustic but well-kept family lodge is secluded on one of the 365 islands on huge, unspoiled Lake Vermilion. The lake, outside the town of Cook, has 1,200 miles of shoreline and is a four-hour drive from Minneapolis/St. Paul. The cabins, which range from one to five bedrooms, have kitchens. Enjoy sailing, fishing, canoeing, tennis, racquetball, and kids' activities.

YEAR-ROUND FAMILY FUN AT SKI RESORTS

Ski slopes and resorts have such beautiful and varied facilities that they make excellent family vacation spots in spring, summer, fall, and winter.

Summer on the Slopes

When the powder has melted and the temperature has risen, many ski resorts gear up for their second season. The fact that more ski areas are keeping their doors open in summer and fall means that you can book a chalet or lodge at cut-rate prices and participate in a wide range of warm-weather, outdoor activities. Call your favorite or nearest ski resort and ask about summer packages for families. You'll find organized children's activities, health clubs, golf and tennis programs, hiking, river rafting, and even outdoor concerts at typically 20 to 50 percent less than when the snow flies.

Our favorite family-friendly resort is The Inn at Prospector Square, Park City, Utah (800–453–3812). In the heart of the Wasatch Mountains, 50 miles from Salt Lake City, this quaint town, home of the U.S. Ski Team and Mrs. Fields' Cookies, turns into an old-fashioned resort in summer with plays, writers' workshops, biking, hiking, and golf. On the property: croquet, badminton, volleyball, tennis, racquetball, and swimming. The hotel has free shuttle service to town, a kids' activity program, teen outings, baby-sitting, and games for all ages.

The following popular resorts also have good family plans and are good values.

- *WATERVILLE VALLEY RESORT,* Waterville Valley, New Hampshire; (800) 468–2553.

- *VILLAGE AT SMUGGLER'S NOTCH,* Jeffersonville, Vermont; (800) 451–8752.

- *WINTERGREEN RESORT,* Wintergreen, Virginia; (800) 325–2200.

- *KEYSTONE RESORT,* Keystone, Colorado; (800) 451–5930.

- *SNOWBIRD SKI & SUMMER RESORT,* Snowbird, Utah; (800) 453–3000.

- *Northstar-at-Tahoe,* Lake Tahoe, California; (800) GO-NORTH.

All of these resorts provide baby-sitting plus organized programs for tots, teens, and those in between.

More Skiing Information

These organizations will help you locate ski resorts, bed and breakfasts, and inns, and will send you literature.

Aspen, (907) 925–1940; www.skiaspen.com

California Ski Industry Association, (415) 543–7036

Central Vermont Ski Information, (800) 223–2439;
    www.linkvermont.com/vermontskiinformation_central.htlm

Colorado Springs, (800) 368–4748; www.springslife.com/skiing

Killington, Vermont, (800) 621–MTNS; www.killington.com

Lake Tahoe, (800) 288–2463; www.tahoesbest.com

New York State Ski Information, (800) 225–5697; www.nuwebny.com/skiinfo

Pacific Northwest Ski Areas Association, (206) 623–3777

Park City, Utah, (800) 453–1360; www.parkcitymountain.com

Reno, (800) 443–1482; www.reno.net

Ski Central, www.skicentral.com (Lists over 500 resorts in the United States, Canada, Europe, Argentina, Chile, Australia, and New Zealand.)

Ski Banff/Lake Louise, (403) 762–4561

Ski Guide, www.ski-guide.com. (The ultimate guide to ski areas in both Canada and the United States, with information on resorts, lift ticket prices, road maps, where to stay, dine, and shop.)

Ski Utah, (800) 534–1779

Vail, (888) 830–SNOW; www.snow.com

Vermont Ski Areas Association, (802) 223–2439

Winter on the Slopes

These same resorts also cater to families when snow is falling, but at higher rates. Steamboat, Colorado, however, often lets children ages twelve and under ski, sleep, and rent equipment free, one-on-one per paying adult. For information call (800) 922–2722. At Purgatory, Colorado, kids twelve and under ski half price with parents any day of the week. This resort also offers midweek lodging specials and has other well-priced deals. Call (970) 247–9000. In Idaho, Sun Valley's "Kids Stay & Ski Free" program extends to age fifteen but excludes holidays. Call (800) SUN–VALY. At Okemo Mountain Ski Resort in Ludlow, Vermont, children twelve and under stay free in a condo, and kids six and under ski free. For more information call (802) 228–4041.

FAMILY CRUISES

Cruise ships are floating playgrounds for children, allowing parents and grandparents to spend their time doing adult things. Some ships provide free baby-sitting, whereas others charge an hourly rate; all have supervised programs for children from tiny tots to teens.

 Keep in mind that newer ships have larger cabins and more for children to do. These nine are leaders in this area.

- *AMERICAN HAWAII CRUISES.* During summer months children get reduced rates when sharing a cabin with two full-fare adults. Call (800) 765–7000.

- *CARNIVAL CRUISE LINES.* The "Camp Carnival" program is available year-round, with daily activities for children ages four to seventeen. Counselors must have professional child-care experience or a college degree in a related field. At various times kids go half-price or even free if traveling with two adults. Also offers baby-sitting on board and on shore. Call (800) 327–9501.

A Freebie For a free copy of *Family Cruising*, which lists cruises with special activities and services for children, send a stamped, self-addressed business-size envelope to World Wide Cruises, 8095 West McNab Road, Fort Lauderdale, FL 33321.

- *CUNARD'S QUEEN ELIZABETH II.* The *QE II*'s nursery is open from 9:00 A.M. to 5:00 P.M. every day; attached to the nursery is a playroom, which is staffed by two counselors. There's also a Teen Center, open twenty-four hours a day, with video games, a juke box, Ping-Pong, etc. Arts and crafts and other organized activities for all ages are supervised. The ship's library has a children's section. Also on board are radio and TV programming, basketball, paddle tennis, volleyball, and four swimming pools. To give parents and grandparents time off, there's a special early-dinner seating as well as baby-sitting at a nominal fee. Children who stay in a cabin with two adults pay less; the amount varies, so ask. Call (800) 528-6273.

- *HOLLAND AMERICA.* Recently tripled its kids' sailing programs. Ask about special deals for kids and grandchildren on this line's well-known Alaskan cruises— sometimes you can save up to 40 percent. Call (800) 426-0327.

- *KD RIVER CRUISES OF EUROPE.* In July and August, KD River Cruises lets children under fourteen, when accompanied by at least one adult, travel free on a number of the company's sailings on the Rhine, Danube, and Elbe Rivers. The line operates twenty-five itineraries on the three rivers, with a total of 130 departures during those two months. Call (800) 346-6525 (eastern United States) or (800) 858-8587 (western United States).

- *NORWEGIAN CRUISE LINE.* The "Kids Crew" program has separate activities for children ages three to five, six to eight, and nine to twelve, and for teens. Counselors are carefully selected from leading universities. Call (800) 327-7030.

- *PREMIER CRUISE LINE.* The Big Red Boat, the official cruise line of Walt Disney World, sails with cartoon characters on board—Mickey Mouse, Goofy, Pluto. It combines three- or four-day cruises to the Bahamas with several days at Disney World. Organized activities are offered for children two and older. Kids sail free at nonholiday times. The ship specializes in family reunions and single-parent arrangements. Call (800) 327-7113.

- *REGENCY CRUISES.* We like this line's easy and not-too-pricey "Family Reunion Package," in which all meals, activities, and entertainment are included. When eight adult family members cruise together, the ship hosts a free champagne Bon Voyage party and gives each relative a family photograph and a special reunion cake. If you've got ten or more adults, fares may be discounted; if fifteen of you sign up, a sixteenth relative can sail free. Regency also has occasional reduced rates for single parents or single grandparents traveling with a child twelve or younger. Call (800) 341-5566 or (212) 972-4499.

- *ROYAL CARIBBEAN CRUISE LINE.* Among this line's specials are a children's dinner menu for children ages four to twelve, coloring books and games, plus shore activities for kids. Call (800) 327-6700.

TRAIN TRAVEL WITH KIDS

Children usually love watching the countryside whoosh by, eating in a dining car, sleeping in an upper berth. On Amtrak children ages two to fifteen travel half-price with an adult. You should also investigate one of the many "Family Adventure" packages, whereby a family of four gets reduced fares and special hotel rates for overnight stays. The four most popular family adventure trips are Washington, D.C., to New York; Sacramento to San Francisco, Chicago to the Grand Canyon; and the auto train from Lorton, Virginia, to the Orlando, Florida, area. Although these packages are available year-round, the majority of them run through the summer and at holiday time, so book well in advance. Grandparents: Ask about the discount for seniors. Call (800) USA-RAIL.

Train Tips for Tots Not all children are always angelic when riding the rails. We suggest that you do the following:

- Bring drawing paper and crayons to record the colors of landscapes along the way. (Trace the route on a blank sheet of paper before leaving home, taking it from an Amtrak publication or an atlas.)

- Encourage older children to tape-record or write about their experiences in a diary.

- Bring a camera along for them to take snapshots for illustrating their diary when they get home.

- Have pens, postcards, stationery, stamps, and addresses to use for writing to grandparents and friends.

- Bring resource books, maps, timetables, and history books of the area to help them to keep track of how far they've traveled and what they've seen.

- Encourage your children to meet other youngsters on the train and to share games and toys.

- Let them dine alone now and then if they are old enough and wish to do so.

LIVING-HISTORY MUSEUMS THAT KIDS LIKE

A terrific way to teach your children or grandchildren about America's heritage outside the traditional classroom is by spending time at an "action" museum, where old-time skills and traditions come alive in authentic historical settings. Here are some favorite ways for kids to glimpse into an earlier America.

- *GREENFIELD VILLAGE*, Dearborn, Michigan; (313) 271–1620. On eighty acres outside Detroit, more than one hundred historic buildings are filled with contents that date from 1650 to the twentieth century. You can show your kids an original Model T Ford, Thomas Edison's laboratory, and the Henry Ford Museum with acres of cars, planes, and boats. They can also ride an 1873 steam locomotive and see the Wright brothers' bicycle shop.

- *PLIMOTH PLANTATION,* Plymouth, Massachusetts; (508) 746-1622. All children delight in peeking inside John Alden's rough-hewn house, with its thatched roof, and seeing where the other Pilgrims first lived, back in 1627. Take time to visit the adjoining Wampanoag encampment, where Native American guides speak about their history; then stop at the *Mayflower II,* a full-size replica moored a few miles away in Plymouth Bay.

- *COLONIAL WILLIAMSBURG,* Williamsburg, Virginia; (800) HISTORY. Located 50 miles east of Richmond, on 173 rolling acres. There's something here for everyone: Revolutionary-era relics, a restored Virginia capital, 500 historic buildings, museums, plays, tours, hikes, and games. Be sure to take the kids for lunch or dinner in one of the historic taverns.

- *OLD STURBRIDGE VILLAGE,* Sturbridge, Massachusetts; (800) 733-1830. This is an authentic representation of rural New England life from 1790 to 1840, with village schoolhouses, farms, and other buildings. Don't miss the Folk Art Gallery, the Clock Gallery, and the reconstructed 1830s Freeman Farm, where life before the Industrial Age comes alive.

- *MYSTIC SEAPORT,* Mystic, Connecticut; (860) 572-5315. Situated on the shores of the Mystic River, the Mystic area is famous for its nineteenth-century ship-building industry and whaling. You'll learn much about U.S. maritime history. Board several moored ships including the *Morgan,* an 1841 wooden whaling bark, and ride through the harbor on a coal-fired steamboat. A must for serious seafaring scholars is the Henry B. DuPont Preservation Shipyard. In addition to its one hundred vessels and exhibits of nineteenth-century homes and shops, Mystic has daily demonstrations of rope making, lifesaving, and boat building.

- *CONNER PRAIRIE,* Noblesville, Indiana; (317) 776-6000. Conner Prairie demonstrates what life was like on the frontier in 1836, with stories, craft demonstrations, conversations, and talks in thirty-nine authentic buildings.

- *LIVING HISTORY FARMS,* Urbandale, Iowa; (515) 278-5286. Here you'll find four working farms, each filled with old tools and techniques that take you through 300 years of agricultural history, as well as gardens, windmills, livestock, and solar-heated barns. All aspects of Indian and pioneer life are well exhibited. Located near Des Moines.

To learn what it was like to live in another era, here are some other good places.

- *AMISH AND MENNONITE FARMS*, Lancaster, Pennsylvania (call Mennonite Information Center; 717-299-0954). Visit actual working farms and enjoy homegrown products. Call for detailed brochure and map.

- *THE C & O CANAL*, Washington, D.C. Ride a mule-drawn barge—just as it was in the nineteenth century. For information contact the D.C. Convention and Visitor's Association, (202) 789-7000.

- *ROANOKE ISLAND*, Manteo, North Carolina; (252) 473-2127. An outdoor drama about the famous Lost Colony, which was settled by the English and "lost" in the 1500s.

- *KENNEDY SPACE CENTER*, Cape Canaveral, Florida; (407) 452-2121. Tour the facility or attend space camp.

- *THE HALE FARM AND WESTERN RESERVE*, Bath, Ohio; (440) 666-3711. All ages can study Midwestern pioneer life.

- *HENSLEY SETTLEMENT*, Cumberland Gap National Historical Park, Middlesboro, Kentucky; (606) 248-2817. This restored village shows how pioneer and mountain people lived in the late 1800s.

- *BOOT HILL MUSEUM*, Dodge City, Kansas; (316) 227-8894. Discover what cowboy life in the Old West was really like.

- *BROKEN BOOT GOLD MINE*, Deadwood, South Dakota; (605) 578-1876. An old mining town is now an enjoyable educational experience.

- *DURANGO & SILVERTON NARROW GAUGE RAILROAD*, Durango, Colorado; (970) 247-2733. Day trips with lunch aboard this authentic historic train.

- *TSA-LA GI*, Tahlequah, Oklahoma; (918) 456-6007. Re-creation of a Cherokee Indian village, plus a museum devoted to Indian artifacts.

- *RANCHING HERITAGE CENTER*, Lubbock, Texas; (806) 742-2498. Everything you ever wanted to know about ranching in the Old West.

PLAN A TRIP TO A NATIONAL PARK

Sleeping and touring our great national parks can mean roughing it in a tent or rustic cabin, or staying in a comfortable historic landmark lodge or Victorian hotel. Either way it's not only a great family experience, but also a way to see some of the United States' most spectacular and dramatic sites, and you'll find it doesn't cost an outrageous amount.

Keep in mind that most lodges in the national parks are open only from spring until late fall, and many are filled months in advance. That means you need to make reservations early; however, as with most bookings, you can also get space by calling on a regular basis and landing a cancellation—after all, people's plans change and last-minute requests can often be filled. Listed here are several of our favorite parks.

Glacier National Park, Montana

This park is the home of one of America's most spectacular drives, "Going to the Sun Road," a 15-mile dramatic experience that starts in West Glacier and ends at the Continental Divide.

 Vehicles over 21 feet long are not permitted.

All lodging at Glacier is booked through a central number: (602) 207-6000. If you find that there's absolutely no room when you call these numbers, check with Glacier Country Tourism, (406) 756-7128, for lodging nearby in Kalispell or Whitefish.

Insider Tip The National Park Services new on-line reservation system (reservations.nps.gov) lets you make reservations at twenty-six parks up to five months in advance. For phone reservations at many but not all camps, call (800) 365-2267.

Published every year, the free *Glacier Country Travel Guide* covers lodging and events in areas beyond the park and has useful maps. Contact: Glacier Country Regional Tourism Commission at (800) 338-5072.

Following are some recommended lodgings at Glacier.

- MANY GLACIER HOTEL, the largest hotel inside the park, is on the shores of Swiftcurrent Lake. Ask for a lake or mountain view in this Swiss-style building.

- LAKE MCDONALD LODGE is a cozy inn built in 1913, with cabins and motel units in addition to the hotel. Be picky about your room—the motel units have little character. Opt for the lodge and insist on a lake view. The dining room also overlooks the lake; if you're having lunch or dinner, check the hours and arrive early or late to get a window table.

- *GLACIER PARK LODGE* is more luxurious in style and has hosted many U.S. presidents. It has a golf course, a heated swimming pool, cookouts, and other activities, plus a playground for children and evening fireside talks.

 Another option is to stay on the Canadian side in Waterton Lakes National Park. The Prince of Wales Hotel, on a bluff overlooking the lake, is charming and feels quite English, with daily tea. At the Village Inn, every room has a view of Lake McDonald, although the architecture is dull.

Yellowstone National Park, Wyoming

This is a longtime favorite of Americans who love the geyser affectionately known as Old Faithful and the world's most active thermal area.

All park lodgings are booked by calling (307) 344-7311. If there's no space in the park, ask for the telephone numbers of local chambers of commerce, as they can often find you room in neighboring villages.

 September and October are the least crowded months. If you have children in tow, remember that those under age twelve stay free with their parents while those twelve and older are charged $8.00 per night.

Following are some lodging options at Yellowstone.

- *ROOSEVELT LODGE* is located at the western end of the park in a quiet area and is a favorite with horseback riders. There are nightly cookouts, a dining room, and bar. Rooms and cabins have views of open fields. Ask for one of the cabins with a wood-burning stove.

- *CANYON LODGE AND CABINS,* located near the Lower Falls waterfalls, has 600 units and a dining room and cafeteria.

 Mosquitoes abound in June.

- *LAKE YELLOWSTONE HOTEL AND CABINS,* built in the 1890s and listed on the Register of Historic Places, has views of the lake. If you don't stay here, have cocktails in the Sun Room or dinner in the dining room.

- *OLD FAITHFUL INN* is one of the largest log structures in the country and is a famous national landmark. It's right next to the upper geyser basin.

- *THE OLD FAITHFUL LODGE AND THE OLD FAITHFUL SNOW LODGE* are less expensive than other facilities, although both are farther away from the geysers. The Snow Lodge is the only facility in the Old Faithful area open during the winter.

Attend School at Yellowstone The Yellowstone Institute

has more than eighty-five courses for adults, children, and families that last one to five days and cover such topics as wildflowers, fly-fishing, grizzly-bear ecology, and mountain-man history. You can either stay in a cabin and share a central kitchen in the remote northeast Lamar Valley section of the park, or you can stay in nearby campgrounds and motels. Tuition averages about $50 to $70 a day. Courses that require outfitting, canoes, horses, or lla-mas cost more. For information contact Yellowstone Institute, Box 117, Yellowstone National Park, WY 82190; (307) 344–2294.

 Because of budget cuts, it is sometimes difficult to get information on the national parks. First, call the individual park. If that doesn't work, try the National Park Service's public inquiries department at (202) 208-4747. For maps and brochures, write the National Park Service, Box 37127, Washington, D.C. 20013.

Yosemite National Park, California

To make reservations, call (800) 967-2283 or (209) 372-0200. The four places within the park that we like are:

- THE AHWAHNEE, 1 mile from the village, and decorated in Native American style, has excellent views of Half Dome, Glacier Point, Royal Arches, and Yosemite Falls. In addition to the main hotel and dining room, there are a number of attractive cottages.

- YOSEMITE LODGE, built in 1915, is less expensive, but because it's at the base of Yosemite Falls, there's lots of tourist traffic. Ask for a room from which you can see the falls.

- CURRY VILLAGE has rustic, cool, shaded cabins that are not much advertised, so space is often available here when all other lodging is booked. The Village is ideal for children and those who like sleeping in tents.

- WAWONA HOTEL, another elegant historic landmark, is located just inside the south entrance to the park and has a golf course. This hotel has a stately, slow-paced ambience.

Tour the National and State Parks

Organized trips thoughout the West that include many of our national parks are run by Venture West, Box 17163, Milwaukee, WI 53217 (414–224–5440); and by Passport Travel (800–549–TOUR); and by Corliss Tours (800–456–5717).

More National Park Information

For copies of the following helpful publications, mail your order, with a check payable to "Superintendent of Documents," to R. Woods, Consumer Information Center, Pueblo, CO 81002.

- *A GUIDE TO YOUR NATIONAL FORESTS.* Map and information to help you plan your visit; $1.00. #136A.

- *LESSER KNOWN AREAS OF THE NATIONAL PARK SYSTEM.* Lists 170 parks, their accommodations, locations, and historical significance; $1.50. #137A.

- *NATIONAL PARK SYSTEM MAP & GUIDE.* Lists activities at 300 parks, monuments, and historic sites; $1.25. #138A.

- *NATIONAL TRAILS SYSTEM MAP & GUIDE.* Fold-out map of sixteen scenic or historic national trails; $1.25. #139A.

- *THE NATIONAL PARKS INDEX.* Lists all parks with addresses, acreages, and dates open; $3.75. #024-005-01094.

- *THE NATIONAL PARKS CAMPING GUIDE.* Covers 100 places with charts and illustrations; $4.00. #024-005-01080-7.

GREAT STATE PARKS

America's 2,040 state parks are largely unspoiled, undiscovered, and often less crowded than our national parks. They have campsites, fishing, hiking, cabins, boat rentals, sailing, and a host of activities. Call your state's department of tourism for a list.

The twelve listed on pages 130 and 131 are among the best. We've given the main telephone number plus one for reservations when needed. Expect to pay $10 to $40 or more for a fishing fee. Boat rentals start at $2.50 per hour for canoes and go up to about $30 an hour for powerboats.

A POTPOURRI OF OTHER FAMILY TRAVEL IDEAS

- *ORGANIZE AN OUTDOOR FAMILY ADVENTURE.* For help in picking the right biking, hiking, rafting, wildlife, or nature trip, get a free copy of Backroad's latest brochure. It covers more than eighty adventure-tour operators from around the world and rates their trips by physical challenge, comfort level, and appeal to families, singles, or persons over age fifty. Call (800) 537-4025 for details.

- *PET THE COWS.* For a free descriptive list of family farm vacations in the Pennsylvania Dutch country, call (800) PA-DUTCH. You and your children can stay one to seven days at many of the farms listed and help feed the animals, collect the eggs, pick and cook vegetables and berries. The communal meals and daily activities make it easy to meet other farm guests—and in that respect these vacations are ideal for single parents and their children.

- *ENJOY THE BIG SKY.* Custer Country, Inc., offers a free guide to Custer Country, land of Lewis and Clark and Sitting Bull. Call them for information on tours, working farm and ranch vacations, wagon-train trips, Indian powwows, fishing, camping, and festivals; (800) 346-1876.

- *LEARN TO SAIL.* Specially priced family packages are offered at various times of the year at the Offshore Sailing School, South Seas Plantation, on Captiva Island, Florida. Among the packages: "Teens at the Helm," which includes sailing lessons plus golf, tennis, fishing, and planned activities. Call (800) 221-4326 for details.

- *BE A DUDE.* American Wilderness Experience, a highly respected and experienced tour operator, will locate the right dude ranch for your family's vacation. It also runs covered-wagon trips in the West. Call (800) 444-DUDE.

A Freebie For a free copy of *The Official Directory of Dude Ranchers Associations*, an annual that lists one hundred ranches, their nearest airports, activities, and accomodations, call (970) 223–8440.

- *VISIT NATIVE AMERICAN COMMUNITIES.* Discovery Passages has tours/stays at Hopi, Navajo, Apache, Sioux, and other Native American lands. Share meals, attend ceremonies, learn their history. Call (520) 717-0519.

Best U.S. State Parks

PARK	FEES/RESERVATIONS	FACILITIES
Adirondack Upstate New York (518) 457–2500 (800) 456–2267	Day $5 Overnight: $10–$20	6 million acres; 500 campsites, cabins, lodges; no hookups; stores, restaurants
Denali 132 miles north of Anchorage, Alaska (907) 745–3975	Overnight: $7–$15 No reservations	324,240 acres; 88 tent sites; no water or hookups; store 32 miles
Devil's Lake 45 miles northwest of Madison, Wisconsin (608) 356–6618 (608) 356–8301	Day: $8 Overnight: $10–$15	12,000 acres; 413 campsties; 125 with hookups; no water; grocery 4 miles north
Eugene Mahoney 20 miles southwest of Omaha, Nebraska (402) 944–2523	Day: $5 Tent: $7 RV: $13; Lodge or cabin: $55–$177/night	620,000 acres; 41 cabins; 149 RV or tent sites; grocery 3 miles west
Franconia Notch White Mountains, New Hampshire (603) 823–5563	Day: free Overnight: $15/two RV: $30	6,765 acres; 98 campsites; no water or hookups; store in parking lodge
John Pennekamp Coral Reef, on Key Largo, Florida (305) 451–1202	Day: $5 Overnight: $25–$30	2,349 acres; 53,660 acres underwater; 46 sites, all with water and hookups; grocery 2 miles south in Key Largo
Lake Barkley Cadiz, Kentucky, 90 miles northwest of Nashville, Tennessee (502) 924–1131 (800) 325–1708	Day: free Overnight: $8.50–$10.50 Lodge: $35–$120/night	3,600 acres; 13 cottages, 135 lodge rooms; 79 campsites with hookups and water; grocery 8 miles east

PARK	FEES/RESERVATIONS	FACILITIES
Mackinac Island on Lake Huron, 285 miles north of Detroit, Michigan (616) 436–5563	$5–$35; call for details	1,800 acres; no camping; no cars on island; access by ferry
Mendocino Headlands, California, 12 miles south of Fort Bragg (707) 937–5804	Day: free	350 acres; no camping in park but in nearby Russian Gulch and Van Damme (800) 444–7275
Moran on Orcas Island, 75 miles northwest of Seattle, Washington (360) 376–2326	Day: free	4,605 acres; accessible by ferry (206–464–6400); 151 campsites; no water or hookups; grocery 7 miles northwest
Steamboat Lake Steamboat Springs, Colorado (303) 879–3922 (800) 678–2267	Day: $5 Overnight: $10	2,500 acres; 184 campsites; no water or hookups; grocery ¼ mile away
Valley of Fire 65 miles north of Las Vegas, Nevada (702) 397–2088	Day: $5 Overnight: $12	36,000 acres; 51 campsites, 19 with water, none with electric hookups; grocery 15 miles north in Overton

Free Factory Tours

These all-American factories welcome visitors, young and old. Call ahead for hours.

- *CALIFORNIA.* Bradbury & Bradbury, 940 Tyler Street, Benica; (707) 746-1900. Watch printers and artists make Victorian wallpaper and ceiling designs used in movies and restored inns.

- *CALIFORNIA.* Sun-Maid Growers of California, 13424 South Bethel Avenue, Kingsburg; (800) 7-SUNMAID. See where thousands of raisins are washed, sorted, and packaged.

- *CALIFORNIA.* Anchor Brewing Company, 1705 Mariposa Street, San Francisco; (415) 863-8350. Watch brew being made, with free samples in the taproom.

- *CALIFORNIA.* Levi Strauss & Co., 250 Valencia Street, San Francisco; (415) 565-9159. Victorian building where leg pieces are sewn.

- *COLORADO.* Stephany's Chocolates, 6770 West 52nd Avenue, Arvada; (800) 888-1522. See candy makers mix and cook chocolate in melting pots that hold 500 pounds of chocolate.

- *COLORADO.* Celestial Seasonings, Sleepytime Drive, Boulder; (303) 581-1202. Watch how all those herbs get packed into tea bags.

- *FLORIDA.* Davidson of Dundee, Inc., 210 U.S. 27 North, Dundee; (941) 438-1698. See how sixty kinds of jelly, juices, and citrus fruit candies are made.

- *FLORIDA.* E-One, Inc., 1601 SW 37th Avenue, Ocala; (352) 237-1122. Manufactures fire engines and sirens.

- *HAWAII.* Mauna Loa Macadamia Nut Corp., Highway 11, Hilo; (808) 966-8640. Drive through the macadamia orchards to reach the plant where raw nuts are roasted, salted, canned, and packed.

- *HAWAII.* Dole Pineapple, 64155 Com Highway, Honolulu; (808) 621-8408. Watch pineapple being diced, sliced, and juiced.

- *KENTUCKY.* Hillerich & Bradsby Co., 800 West Main Street, Louisville; (502) 588-7227. See custom baseball bats made for the pros.

- *LOUISIANA.* McIlhenny Co., Avery Island; (318) 365-8173. Tabasco is made here from fermented peppers and vinegar.

- *MASSACHUSETTS.* Yankee Candle Company, Route 5, South Deerfield; (413) 665-8306. Museum plus candle making.

- *MASSACHUSETTS.* Pairpoint Crystal Company, 851 Sandwich Road, Sagamore; (508) 888-2344. Watch glassblowing of bowls, vases, limited editions, and pieces for the Boston and New York art museums, using the same tools and processes as in 1837 when the company was founded.

- *MICHIGAN.* DeKlomp/Veldheer, 12755 Quincy Street, Holland; (616) 399-1900. the only Delftware factory in the United States. Also makes wooden shoes.

- *MICHIGAN.* Iverson Snowshoes, 95 Maple Street, Shingelton; (906) 452-6370. Watch white ash heated and bent into snowshoes.

- *NEW YORK.* Steuben Glass, 1 Museum Way, Corning; (607) 974-8173. Watch artisans working with molten glass and blowing out fine, artistic pieces.

- *PENNSYLVANIA.* Julius Sturgis Pretzel Co., 219 East Main Street, Lititz; (717) 626-4354. America's oldest pretzel factory and still family run. They'll let you twist your own.

- *SOUTH DAKOTA.* Homestake Mine, 160 West Main Street, Lead; (888) 701-0164. One of the largest producing gold mines in the Western Hemisphere.

- *VERMONT.* Ben & Jerry's, Route 100 North, Waterbury; (802) 244-5641. Watch your favorite flavor of ice cream being made.

- *WASHINGTON.* Boeing, 3303 West Casino Road, Everett; (425) 342-4805. Watch the 6,000+ employees ride bikes from one partially assembled plane to another. Each factory is the size of a football field. This is the world's largest aircraft company, covering almost one hundred acres.

- *WASHINGTON, D.C.* Bureau of Engraving & Printing, (202) 874-3188. Watch huge printing presses turn out billions of U.S. currency.

- *WISCONSIN.* Kohler Co., 10 Upper Road, Kohler; (920) 457-4441. This factory turns out toilets and bathtubs.

WHERE TO TAKE THE GRANDCHILDREN

When school doors close, grandparents across the nation whip into action and arrange to spend time with their grandchildren. Because grandparents live longer and remain in better health than they did in the past, many are interested in doing something different with their grandchildren, something beyond a sleep-over and a picnic. This situation has led to the birth of some excellent pre-planned trips—just show up with comfortable shoes, your camera, the children, and, of course, your wallet. Grandparent-grandchild tour operators have trips that range from gentle cruises and historic tours to biking trips and white-water rafting. Here are three of the best.

- *INTERHOSTEL.* This organization's "Grandparents/Family Hostel" program permits parents to tag along, too. Programs, designed for kids of all ages, are held at co-sponsoring universities abroad and feature workshops, lectures, field trips, and attractions that kids really like. Among the destinations are Prague,

Holland, the Czech Republic and Slovakia, Madrid, and Mexico. The cost for ten days is about $2,250 for adults and $1,800 for kids, including airfare from the East Coast, all meals, lodging, and activities; Mexican trips are slightly less. Interhostel is for those fifty and older; companions must be at least forty. For information contact Interhostel, University of New Hampshire, at (800) 733-9753 or (603) 862-1147.

- *ELDERHOSTEL.* More than sixty of Elderhostel's domestic summer programs are designed for persons ages fifty-five and over and their grandchildren. Most programs involve outdoor learning experiences; for example, the two-week Alaska program, with a week at Alaska Pacific University in Anchorage, followed by a week in a log cabin on the Nenana River in Denali National Park with lectures and field trips, costs about $900 for adults and $800 for kids but does not include airfare. Other learning trips focus on cowboys, Indian culture, music, nature, and the like. For information write to Elderhostel, 75 Federal Street, Boston, MA 02110 or call (617) 426-8056.

- *GRANDTRAVEL.* This firm has some sixteen to twenty vacations to such places as Washington, D.C., New England, the Southwest Indian country, the Grand Canyon, national and state parks, California, Hawaii, and Alaska as well as international trips, such as barging in Belgium and Holland, visiting English and Scottish castles, or going to Kenya on a safari. The average cost is about $2,800. Call Grandtravel at (800) 247-7651.

A Freebie

For a free copy of *Family Adventure Travel Directory*, which lists tour operators and packagers specializing in family vacations, send a stamped, self-addressed, business-size envelope to Family Adventure, Box 469, Woodstock, NY 12498.

Here are some other operators that run similar programs.

- *VISTATOURS,* 1923 North Carson Street, Carson City, NV 89701; (800) 248-4782

- *WARREN RIVER EXPEDITIONS,* Box 1375, Salmon, ID 83467; (800) 765-0421

- *NAGGAR TOURS,* 605 Market Street, San Francisco, CA 94105; (800) 443-6453. Ask about their "Grand Tag-Along Discount" of 50 percent on certain tours for grandkids accompanied by their grandparents.

- *TRAVEL THE WORLD WITH TURNER,* 2135 Margaret Avenue, Terre Haute, IN 47802; (800) 873-5252

Riding the Trolley Cars

Young and old alike love trolley cars, but they're not easy to find. New Orleans, San Francisco, Lowell (Massachusetts), Yakima (Washington), Detroit, and Philadelphia still have a few—either vintage or new ones—and a handful of museums offer 1-to-5-mile rides on old trolleys. Use this list when grandchildren come to visit or when you have the urge to climb aboard yourself.

- *Western Railway Museum,* Suisun, California; (707) 374–2978

- *Connecticut Trolley Museum,* East Windsor, Connecticut; (860) 627–6540; www.iconn.net/trolley

- *Seashore Trolley Museum,* Kennebunkport, Maine; (207) 967–2712; www.biddeford.com/~carshop/trolley

- *National Capital Trolley Museum,* Wheaton, Maryland; (301) 384–6088

- *Illinois Railway Museum,* Union, Illinois; (815) 923–2488

- *Fox River Trolley Museum,* South Elgin, Illinois; (847) 697–4676; www.foxtrolley.org

- *Baltimore Streetcar Museum,* Baltimore, Maryland; (410) 547–0264

- *Rockhill Trolley Museum,* Orbisonia, Pennsylvania; (814) 447–9576

For more information read *Steam Passenger Service Directory,* available at libraries or from Seashore Trolley Museum, Box A, Kennebunkport, ME 04046 ($14.95 plus $2.00 shipping).

- SPORTS LEISURE TRAVEL, 9527-A Folsom Boulevard, Sacramento, CA 95827; (916) 361-2051

- CLUB MED; (800) CLUB-MED. This resort's "mini clubs" for children at many but not all resorts have scuba diving, acrobatics, and tennis and golf lessons. At various times of the year, kids ages two to five stay free. Several times during the year, kids up to age six stay free, and grandparents (age sixty and over) get a discount on week-long packages at Club Med's Family Villages in the Bahamas, West Indies, Mexico, Dominican Republic, and Sandpiper, Florida.

WHEN KIDS GET SICK ABROAD

A broken arm, the flu, a bad cold ... it can happen, but with a little preparation ahead of time, your child's illness need not turn into an international disaster.

Before You Go

1. *Contact your pediatrician* or family doctor about appropriate shots. Don't delay; some immunizations must be given weeks beforehand. Double-check with the Public Health Service's Centers for Disease Control, (404) 332-4559 (a twenty-four-hour helpline).

2. *If your child has allergies,* a preexisting condition, or a unique medical problem, he or she should wear a medical alert tag; contact Medic Alert Foundation, Box 1009, Turlock, CA 95381; (800) 344-3226. Cost: $35 and up depending on whether you want a stainless steel, silver, or gold tag.

3. *Get the telephone numbers and addresses* for the U.S. consulates in all cities you're visiting by calling the U.S. State Department, (202) 647-5225.

4. *Call your credit-card issuer.* Some provide emergency travelers' assistance, such as names of English-speaking doctors and facilities. Some assign a doctor or dentist from the United States to consult by phone with local medical personnel abroad. Others help you fill a prescription or arrange for an air ambulance.

    Note: American Express provides some coverage on all cards; Visa and MasterCard on gold cards only.

    Access to help through your credit card is usually by telephone, and many accept collect calls, but be sure to take the telephone number with you.

5. *Join the International Association for Medical Assistance to Travelers,* a nonprofit organization. There's no fee, but a tax-deductible donation is welcomed. Members receive a booklet listing locations and phone numbers of IAMAT-affiliated, more than English-speaking doctors, hospitals, and clinics in over 130 countries and territories. These doctors have already agreed to an approved fee schedule. IAMAT, 417 Center Street, Lewiston, NY 14092; (716) 754-4883.

6. *Check your health insurance policy* regarding overseas coverage. If you have coverage, take along claim forms so they can be filled out on the spot. *Note:* Blue Cross requires only an itemized bill for reimbursement.

7. *If your policy has skimpy coverage,* consider purchasing a one-time temporary policy; make certain it covers medical evacuation back to the United States and will guarantee payment of bills. Get rates and coverage from Travmed (800-732-5309) and Access America (800-284-8300), or check with your own agent.

8. *Pack first-aid supplies.* Your first-aid kit should contain baby aspirin or other pain killer, safety pins, motion-sickness medicine, sunscreen, talcum powder, antiseptic, water purifier, cough medicine, special foods and formulas, diapers, Q-tips, handiwipes, Band-Aids, toothbrush/paste, flashlight, insect repellent, gauze and tape, thermometer.

9. *Assemble a medical folder* that includes a copy of your itinerary, a copy of passports and tickets for you and your children, blood types, your pediatrician's phone and fax number, copies of vaccination certificates, numbers of your traveler's checks and credit cards, and a bank-deposit slip. Make a copy to leave in your office or with a friend or relative; take the other with you.

10. *Bring an adequate supply of prescription medicines* for the entire trip. If any are unusual or contain narcotics, ask your doctor for a written statement describing the child's condition to show to customs officials. Also bring along written prescriptions, using the generic names—not trade names—in case you need a refill or lose the medications. (Trade names may be different overseas; generic names are not.) Carry prescriptions separate from the medicines they are for. Carry medicines with you, not in checked luggage, and be sure to leave all medicines, including nonprescription ones, in their original containers to ease your way through customs. Lastly, take extra glasses and contact lenses, as well as prescriptions for both.

For Emergency Help

If you have not taken the above steps and your child needs medical attention, for emergency help, if you're staying in a first-class hotel the hotel doctor can be your first call. Check, too, with the American embassy or consulate for names of local hospitals and doctors. If all else fails and you cannot find help any other way, call the State Department's Citizens Emergency Center in the United States, (202) 647-5225; they will contact the nearest U.S. consulate for you.

8
Great Bargains for the Fifty-Plus Crowd

Travel is one way of lengthening life.

—Benjamin Franklin

And in the world of travel it literally pays to get older—and to tell people about it. One of the really nice things about turning fifty, fifty-five, sixty, sixty-two, or sixty-five is that you can get myriad discounts on hotel and motel rooms, on cruises, packaged tours, trains, buses, planes, and rental cars. Even museums, historic homes, and tourist sites will let you through the door for less money than the rest of the world pays—so how can you afford to stay home? Whenever booking a ticket or reservation, ask for a senior discount whether one is offered or not. Most reduced rates apply only if you request them at the time you make your reservation. Be prepared to provide proof of your age: your passport, driver's license, Medicare card, or membership in the American Association of Retired Persons (AARP). Make certain that the senior citizens' rate is the lowest one available; short-term promotions may be even lower. Finally, if you can, travel in nonpeak seasons and at hours when rates are already lower.

Here's what you need to know to save money when you hit the road.

HOW TO PAY LESS FOR BEING OLDER

Her's a listing of the key organzations in the field.

- *AARP,* (800) 424-3010; www.aarp.org. Membership is $8.00/year or $20.00 for three. Minimum age: 50. Benefits: Has official discounts with over twenty hotel and motel chains; many more unofficially honor AARP members' discounts. Ask about the deal with Virgin Atlantic—you get 12 to 25 percent off on advance economy fares to London and $50 off any Virgin Atlantic package to Great Britain.

- *Canadian Association of Retired Persons,* (800) 363-9736 (in Canada only); (416) 368-8748; www.fifty-plus.net. Memberships C$15.95/year or C$43.95 for three; double fee for non-Canadians. Minimum age: 50. Benefits: From 10 to 30 percent off at ten hotel chains, on airfares and vacation packages through its own travel service, including 15 percent off on Canadian Airlines.

Has travel insurance at competitive rates and the Worldwide Emergency Assistance hotline for help anywhere in the world.

- *National Association for Retired Credit Union People,* (800) 840-3491. Membership: $12/year; $32 for three. Minimum age: 50. Benefits: 10 to 30 percent off at Choice, Days Inn, and Howard Johnson.

- *Retired Enlisted Association,* (303) 752-0660. Membership: $15/year. For any retired military people or those on active duty for at least ten years. No minimum age. Benefits: 10 percent discount on airlines and hotels.

AIRLINE DISCOUNTS

Just about every airline, foreign and domestic, has discounts of 10 percent or more for the fifty-plus crowd. When you make a reservation, ask about the senior discount, but remember that it may not always be the lowest fare. After you get a quote, study the restrictions: Do you have to fly in the middle of the night? Stay so many days? Are there blackout periods when your ticket won't work? How stiff is the penalty for changing your flight?

If you're thinking of buying a yearly pass or booklet of coupons, make certain that you're really going to take that many flights within 365 days. And don't use up your coupons on short flights— the longer the flight the greater your savings. Only a limited number of seats are put aside for discounted fares, so book early in order to get on a specific flight. Whatever discount you can get, try to combine it with supersaver fares, which require a thirty-day advance purchase.

Each airline has a slightly different version of discount or senior coupon booklets, so you'll have to check with the line you're most apt to fly.

Domestic Airlines
WITH SPECIAL DEALS FOR SENIORS

Alaska Airlines	(800) 426–0333
American Airlines	(800) 237–7981
America West	(800) 235–9292
Continental	(800) 248–8996
Delta Airlines	(800) 221–1212
Delta Shuttle	(800) 221–1212
Hawaiian Air	(800) 367–5320
Midwest Express	(800) 452–2022
Northwest Airlines	(800) 225–2525
Southwest	(800) 435–9792
TWA	(800) 221–2000
United Airlines	(800) 633–6563
USAirways	(800) 428–4322
Virgin Atlantic	(800) 862–8621

CRUISE DISCOUNTS

Take time to read Chapter 5 for general tips on cruise discounts. In general, booking far in advance or at the last minute will give you a good deal. Here are some senior specials.

- *BERGEN LINE CRUISES* (800-323-7436 or 212-319-1300): Scandinavian cruises on the Color Line, Silja Line, and Norwegian Coastal Voyages all offer senior discounts. The Color Line cruises the North Sea and to England and the Continent. The Silja Line cruises Finland, Sweden, and Germany. Norwegian Coastal Voyages goes along the Norwegian coast from Bergen to Kirkenes.

- *CELEBRITY CRUISES* (800-423-2100). The Senior Saver cruise, for persons sixty-five and over, lets you take a companion along for half price. Departures are from San Juan and Miami for Caribbean cruises.

- *PREMIER CRUISE LINES* (800-327-7113). Some discounts are available on the Big Red Boats to Nassau, Key West, and Cozumel and on packages to Orlando theme parks for persons age sixty and over plus a companion. Ask about rental-car discounts as well.

- *FOR MEN ONLY.* Free cruises are available for single men. Unattached men over the age of fifty are considered a rare item; if you're one of them, you just might be able to get a free cruise, as long as you're willing to dance, dine, and mingle with female passengers. You'll also be asked from time to time to play cards and escort them on shore excursions. Check with the "host program" division of the cruise lines listed below and contact Working Vacation,

Foreign Airlines
WITH SPECIAL DEALS FOR SENIORS

Aeromexico	(800) 237–6639
Air Canada	(800) 776–3000
Air France	(800) 237–2747
Air New Zealand	(800) 262–1234
Alitalia	(800) 223–5730
British Airways	(800) 247–9297
Canadian Airlines	(800) 426–7000
El Al	(800) 223–6700
Finnair	(800) 950–5000
Iberia	(800) 772–4642
KLM Royal Dutch	(800) 225–2525
Lufthansa	(800) 645–3880
Mexicana	(800) 531–7921
Sabena (Belgian)	(800) 950–1000
SAS (Scandinavian)	(800) 221–2350
Swissair	(800) 221–4750
TAP Air Portugal	(800) 221–7370

(815) 485-8307. This company interviews and places men on cruises. Although the cruises are free, the men must pay the company a placement fee of $25/day.

- The following cruise lines also use single men: Crystal Cruises (800-446-6620), Cunard (800-528-6273), Delta Queen Steamboat Co. (504-543-1949), Holland America Line (800-544-0443), Merry Widow Dance Cruises (800-374-2689), and Royal Olympic (800-872-6400). Call for details.

- *FOR WOMEN ONLY.* If you like to dance and are at least fifty years old, check out The Merry Widows Dance Tours, which has several cruises each year. They have one male dancer for every five women, and you're guaranteed to dance the night away. (You don't have to be a widow to sign on.) This group also has tours and packaged vacations for older, single women at major resorts. Call (800) 374-2689 or (813) 289-5000.

TRAIN DISCOUNTS

When you're riding the rails, you can often get a discount, but you need to speak up because they're not well advertised.

Domestic

- *AMTRAK* (800-872-7245) gives persons ages sixty-two and older a 10-percent discount on many trips, although not on Metroliner trains. Additional savings are offered seasonally. (See Chapter 3.)

- *OMNITOURS* (800-962-0060 or 708-374-0088) offers escorted tours of the United States and Canada that combine rail travel with stays at hotels and inns and local sightseeing by motorcoach. Trips to such popular destinations as the national parks, Quebec, and parts of California are designed for persons ages fifty and older.

Abroad

- *UNITED KINGDOM.* A BritRail pass covers unlimited first-class travel throughout England, Scotland, and Wales.

 You must purchase the pass through an agent in the United States. For information contact BritRail, 1500 Broadway, New York, NY 10036 or call (212) 575-2667.

- *CANADA.* Via Rail gives up to 50 percent off to travelers age sixty or more in the off-season and 10 percent off in season. Call (800) 561-9181 for information.

- BELGIUM. If you're sixty or older, you can buy a Golden Rail Pass in the United States and get six free trips anywhere in Belgium. For details call the Belgium Tourist Office at (212) 758-8130.

SIGHTSEEING DISCOUNTS

Ask about discounts wherever you go: at museums, historic houses, ruins, and other sights. Foreign tourist bureaus and U.S. chambers of commerce or state tourist offices (see Appendix) can tell you about their local discounts for the over-fifty crowd. Call before you leave home.

 For a free list of all U.S. state tourism offices, with their 800 numbers, send a self-addressed, stamped envelope to Discover America, Travel Industry Association of America, 2 Lafayette Center, 1133 Twenty-first Street, NW, Washington, DC 20036.

Here are two especially good deals.

1. GREAT BRITAIN. The Great British Heritage Pass can be used at more than 600 castles, palaces, homes, and gardens, including the Tower of London and Windsor Castle. For current information and reduced prices, contact British Tourist Authority at (212) 986-2200 or (800) 422-2748.

2. U.S. NATIONAL PARKS. The Golden Age Passport provides free admission to all of the U.S. federal government's parks, monuments, and recreation areas if you're over age sixty-two. You also get half off on fees for camping, boat launching, parking, and tours. Although not available by mail, you can get a Golden Age Passport at any national park where an entrance fee is charged. You'll be asked for proof of age; the cost is $10. For more details write to the National Park Service, Box 37127, Washington, DC 20013.

HOTEL, MOTEL, AND RESTAURANT DISCOUNTS

Just about all hotels and motels will give senior citizens some discount some of the time. Read chapter 6 for tips on how to get the best discounts on accommodations. Remember that senior discount may not always be the lowest one available. Establishments that boast about their rates for seniors are listed on the following pages.

 Ask about restaurant discounts. Some chains give seniors something off on their meals, especially to members of the hotel's travel club or program, or to those who belong to AARP.

Hotel Discounts for Seniors

In addition to the discount information given below, some of these hotels also offer free breakfasts and parking, weekend deals, longer-stay discounts, and free stays for kids or grandkids. Call to find out about their current promotions.

Aston Hotels & Resorts, (800) 922-7866. The Aston chain is located on Hawaii's major islands. Sun Club members age 50+ get 20 to 30 percent discounts plus free or discounted auto rentals.

Best Inns, (800) 237-8466. Midwestern and Southern inns give $5.00 or $10.00 off room rates to persons 50+ if they belong to the Senior First Club; membership is free.

Best Western, (800) 528-1234. Travelers 55+ and AARP members (age 50+) get 10 percent off regular rates at some Best Westerns.

Calinda, (800) 228-5151. These inns throughout Mexico, affiliated with Choice Hotels, offer discounts of 10 to 30 percent for those 50+.

Canadian Pacific, (800) 441-1414. These Canadian hotels and motels give 10 to 30 percent off if you're 65+; weekend rates are often lower than weekday rates.

Chimo Hotels, (800) 387-9779. This small eastern Canadian chain gives AARP members at least 20 percent off and/or special weekend family deals.

Choice Hotels, (800) 424-4777 or (800) 221-2222. If you're 50+, you get up to 30 percent off regular rates *if* you have an advance reservation. Among the hotel chains under Choice Hotels are Comfort, Quality, Clarion, Sleep, Rodeway, Econo Lodge, and Friendship, plus Calinda in Mexico.

Clarion (See Choice Hotels.)

Colony Hotels & Resorts, (800) 777-1700. Hawaiian and mainland motels with 20 to 30 percent off for AARP members; others age 60+ get 20 percent off.

Comfort Inns (See Choice Hotels.)

Courtyard by Marriott, (800) 321-2211. AARP members get 15 percent discounts; some discounts offered to other seniors.

Days Inns, (800) 241-5050. Members of the September Days Club get discounts of 15 to 50 percent; you must be 50+. Days also offers discounts on car rentals and local attractions. For membership information call (800) 241-5050. Non-AARP members get 10 percent off, and grandchildren eat free at many Days Inns. Membership is $15/year or $25/two years.

Doral Hotels, (800) 22-DORAL. AARP members and persons 60+ get up to 25 percent off weekday room rates at the four Dorals in Manhattan; continental breakfast is included.

Doubletree Inns, (800) 426-6774. AARP members and other persons 60+ get 10 to 30 percent off.

Econo Lodges (See Choice Hotels.)

Embassy Suites, (800) 362-2799. Persons 55+ get 10 percent or more off room rates and free breakfast and cocktail.

Fairfield Inns by Marriott, (800) 228-2800. Economy-style motels give 15 percent discounts to AARP members and 10 percent discounts to persons 62+ on rooms that start at $40 a night.

Friendship Inns (See Choice Hotels.)

Hampton Inns, (800) HAMPTON. Ask for the LifeStyle 50 deal—a four-for-one plan: four guests in a double room for the single rate, with continental breakfast. Call for an application.

Hawaiian Hotels & Resorts, (800) 222-5642. Discounts vary widely; ask.

Hilton Hotels, (972) 788-0878. Senior HHonors Club for persons 60+ entitles you to room discounts of 25 to 50 percent at many Hiltons and 20 percent off at most Hilton restaurants; also discounts on Hertz cars and other perks. Dues are $95/year or $290/lifetime. Allow three weeks for processing.

Holiday Inns, (800) 465-4329. Get 10 to 20 percent off rooms, if you're an AARP member.

Hyatt, (800) 233-1234. Get 25 percent off if you're 62+ and meal discounts at some hotels.

Marriott, (800) 228-9290. Some Marriotts give AARP members 10 percent off rooms.

Novotel, (800) 221-4542. Guests 60+ get discounts of varying amounts at hotels in Toronto, Ottawa, Montreal, New Jersey, and New York.

Omni Hotels, (800) 843-6664. Discounts of 10 percent to AARP members.

Outrigger, (800) 462-6262. These Hawaiian hotels give persons 50+ 20 percent off room rates; 25 percent to AARP members.

Quality International (See Choice Hotels.)

Radisson Hotels, (800) 333-3333. Most Radisson Hotels give "Senior Breaks" discounts, 10 to 25 percent off, but call local properties to find out about even bigger discounts. Must be 50 in the United States and age 65 abroad.

Ramada, (800) 766-2378. The "Best Years" Club at more than 700 inns gives members of senior organizations and anyone age 50+ discounts of 20 to 25 percent. Must be 60; $15 one time fee.

Red Carpet Inns, (800) 251-1962. Discounts vary; ask.

Red Lion Inns, (800) 547-8010. "Prime Rate Discount" at most Red Lion & Thunderbird Inns gives AARP members 20 percent off, 10 percent off some meals.

Red Roof Inns, (800) 843-7663.With a RediCard get 10 percent discount, three coupons worth $5.00 each, and other goodies. Lifetime membership is $10 plus $2.00 for spouse; you must be 60.

Renaissance Hotels & Resorts, (800) 228-9898. Various discounts if you're 60+ or an AARP member.

Residence Inns, (800) 331-3131. All-suite chain run by Marriott; 10 to 40 percent discount to AARP members and other persons age 62+.

Rodeway Inns (See Choice Hotels.)

Sandman Motels, (800) 726-3626.Western Canadian motels give persons 55+ a 25 percent discount. Get free Club 55 card first.

SAS International Hotels, (800) 221-2350. European and Middle Eastern hotels give weekend discounts related to your age starting at 65 percent off if you're 65; 75 percent off if you're 75, etc.With a couple, the older person gets the discount; includes breakfast.

Sheraton, (800) 325-3535. Most Sheratons give 25 percent discount to persons age 60+ and to members of AARP. Grandkids stay free in your room.

Sleep Inns (See Choice Hotels.)

Sonesta International Hotels, (800) 766-3782. If you're 65+ or belong to AARP, get 10 or 15 percent off if you request special rate in advance.

Stouffer, (800) 468-3571. A 25 percent discount for AARP members.

Super 8 Motels, (800) 843-1991. Budget motels give 10 percent off if you're over 50; deals vary widely.

Thunderbird Inns (See Red Lion Inns.)

Travelodge, (800) 578-7878. Travelodges, Viscount Hotels, and Relax Inns in United States and Canada give 15 percent to persons 49+ who join their "Classic Travel Club." No membership fee.

Vagabond Inns, (800) 522-1555. Western United States inns offer "Club 55" discounts of 10 percent or more off single room rates; up to four can stay in a room; discounts on trips and events.

Viscount Hotels (See Travelodge.)

Welcome Inns, (800) 387-4381.This Canadian chain gives those 55+ a 10 percent discount.

Westin Hotels & Resorts, (800) 228-3000. Each Westin hotel has its own discount policy for seniors and/or good weekend deals, often 50 percent off.

Woodfin Suites, (800) 237-8811. All-suite hotels near major U.S. airports give AARP members sizable discounts.

Wyndham Hotels & Resorts, (800) WYNDHAM. Wyndham—with resorts in Jamaica, Aruba, and St. Thomas—often gives a 50 percent discount if you're 62+ or an AARP member.

LEARNING VACATIONS

Go back to college and study while traveling. The groups listed below offer low-cost academic trips for older travelers through a worldwide network of schools, colleges, and universities. You usually sleep in dormitories, dine on cafeteria chow, and attend courses taught by the host institution's faculty. Prices for one-to two-week trips are amazingly reasonable. Get the current catalogs well in advance of when you wish to travel, as these programs are popular and often filled way ahead of departure date.

 Ask to be placed on the waiting list if the trip you want is filled. Cancellations among older travelers are fairly common.

- *CHAUTAUQUA INSTITUTION.* On Lake Chautauqua north of Buffalo, New York, this summer learning institute, in a Victorian village, offers special classes and weekends for persons over fifty, including lectures, films, entertainment, discussion groups, activities. Ask about the 55 Plus Weekend and Residential Week for Older Adults, which is priced around $400 and includes room and meals. Contact the Program Center for Older Adults, Chautauqua, NY 14722; (800) 836-ARTS.

- *ELDERHOSTEL.* This educational travel program is for people age fifty-five or older; companions must be at least fifty years old. It offers programs in the United States, Canada, and overseas. Participants live in dorms on campus or sometimes other accommodations and take courses. No exams or credit are given. Contact Elderhostel, (877) 426-8056.

- *INTERHOSTEL.* For a moderately priced international study program, contact Interhostel. You stay on campuses or in inexpensive hotels and attend lectures. For people fifty and older; companions must be at least forty. For information write or call Interhostel, University of New Hampshire, 6 Garrison Avenue, Durham, NH 03824; (800) 733-9753.

- *TRAVELEARN.* College professors escort these luxury tours to overseas destinations. All accommodations are first class. Tours run two to three weeks. All-inclusive prices start at $3,000 including airfare. The average age of participants is fifty. For information contact TraveLearn, Box 315, Lakeville, PA 18438; (800) 235-9114.

- *GO AHEAD VACATIONS.* This organization arranges worldwide cruises, tours, and independent travel for people ages fifty-five and older. The focus is on good value. Trips run from eight to twenty-one days and cost from $765 to $3,000, with an average price of $2,000. There is a roommate matching service.

 Get seven people together, and the eighth travels free.

Contact Go Ahead Vacations, 1 Memorial Drive, Cambridge, MA 02142; (800) 242-4686; or (617) 252-6262.

ADVENTURE TOURS

If your idea of a vacation involves a wilderness trip or an outdoor activity, you don't have to sacrifice creature comforts such as hot showers and real beds. Here are some outfitters and organizations that have active trips and events done with style and panache and at a slightly slower pace.

- Alaska Wildland Adventures, Girdwood, Alaska; (800) 334-8730

- Backroads Bike Trips, Berkeley, California; (800) 462-2848

- Elderhostel's Bicycle Tours, Boston, Massachusetts; (877) 426-8056

- Eldertreks, Toronto, Canada; (416) 588-5000

- International Bicycle Tours, Essex, Connecticut; (860) 767-7005

- Outdoor Vacations for Women Over 40, Groton, Massachusetts; (508) 448-3331

- Roads Less Traveled, Longmont, Colorado; (800) 488-8483

- U.S. Lighthouse Society, San Francisco, California; (415) 362-7255

- Walk About the West, Colorado Springs, Colorado; (719) 531-9577

- Walking the World, Fort Collins, Colorado; (970) 225-0500

- Warren River Expeditions, Salmon, Idaho; (800) 765-0421 or (208) 756-6387

SPORTING VACATIONS

Just because you've joined the over-fifty crowd doesn't mean you have to hang up the bat or turn in your racquet. Physical activity is more important than ever, and here are some groups that will help you avoid becoming a couch potato. In addition, check your favorite ski spots; most of them, even the most luxurious, have either days when seniors ski for free or reduced tickets—often on weekdays when slopes are less crowded.

- *NATIONAL ASSOCIATION OF SENIOR CITIZEN SOFTBALL.* Hundreds of U.S. and Canadian teams are made up of men fifty and older and women forty-seven and older, with no age cap. Contact NASCS, Box 1085, Mt. Clements, MI 48046; (810) 791-2632.

- *NATIONAL SENIOR SPORTS ASSOCIATION.* This nonprofit group, for people over fifty, sponsors golf tournaments and vacations all over the United States and to foreign golf courses. It also organizes bowling trips and assorted cruises for members and gives you discounts on equipment and names of other members so that you can find fellow players when you're traveling. Membership costs $25 for one year, $65 for three, or $150 for life. Write or call NSSA, 1248 Post Road, Fairfield, CT 06430; (800) 282-NSSA.

- *SENIOR SOFTBALL-USA.* This group organizes tournaments throughout the United States as well as international events. Once a year there's a trip abroad so that members can play ball in foreign countries. Men and women can join once they turn fifty. Contact Senior Softball-USA, 9 Fleet Street, Sacramento, CA 95831; (916) 393-8566.

- *U.S. TENNIS ASSOCIATION.* The Senior Division of this organization arranges competitions on a local and regional basis and will put you in touch with players throughout the U.S. Contact U.S. Tennis Association, Senior Division, 70 West Red Oak Lane, White Plains, NY 10604; (914) 696-7000.

- *CANYON RANCH.* Canyon Ranch has two fitness resorts, one in Tucson, Arizona, and one in the Berkshires in Massachusetts, where special times are set aside for persons sixty and older. Lectures, exercise, walks, sports, time with nutritionists, medical studies, and nonfat meals are featured. At various times there's a 10 percent discount. For information call (800) 726-9900.

- *OVER THE HILL GANG.* This international club organizes local units for skiing, hiking, scuba diving, camping, fishing, canoeing, ballooning, surfing, and just about everything else in between. You must be at least fifty to join; membership costs $40 for a single person, $60 for a couple. If there's no chapter in your area, join anyway and participate as you travel. Contact Over the Hill

Gang International, 3310 Cedar Heights Drive, Colorado Springs, CO 80904; (719) 685-4656.

OLDER AND SINGLE

If you want to travel but don't have anyone to go with, there's no need to stay home. Organizations, clubs, and packagers are waiting for you. Check out our suggestions in chapter 9, Traveling Solo, as well as these.

- *CLUB MED.* Through Club Med's "Forever Young" program, you can get discounts on stays of a week at about six Club Med resorts deemed to be suitable for persons ages fifty-five and older, including ones in Cancun and Ixtapa in Mexico, Eleuthera in the Bahamas, Paradise Island in Nassau, and Sandpiper in Florida. There are shopping, excursions, golf, swimming, etc., all in a setting that requires little climbing. Call (800) CLUB-MED.

- *SANDALS RESORTS.* These all-inclusive resorts, located throughout the Caribbean, for couples only, have a Golden Players Club that is geared toward the interests and physical stamina of persons ages fifty and older, with social and athletic events, group sightseeing, etc. Call (800) SANDALS.

- *GOLDEN COMPANIONS.* This organization finds travel companions for persons over age forty-five through its extensive U.S. and Canadian network. You first must fill out a form describing your interests and the type of person with whom you wish to travel. There are about 1,000 members, and you do your own matchmaking through the mail. You'll also get some travel discounts; annual dues are $85. Contact Golden Companions, Box 5249, Reno, NV 89513; (702) 324-2227.

OFF THE BEATEN PATH

In addition to matchmaking services, there are tour operators that specialize in escorted tours for older people. Many also try to locate a roommate for you in order to avoid the single supplement. Our favorites, in alphabetical order, are these:

- *EVERGREEN CLUB.* This B&B club is for people over age fifty who are willing to have fellow members stay in their house or apartment. There's a flat rate of $10 per night for a single; $15 for a double. It's a great way to meet other people and, at the same time, make or save a little money. Annual dues, which are $50 for a couple and $40 for a single, include a directory with names, addresses, and occupations of members, plus information on local attractions and sites. Contact Evergreen Club, 404 North Galena Avenue, Dixon, IL 61021.

- GOLDEN AGE TRAVELLERS. This group is for people more than fifty years old. When you join ($10 a year for singles), you get a quarterly listing of forthcoming trips, discounts, and deals on cruises. If you want to stay several weeks in one place, ask about packages that include your airfare, hotel, and some extras. Write or phone them at Pier 27, The Embarcadero, San Francisco, CA 94111; (800) 258-8880.

- GRAND CIRCLE TRAVEL. This company designs packages for the over-fifty crowd and will try to match roommates if you so request. If no roommate is available, you're charged just half the single supplement on some trips. Contact them at Grand Circle Travel, 347 Congress Street, Boston, MA 02210; (800) 221-2610.

- SAGA HOLIDAYS. This company specializes in tours for persons ages fifty and older. They will try to find a roommate so that you can avoid the single supplement. Write or phone them at 222 Berkeley Street, Boston, MA 02116; (800) 343-0273.

- SENIORS ABROAD. This homestay program (see page 102) enables travelers over age fifty to stay in the homes or apartments of host families in foreign countries, including many in Europe, as well as Japan, Australia, and New Zealand. Prices are extremely reasonable. Contact Seniors Abroad, (619) 485-1696.

- SERVAS. Aimed at promoting goodwill among people, this nonprofit organization is open to all ages, all over the world. Members get a list of hosts with whom they can stay and then make their own arrangements. The only cost is an annual membership fee of $55. Hosts are interviewed, and guests must provide letters of reference. For details contact U.S. Servas, 11 John Street, Suite 407, New York, NY 10038; (212) 267-0252.

- MATURE TOURS. A division of Solo Flights, this company has many interesting, reasonably priced trips geared toward the over-fifty traveler. Their annual New York City outing is one of the best we know of. Also: cruises, trips to other cities, steamboating. Call (800) 266-1566 or (203) 445-0107.

Be a Volunteer

If you think you'd like to combine travel with involvement in some kind of volunteer work, send for the *Guide to Volunteering for Older Americans* (publication #638Z). It lists types of activities, experiences, and training required, and the names and contact information of the sponsoring organizations. Write to Consumer Information Center, Dept. 638Z, Pueblo, CO 81009.

9
Traveling Solo

He travels the fastest who travels alone.

—Rudyard Kipling

And indeed, there are many wonderful aspects to traveling alone. You're certainly more apt to meet the natives and fellow travelers. You have time to absorb the culture. You can set your own itinerary, decide how much to spend, where to sleep, and when and what to eat. You can even snack on crackers in bed.

Traveling solo, however, does come with its own set of idiosyncrasies and issues. The key problem single travelers must face, of course, is the single-room supplement: Most hotel rooms and ship cabins are geared (and sold) on the basis of occupancy by two persons. The single-room supplement can be as much as 50 to 75 percent of the rate paid for a double accommodation or space.

Another concern for some people is loneliness. Women in particular tend to feel uncomfortable eating alone in restaurants, especially upscale or famous eateries, although this, too, is changing as more women travel for business and become accustomed to being on their own away from home.

If you don't want to dine alone every night or sight-see as a single, you absolutely don't have to. Consider the alternative trips described in chapter 11. Volunteer vacations sponsored by Earthwatch and Habitat for Humanity, for instance, are filled with singles (couples, too) all focusing on the common goal of helping other people.

Tennis and sailing camps, golf and cooking schools, and other programs in which you study, learn something new, or gain a skill are also ideal for singles, as are spas and health retreats and selected cruises. Of course there are also hundreds of regularly packaged vacations and trips available, although you'll have to pay the single supplement in most cases.

We also suggest that you check out gourmet, architectural, or museum tours and trips sponsored by local and national alumni groups, museum guilds, food and wine societies, and sports clubs. Keep in mind that B&Bs and small hotels are friendly places in which to stay.

Women's Travel Groups

Adventure Associates, (800) 527–2500, has both women-only and coed trips, mainly in the Pacific Northwest but some international. Focus is on sea kayaking, backpacking, river rafting, hiking.

Merry Widows, (800) 374–2689, c/o AAA, a traveling group for women ages fifty and over, brings along its own gentlemen dancers—generally one man for every five women—on cruises. It also has land trips in the United States and abroad and will try to make roommate assignments.

Rainbow Adventures, (800) 804–8686, is a creative company that arranges interesting, outdoor-style tours for women ages thirty and older. Although not aimed specifically at singles, it's obviously not for mixed couples. Rainbow Adventures will pair off women in double rooms, if they wish, so that they can avoid paying the single supplement. Among its trips are cross-country skiing in Yellowstone and safaris in Kenya.

Woodswomen, (800) 279–0555. This Minneapolis group offers seventy adventure and wilderness journeys by canoe, kayak, raft, and backpack, all over the world.

Women in the Wilderness, (800) 621–4727. Established in 1987 in St. Paul, this group focuses on canoe/hiking trips, dogsledding, snowshoeing, and kayaking.

Women's Travel Club, (800) 480–4448 or (305) 936–9669, has a newsletter with the names of members seeking travel companions as well as a list of group trips, meeting dates, and general information. Membership is $35/year. Geared to both married and single women of all ages, it organizes unique, discounted trips with room-share guarantees to all parts of the world.

MATCHMAKERS, CLUBS, AND SINGLES TOUR OPERATORS

A handful of organizations arrange trips specifically for singles or find roommates for single travelers. Our favorites, in alphabetical order, are these:

- BALLROOM DANCERS WITHOUT PARTNERS (800-778-7953), c/o Vacations Plus, is a travel group that caters to single men and women and provides dancing on luxury cruises. It's aimed at those over age fifty with the average age about sixty. Group and private lessons are often offered, and there's no need to bring along a partner. Cabin share arranged if you wish to avoid the cruise line's single surcharge. The most popular cruises are to the Caribbean and Alaska.

- *CLUB MED* (800-CLUB-MED), a large, well-known company that runs all-inclusive resorts around the world as well as two cruise ships, will double up single travelers at random so that they can avoid the extra single fee.

- *CUNARD LINE* (800-5-CUNARD), a cruise company that owns the venerable *QE II*, offers standby fares for singles on transatlantic crossings of this elegant ship from New York City to England. Singles are notified thirty days prior to sailing whether or not they will get a cabin to themselves at the regular per-person rate plus $200. *Note:* This rate includes return airfare to the United States.

- *GOLDEN AGE TRAVELLERS* (800-258-8880), a travel club, based in Reno, Nevada, for those over age fifty, has a roommates-wanted listing.

- *GOLDEN COMPANIONS* (702-324-2227) is a group that matches people over age forty-five for cruises, trips, and tours. Annual membership ($85) entitles you to a bimonthly newsletter, a members directory with information on its 1,000 members, plus an anonymous mail exchange through which you can do your own matchmaking.

- *GRAND CIRCLE TRAVEL* (800-221-2610), for persons ages fifty and older, will try to match singles if you ask for its trips and tours.

- *ORIENT FLEXI PAX TOURS* (800-545-5540) will seek roommates of the same sex if you ask. If it is unable to find a roommate near departure time, the company gives a full refund of the tour price on its escorted tours. It has trips to China, the Orient, Australia, New Zealand, and Fiji.

- *PASSPORT TRAVEL* (800-549-8687) organizes several single-parent family vacations every year with activities for kids, so if you're a single parent, get in touch with this tour operator. A nice touch: There's baby-sitting or child supervision in the evening so that parents can socialize with other parents.

- *SAGA HOLIDAYS* (800-921-9291) organizes tours for persons age sixty or more here and abroad and will try to find roommates on its escorted trips and cruises; sometimes there's no single supplement if space is available.

- *SOLO FLIGHTS* (800-266-1566 or 203-443-0107) is a twenty-two-year-old travel agency that has interesting, well-priced tours with excellent accommodations, sightseeing excursions, and tickets to special events, concerts, and theater. Destinations include London, New York, San Francisco, and Mississippi steamboat cruises. Some trips are for senior solo travelers, whereas others are for all ages.

Tips for the Best Solo Trips The best trips to
make alone are those in which you can do the following:

- Immerse yourself in a subject: art architecture, music, sports, history, or a foreign language.

- Remain in one place long enough to meet people.

- Join a group for a specific purpose, such as a dig in Turkey or a writing class in Iowa.

- Stay at a resort or take a cruise that is specifically organized for singles.

BEING PAID TO GO: THE ESCORT WORLD

If you're a single man, can dance, and are well mannered, you may be able to land a free cruise. In some cases you receive a small stipend in exchange for serving as a host. You'll be asked to dance with single women on the cruise, join them for card parties, and generally escort them about the ship and on shore excursions. You're not asked to be a Romeo; in fact seduction is not part of an escort's official assignment. For detailed information contact Working Vacation, (815) 485-8307. This group places men over age forty-five on cruises. Although the cruise is free, there's a $28/day fee. Also, see pages 81, 150, and 155 for more information on being an escort.

Ten Single CABIN SHIPS

SHIP	NUMBER OF SINGLE CABINS
QEII	110
Royal Odyssey	95
Sagafjord	43
Vistafjord	36
Rotterdam	32
Westward	23
Norway	20
Mermoz	17
Ocean Princess	15
Ocean Pearl	11

TOP TRIPS FOR SOLO TRAVELERS

You'll find it's easy to meet others when you participate in group activities. Try these on for size:

Spas

Canyon Ranch Health and Fitness Resorts (in Tucson, Arizona, and Lenox, Massachusetts), (800) 742-9000

Rancho La Puerta (near San Diego), (800) 443-7565

Rio Callente (in Guadalajara, Mexico), (800) 200-2927

Hiking and Skiing

Sierra Club, (415) 977-5500

Appalachian Mountain Club, (617) 523-0636

Biking

Vermont Bicycle Touring, (800) 245-3868

Backroads and Bicycle Touring, (800) 533-2573

Tennis

Tennis Camps Limited, (800) 223-2442

White-Water Rafting

Outdoor Adventure River Specialists, (209) 736-4677

American River Touring Association, (800) 323-ARTA

Sailing

Offshore Sailing School, (800) 221-4326

Bird-Watching

National Audubon Society, (212) 979-3000

Six Joys of Traveling Solo

1. You don't have to be cheerful at breakfast.
2. You can go where you want, when you want.
3. You can decide if something is too expensive or not.
4. You can eat crackers in bed.
5. You don't have to wait to use the bathroom.
6. You can pack up and go home when you want.

ON THE ROAD

If you like to travel in a motor home or van, you can join with others through Loners on Wheels, a camping club for mature singles that does not do match-making. It has about sixty chapters in the United States and Canada and a membership of about 3,000 people. There are continual camping events at inexpensive sites and a monthly newsletter and directory to keep members up-to-date. Dues are $36 a year ($45 in Canada). Write to Loners on Wheels, Box 1355, Poplar Bluff, MO 63901; or call (573) 785-2420.

10
Travel for the Physically Handicapped

I have traveled a good deal in Concord.

—Henry David Thoreau

I f you have trouble getting about, don't despair. You can see a great deal, learn much, and have a fine time in your own town or even in your own backyard. However, because some thirty-six million Americans have some type of physical disability, it's not surprising that travel for the handicapped is on the upswing. Thanks to the Americans with Disabilities Act, many physical barriers are being eliminated. The act requires public places, including hotels and restaurants, to make their establishments accessible to the handicapped.

The biggest barrier to travel for the physically handicapped is often psychological. There are, however, plenty of useful information sources and groups to help you. The best companies are often those owned by people with disabilities themselves. So if you want to go someplace or see something, you should go. Not only will everyone be rooting for you, they will help you, if you let them.

Preplanning, of course, is important, and discovering that everything isn't perfect should not be a deterrent. Begin by contacting the Society for the Advancement of Travel for the Handicapped (SATH) at 347 Fifth Avenue, Suite #610, New York, NY 10016; (212) 447-7284. You'll find their magazine, *Access,* very useful. They also keep a continually updated list of books about travel for the disabled.

THE PRELIMINARIES

Here are a few parameters to keep in mind as you plan your trip:

* *BE REALISTIC.* No one likes to acknowledge his or her limitations, but don't let your fears about being handicapped get in your way. Travel as much as you can; go where you can. And where you can't go, you simply can't go. Don't try to be a hero.

* *THINK.* Given your particular situation, maybe you should avoid very isolated destinations—such as small B&Bs and inns with many stairs and winding hallways—and instead pick places and tours that are easier to handle and that have medical help on hand or nearby.

159

- *TELL.* Let the travel agent or the companies you're using know you are handicapped when you make your reservations. This will give them adequate time to make your trip more comfortable. If you need a wheelchair, for example, they can make certain one is ready in advance. Most hotels and many motels now have rooms with special features—wheelchair-accessible bathrooms, for example; handrails in the bathroom; phones with enhanced hearing devices; grab bars by the bed; smoke detectors with flashing lights for the hearing-impaired. Cruise lines have cabins with all these extras, too. Ask for one near the dining room. Rental cars now come equipped with hand controls, and there are rental vans that will raise or lower wheelchairs—but they must be reserved at least a week or two ahead of time.

- *PACK RIGHT.* Arrange to take any items or equipment that will make your trip easier: folding wheel chairs, collapsible canes, extra batteries for your hearing aid, portable oxygen, the right medications, and a list of your doctors.

- *SPEAK UP.* There are wheelchairs at airports, and airlines will gladly meet you curbside. If there is no chair when you arrive, ask the baggage handler to get one. When checking in, reiterate your request, so there will be a wheelchair at each stop en route to your destination. Generally you will be pushed by an airline employee, whom you do not tip; however, if you're pushed by a porter, give him a dollar or two. If you are unable to walk to your seat on the plane, ask the attendant for one of the narrow wheelchairs that move up and down the aisles and will take you directly to your seat.

 Folding wheelchairs are handy, but check yours as baggage and use the airline's while you're on the plane. It's much more convenient.

On the Water
Disabled travelers, including those in wheelchairs, can enjoy barging in France and yachting in the Caribbean aboard vessels operated by Le Boat, Inc. For information, call (800) 922–0291.

For a copy of *Cruising for the Physically Challenged,* call World Wide Cruises, (800) 882–9000. This brochure rates the best ships for wheelchair accessibility; an excellent list.

ORGANIZATIONS THAT CAN HELP

Listed here are some helpful organizations and agents.

- *THE SOCIETY FOR THE ADVANCEMENT OF TRAVEL FOR THE HANDICAPPED* has a list of tour operators who run trips for the disabled, as well as information on special facilities around the world. It also publishes a quarterly newsletter on travel for the handicapped. Membership is $45/year; $25 for students and seniors. For information contact them at 347 Fifth Avenue, New York, NY 10016; (212) 447-7284.

- *TRAVELIN' TALK* publishes a national directory of members who, as part of a support network, will provide information on facilities for disabled travelers in their hometown or city. The directory costs $35 and can be obtained by calling (615) 552-6670. For a free copy of the quarterly newsletter, send a self-addressed envelope with 50 cents postage to Box 3534, Clarksville, TN 37043.

- *DIRECTORY OF TRAVEL AGENCIES FOR THE DISABLED* lists 360 agencies throughout the world. Contact Disability Bookshop, Box 129, Vancouver, WA 98666; (800) 637-2256 ($19.95 plus $3.50 shipping).

- *FLYING WHEELS TRAVEL* has many tours for persons in wheelchairs. For information, contact them at 143 West Bridge Street, Owatonna, MN 55060; (800) 535-6790.

- *ACCESSIBLE JOURNEYS* arranges domestic and foreign trips for persons who are in wheelchairs or who are slow walkers. For information, contact them at 35 West Sellers Avenue, Ridley Park, PA 19078; (800) 521-0339.

- *WILDERNESS INQUIRY* plans canoe, kayak, and dogsledding trips to all parts of the country for the disabled. Call (800) 728-0719 for information.

- *DISABILITY BOOKSHOP* (800-637-2256) provides a list of companies that rent wheelchair-accessible vehicles.

- *DIALYSIS AT SEA CRUISES.* (800) 544-7604. Has more than eighty sailings on ships that carry equipment and trained personnel.

- *TRAVEL TURTLE TOURS.* (800) 453-9195 or www.accessable.com/tours/turtle. Plans trips around the world for those who are disabled.

- *ACCESSIBLE TRAVEL.* This web site has a wealth of resources for people with special needs. Includes travel agents who plan tours, related organizations and publications, plus links to other resources on the web. Log on to www.access-able.com.

SPECIFIC DESTINATIONS

New York City

If you're coming to New York in a wheelchair, you may find it easier to get to and from the airports by New York Gray Line's vans rather than by taxi. All vans have wheelchair lifts. This service links Manhattan with the area's three airports. There's no additional charge. Vans operate daily with stops at all airline terminals, some Manhattan hotels, and two Gray Line terminals: one on West 46th Street and one at 8th Avenue at 49th Street. For information, call (800) 451-0455.

Etiquette Tips
FOR TRAVELING WITH OR MEETING
A HANDICAPPED PERSON

Handicapped people sometimes worry about how others will treat them when they are away from home and the reassuring comfort of familiar turf. Their concerns are not without reason, for, indeed, they are occasionally ignored—often because people have been brought up not to stare at those who are different. At other times, the handicapped are the victims of oversolicitation. What's best? Here are five guidelines, drawn up by a handicapped person, for the able to follow in dealing with the disabled.

1. *Always address a handicapped person directly.* Do not, for example, talk instead to the person pushing the wheelchair. And never refer to the handicapped in the third person when he or she is right there.

2. *Speak in a normal tone and at a normal level.* Don't resort to baby talk and don't shout. Just because someone is blind, for instance, does not mean he is hard of hearing. Or if someone has physical limitations, it does not mean she is incapable of understanding.

3. *Wait until receiving permission before helping.* Ask if the person would like you to open or hold the door. (Some handicapped people use the door or doorknob for support.) If it's a revolving door, he or she may wish to go through it at a slower pace, and helping could be disastrous. When you're with someone who is blind, first ask if he or she would like assistance in crossing the street or a room; if the answer is yes, let the person take your arm, and talk as you move forward, explaining the situation or conditions. Never leave the person at the other side of the road or room without telling him where he is and asking if you can do anything else.

4. *If you are at a hotel, a restaurant, or on a ship where food is served buffet style,* ask if you can bring a tray of food directly to the table for someone who is in a wheelchair or walking with a cane or who has difficulty seeing. Let them select, or at least ask them what they would like.

5. *On cruise ships or at tour receptions and welcome parties,* where most people will be standing or dancing, make a point to talk to those who must remain seated.

A rule of thumb: Help unobtrusively and preserve the dignity of the handicapped traveler.

Before your trip order a copy of *Access for All,* a guide for people with disabilities to more than 190 New York City cultural institutions. This is available free from WCBS News Radio 88, Department of Public Affairs, 51 West 52nd Street, New York, NY 10019; send a stamped, self-addressed business-size envelope.

London

London Theatre Guide for the Disabled describes facilities, parking, discounts for wheelchair users and contains a list of helpful contacts. It is available at no charge from Artsline, 5 Crowndale Road, London, NW1 1TRU, England.

A Freebie For a free copy of *Ten Simple Tips for Travelers with Disabilities,* call (800) 637-2256.

11
Special Interest Vacations

In doing, we learn.

—*George Herbert*

And in fact, it's fun to do something different—to learn a new language, to improve your physique, to climb to the top of a mountain, or to study nineteenth-century literature. You can arrange some of these experiences on your own, but doing so can be time-consuming and expensive. The staff at *Travel Smart Newsletter* specializes in telling its readers about the unusual. Here are some of our favorites. You'll find more listed in chapter 7, Traveling with Children; chapter 8, For the Fifty-Plus Crowd; and chapter 9, Traveling Solo. We've arranged these smart deals alphabetically by category.

ARTISTIC RETREATS

Peace, quiet, beauty, and professional workshops—the ideal working/thinking vacation for writers, musicians, artists, sculptors, and other artistic types who need a nurturing environment.

- ANDERSON RANCH ARTS CENTER, Snowmass Village, Colorado (970-923-3181), offers workshops for twelve to sixteen people for one or two weeks at a time. Tuition ranges from $350 to $1,000; lodging is $300 per week. You live in a condo or dormitory room; meal plan is optional. There are workshops in painting, drawing, ceramics, sculpture, and furniture design.

- DJERASSI RESIDENT ARTISTS PROGRAM, Woodside, California (650-747-1250), offers programs for ten artists (writers, painters, composers, dancers) at a time. Tuition and room and board are free (provided you qualify). Stay one or two months in a seven-bedroom house and a barn that overlook the Pacific Ocean.

- THE MACDOWELL COLONY, Peterborough, New Hampshire (603-924-3886), has room for thirty-two writers, artists, composers, photographers, and architects at a time. Admission is selective. You must make a voluntary contribution; stay up to four weeks. Accommodations are in an eighteenth-century farm on 450 acres, with shared baths. Dinner and breakfast are served in the dining room (lunch in your studio).

- *WRITING SCHOOLS.* If you want to learn to write or improve your writing abilities, the University of Iowa in Iowa City, Iowa, and Bennington College in Bennington, Vermont, are considered the two best in the country. They run a variety of programs; you live on campus and attend lectures, workshops, and readings. Contact them in January or February for attendance during the summer. You will be asked to submit published works or writing samples and letters of reference. For details call University of Iowa at (319) 335-3500 and Bennington College at (802) 442-5401.

- *OX-BOW,* Saugatuck, Michigan (312-899-5130), accommodates eight to twenty-four painters, writers, glassblowers, and potters per workshop. Tuition starts at $305 per week; $380 for room and board. Live in a large Victorian house or rustic cabins with shared baths; all meals are served in communal dining room.

- *VIRGINIA CENTER FOR THE CREATIVE ARTS,* Sweet Briar, Virginia (804-946-7236), has space for twenty-three writers, artists, and composers. For $30 per day you get a room, studio, and three meals; stay one week to two months. Accommodations are in a twenty-two-bedroom house situated on 450 acres near Sweet Briar College; shared baths and separate studios; prepared family-style meals.

- *YADDO,* Saratoga Springs, New York (518-584-0746), offers twelve to thirty-five writers, composers, artists, and choreographers a private studio or a room with a private bath in a nineteenth-century estate on 400 acres. There is a voluntary contribution of up to $25 a day; stay five weeks. Communal breakfast and dinner; lunch in your studio.

BASEBALL CAMPS

You can watch your favorite players warm up at spring-training camp. Exhibition games start in March. Send a self-addressed, stamped envelope to the American Baseball League or the National Baseball League and ask for a schedule plus phone numbers for individual teams. Both leagues are at 350 Park Avenue, New York, NY 10022. Tickets must be ordered directly from the teams.

Trips to famous baseball parks across the country are organized by Sports Travel. Call (800) 662-4424.

Every February fans can spend a week with former great New York Mets players at their spring-training facility in Port St. Lucie, Florida. This packaged tour includes round-trip airfare between New York and West Palm Beach, seven nights in a hotel, playing equipment, your own locker, breakfast and lunch daily, and play with and against former Mets greats. For information call Ultimate Week, (407) 788-2222.

BIKING TRIPS

American Youth Hostels runs warming-up trips in its Discovery Tours program. Trips are organized by ages, starting at age eighteen and going on up to the over-fifty crowd. For information call (202) 783-6161.

Bon Voyage Specialty Tours, in Fort Collins, Colorado (800-800-8511), has trips on Cape Cod and in Holland, Denmark, Israel, Ireland, Australia, and New Zealand. In Holland you sleep on a barge.

COOKING SCHOOLS

Rejuvenate your tastebuds with a cooking-school vacation. Weekend and five-day courses range from $300 to about $1,000. Many schools also offer hiking, golf, swimming, biking, and tennis, as well as antiquing nearby. Here are some suggestions.

United States

- *A Taste of the Mountains Cooking School,* Glen, New Hampshire; (800) 548-8007

- *Great Chefs* at the Robert Mondavi Winery, Oakville, California; (888) RMONDAVI

- *Tante Marie's Cooking School,* San Francisco, California; (415) 788-6699

Paris

- *Le Cordon Bleu,* 8, Rue Leon de l'homme; (800) 457-CHEF

- *Ecole de Gastronomie Française Ritz-Escoffier,* 15, Place Vendôme; (888) 801-1126; 011-33-1-43-16-30-50

- *Ecole Princesse* ERE 2001; 18, avenue de la Motte-Picquet; 011-33-1-45-51-36-34

FIELD RESEARCH

In the hands-on programs listed below, you help scientists who are studying nature or conducting research programs. Living arrangements are usually in dormitories, camps, or local institutions. Anyone in good health may participate—you don't need any expertise, just a willingness to work hard and an ability to live in a community setting. You won't get paid, but you'll have an interesting time. Most programs require a modest fee, ranging from $150 to $750 for a week to ten days, but type of experience and level of physical stamina required vary widely. Call these organizations for literature:

- *ARCHAEOLOGICAL CONSERVANCY,* Albuquerque, New Mexico; (505) 266-1540

- *ARCHAEOLOGICAL INSTITUTE OF AMERICA,* Boston, Massachusetts; (617) 353-9361

- *EARTHWATCH,* Watertown, Massachusetts; (800) 776-0188

- *NATIONAL AUDUBON SOCIETY,* New York, New York; (212) 979-3000

- *NATURE CONSERVANCY,* (212) 997-1880

- *SIERRA CLUB,* San Francisco, California; (415) 977-5653

- *SMITHSONIAN INSTITUTION,* Washington, D.C.; (202) 357-4700

- *WORLD WILDLIFE FUND,* Washington, D.C.; (202) 293-4800

FLY-FISHING SCHOOLS

This sport, recently made popular by former President George Bush, is relaxing, quiet, and not too expensive.

- *THE JOAN AND LEE WULFF FISHING SCHOOL,* about 100 miles north of New York City in Lew Beach, New York; (914) 439-4060. Weekend seminars on the Beaverkill River.

- *ORVIS FLY-FISHING SCHOOLS* in Manchester, Vermont; (802) 362-3622

- *L.L. BEAN FLY-FISHING SCHOOLS* in Freeport, Maine; (207) 865-4761

FOREIGN-LANGUAGE PROGRAMS

Brush up on or learn Spanish, French, Italian, Chinese, or other languages, either here or abroad.

- *LANGUAGE STUDY ABROAD* (818-242-5263) arranges for you to live with a native family while learning the language at a nearby school. Prices range from $695 to $800 and include boarding with a family for two weeks, meals, and lessons. You pay your airfare to the foreign country.

- *THE LANGUAGE SCHOOLS,* Middlebury College, Middlebury, Vermont (802-443-5000), is held each summer on the Middlebury campus; you live in a dormitory for a seven-week total-immersion program in one of eight foreign languages.

- *THE NATIONAL REGISTRATION CENTER FOR STUDY ABROAD,* Milwaukee, Wisconsin (414-278-0631), will make arrangements for you to participate in one of more than 800 programs offered by the center.

- FOREIGN LANGUAGE/STUDY ABROAD PROGRAMS, New York, New York (212-662-1090), offers a "Foreign Home Stay" program as well as traditional language schools abroad; the staff will help you pick the program best suited to your needs and budget.

GOLF VACATIONS

Complete Golfing Vacation Guide describes more than one hundred of Europe's foremost golf courses and nearby hotels, with maps and driving distances. To obtain a free copy, call Golf International at (800) 833-1389.

PGA Travel has unique hotel and golf packages to Scotland, Ireland, Spain, the Ryder Cup matches, and more. Call (800) 283-4653.

Three Off-Beat Golf Destinations

- ALABAMA. Think golf, think Alabama? This state has one of the best-kept golf secrets—the Robert Trent Jones Golf Trail, with a number of first-rate golf courses, all with extremely reasonable fees. The trail covers more than 100 miles of championship courses, going from the Appalachians in the northern part of the state to the Gulf of Mexico. All courses, designed by Jones, are open to the public and have greens fees ranging from $35 weekdays to $45 on weekends. You'll also enjoy the brand-new clubhouses, restaurants, and shops done in the "private" golf club style.

  Here's a list of the courses, going approximately from north to south, with the names of nearby hotels with special golfer's rates.

GOLF COURSE	TOWN/CITY	HOTEL
Hampton Grove	Huntsville	Huntsville Hilton; (800) 445-8667
Oxmoor Valley	Birmingham	Tutwiler Hotel; (205) 322-2100
Grand National	Auburn/Opelika	Auburn Hotel; (800) 2-AUBURN
Magnolia Grove	Mobile	Adam's Mark; (800) 444-2326
Highland Oaks	Dothan	Holiday Inn South; (800) 465-4329

 For a Robert Trent Jones Golf Trail Pass, which gives you unlimited play, call (800) 949-4444. You can also book tee times and get information on specific courses through this number. For a map and general information on Alabama's historic attractions, call (800) ALABAMA.

- *LAKE HAVASU, ARIZONA.* These desert courses offer year-round play at reasonable rates and a surefire way to escape winter's chill. Located about an hour from Laughlin, Nevada, and some 150 miles from Los Angeles, you'll find not only golf but also house-boating, fishing, tennis, and horseback riding—and it's seldom crowded. These beautiful courses (one in nearby Laughlin) have lake, mountain, or desert views. Greens fees range from about $20 to $50. You can stay in Lake Havasu for less than $100 per night at the London Bridge Resort (800-624-7939). The Nautical Inn, which is more upscale and resort-like, costs somewhat more (800-892-2141). In all cases ask about special golf packages, which include reduced rates and greens fees. Contact *London Bridge Golf Club, (520-855-1575) or Emerald River Golf Course,* (702-298-0061).

- *CHARLESTON, SOUTH CAROLINA.* The proverbial golf widow is a thing of the past in this historic area of South Carolina. "His & Hers" packages include accommodations, greens fees, and cart. Golf fees are eliminated from the daily rate for those who don't swing a club—for a savings of about $35. Contact Charleston Golf Partners, (800) 247-5786.

Insider Tip If you don't want to lug your clubs, call VIP Golf (760) 776–6866. Their Golf Bag Express program will ship your clubs by UPS to/from your destination.

More Golf Goodies

Almost every major resort in this country, as well as those in the United Kingdom, runs golf packages, with rates varying from season to season and from year to year. We suggest you contact any that interest you for current golfing deals. Our picks:

- *The Homestead,* Virginia, (800) 336-5771

- *Hilton Head,* South Carolina, (843) 785-3673

- *Wild Dunes Resort,* Charleston, South Carolina, (800) 845-8880

 For information on special golf packages around the world, contact Value Golf Vacations (800) 786-7634. They can also get you tickets to the British and American opens, with accommodations and sightseeing. Golf International, (800) 833-1389, and PGA Travel, (800) 283-4653, offer similar programs.

Golf Schools There are more than 200 golf camps around the country, ranging from about $600 for three days to $1,000+ for a week. For a complete list: www.shawguides.com/golf.

- *Academy of Golf Dynamics.* (800) 879–2008 or www.moontower.com/golf-dynamics. Has camps in Colorado, Florida, Texas.

- *Golf Digest Schools.* (800) 243–6121 or www.golf.com/golfdigest/schools. Held at Sea Island Golf Club in Georgia.

- *Nike Parent-Child Golf Camps.* (800) 645–3226 or www.ussportscamps.com. Has fourteen-plus locations around the country.

- *The Golf School.* (800) 240–2555 or www.thegolfschool.com. Has camps in New England and the mid-Atlantic region.

HIKING AND TREKKING TOURS

Depending on the trek, you carry your own gear or have porters, share in the cooking or have catered meals. Regardless, these tours are quite strenuous, so make sure you are in good physical shape. Softer, less demanding treks are run by the Wayfarers—a van follows out of sight, carrying luggage and picking up stragglers.

Here are some of the best groups:

- APPALACHIAN MOUNTAIN CLUB, Boston, Massachusetts; (617) 523-0636

- BOULDERS RESORT, 13 miles from Scottsdale, Arizona; (800) 553-1717

- COUNTRY WALKERS, Waterbury, Vermont; (802) 244-1387

- ENGLISH LAKELAND RAMBLERS AND OUTDOOR BOUND, New York City; (800) 724-8801

- EQUITOUR, Solvang, California; (800) 666-3487

- OUTWARD BOUND USA, Greenwich, Connecticut; (800) 243-8520

- SIERRA CLUB, San Francisco, California; (415) 977-5500

- WAYFARERS, Newport, Rhode Island; (401) 849-5087 or (800) 249-4620

HORSEBACK RIDING AND FOX HUNTING

Cross Country International Equestrian Vacations has well-run, deluxe trips for persons who want to ride or learn to ride. Many trips are to Ireland and England, where you stay in small hotels and inns in picturesque countryside. Horse, equipment, and fees are included in the price as well as accommodations and most meals. For more information call (800) 828-TROT.

ICE FISHING

From Maine to Minnesota to Alaska, ice fishing is an inexpensive way to enjoy the outdoors—and catch dinner. For brochures and information call:

- *Minnesota Office of Tourism,* (800) 657-3700

- *St. Paul Convention & Visitors Bureau,* (800) 627-6101

- *Leech Lake Area,* (800) 833-1118

- *Houghton Lake,* (800) 248-LAKE

- *Saginaw Bay,* (800) 444-9979

- *Tawas,* (800) 55-TAWAS

LEARNING VACATIONS

In addition to the programs listed below, contact your college or university, local museum or historical society, botanical garden, or zoo. Many of these places—including the New York Museum of Natural History (212-769-5100), Chicago Art Institute (312-443-3600), Boston Museum of Fine Arts (617-267-9300), and San Diego Zoo (619-234-3153)—sponsor cultural trips to other countries or run on-campus summer and weekend institutes. They are open to the public, although you may be asked to join the organization or make a donation. (For special learning programs for senior citizens, see page 147.)

 Check, too, with Academic Arrangements Abroad, 50 Broadway, New York, NY 10004; (800) 221-1944. This long-established company, with an excellent reputation, puts together some of the most interesting cultural and academic tours, cruises, and vacations for alumni associations, museum groups, foundations, and other special organizations. Call for a current listing of its unique trips, all of which have experts along for informal lectures and entry to behind-the-scenes activities and events.

- *CHAUTAUQUA INSTITUTION* (800-836-ARTS), on a 17-mile-long lake in far western New York State, is a vacation center for the arts with more than 150

courses in languages, music, painting, dance, etc. Chautauqua also has its own symphony and opera and ballet companies. Sometimes Al Gore lectures, and Ray Charles and Tammy Wynette entertain. There are no cars, alcohol, or wild life in this Victorian village, but there are children's programs, golf, boating, fishing, tennis, hiking, and bird-watching. Stay at one of seven hotels or a quaint guest house. (For special opportunities for senior citizens, see page 147.)

- *CORNELL'S ADULT UNIVERSITY,* Ithaca, New York (607-255-6260), holds week-long seminars on a variety of subjects. The cost includes room and board on campus. Off-campus study tours around the United States and abroad are also available.

- *DISCOVERY PASSAGES* (520-717-0519) organizes visits to Hopi, Apache, Navajo, and other Native American areas.

- *HISTORY AMERICA TOURS* (800-628-8542) specialize in tours of Civil War battlefields, great artists of the American West, and the California Mission Trail.

- *JOURNEYS INTO AMERICAN INDIAN TERRITORY* (800-458-2632) is a group that runs unusual trips, led by both anthropologists and Native Americans, that include sleeping in a tepee, meeting tribal members, and studying the life of the Cheyenne, Cherokee, or Seminole Indians.

- *LANGUAGE STUDY ABROAD,* Glendale, California (818-242-5263), will make arrangements for you to learn Spanish, French, or Italian in Cuernavaca, Seville, Vichy, Sienna, or Rome in total-immersion courses. You'll live with a private family and have time for touring.

- *UNIVERSITY VACATIONS (UNIVAC),* Miami, Florida (800-792-0100), has one- and two-week sessions at Oxford and Cambridge in England, Trinity College in Dublin, and the Sorbonne in Paris.

LIGHTHOUSE TOURS

The U.S. Lighthouse Society has tours each year to some of this country's most beautiful regions; yacht trips or cruises are often part of the deal. For a list send a self-addressed, stamped envelope to the U.S. Lighthouse Society, 244 Kearny Street, San Francisco, CA 94108.

NATURE TOURS

The groups listed below arrange fascinating tours and programs that involve exploring the flora and fauna of a region, such as watching calving whales in Baja, studying wild orchids in Papua, or observing fur seals in Canada. All are led by expert naturalists.

- *American Wilderness Experience,* Boulder, Colorado; (800) 444-0099

- *National Audubon Society,* New York City; (212) 979-3000

- *New York Botanical Gardens,* Bronx, New York; (718) 817-8647

- *Society Expeditions,* Seattle, Washington; (800) 548-8669

  (See also list of hiking associations on page 171.)

PARKS

Many of our national parks are packed during the summer, but these five less-well-known ones are never crowded.

- CUMBERLAND GAP HISTORICAL PARK, in Kentucky and Tennessee, was a favorite of Daniel Boone and a key passage to the Old West. For information call (606) 248-2817.

- NORTH CASCADES is home to 318 glaciers with beautiful mountain scenery; located 125 miles northeast of Seattle. Call (253) 856-5700 for information.

- CAPE LOOKOUT NATIONAL SEASHORE has wide beaches that stretch 55 miles along the North Carolina coast. Hunting, fishing, hiking, and camping are available. For details call (919) 728-2250.

- WIND CAVE NATIONAL PARK, in South Dakota, features limestone caverns with crystal formations and open prairies full of bison, elk, and wildlife. This park has the seventh-longest cave in the world—more than 53 miles long. For information call (605) 745-4600.

- BIGHORN CANYON. In Montana, Bighorn Lake extends 71 miles, including 47 miles through spectacular Bighorn Canyon. Call (406) 666-2412 for information.

SAILING

Various learning vacations, for individuals as well as families, are available from the Offshore Sailing School and are led by certified instructors. Courses are held in Florida and New England. You stay in nearby accommodations, but take lessons on the water. At a certain level of experience, students take overnight sailing trips with an instructor on board. For information call (800) 221-4326.

SPAS

Instead of listing the well-known spas, which advertise heavily and are familiar to most travelers, here are eight less-known but full-fledged spas that have lower rates.

- *MARIO'S INTERNATIONAL AURORA HOUSE SPA,* Aurora, Ohio (330-562-9171); only 30 miles from Cleveland

- *AVEDA SPA,* Osceola, Wisconsin (715-294-4465); one hour from Minneapolis/ St. Paul

- *NEW AGE HEALTH SPA,* Neversink, New York (800-NU-AGE-4-U); on a 160-acre Catskill Mountain farm, with limo/van service from Manhattan

- *GREEN VALLEY HEALTH SPA,* St. George, Utah (800-237-1068); in the mountains of southern Utah

- *NEW LIFE SPA,* at the Inn of the Six Mountains in Killington, Vermont (800-545-9407); in a beautiful New England setting

- *THE OAKS AT OJAI,* Ojai, California (800-753-6257); about a two-hour drive up the coast from Los Angeles

- *DEERFIELD MANOR SPA,* East Stroudsburg, Pennsylvania (800-852-4494); a simple but excellent value in the Poconos

 Before you go, take time to read *Health Spa Tips,* an unbiased booklet available for $1.00 from the Council of Better Business Bureaus, Dept. 023, Washington, DC 20042; enclose a stamped self-addressed, business-size envelope with your order.

SPECIAL EVENTS

Music

Allegro Enterprises is a New York City–based tour operator that specializes in music tours and is the only authorized North American agent for the Kirov, Bolshoi, and Finnish National Opera. It frequently has musical tours tied in with special events to Italy and other European countries. Call (800) 666-3553 for detailed information.

Drama

A helpful directory is the *Directory of Outdoor Historical Drama in America,* which describes more than ninety music, dance, and historical festivals and pageants; it includes a locator map and plot summaries as well as dates and addresses. To get a copy send $5.00 to Institute of Outdoor Drama, University of North Carolina, CB 3240, Chapel Hill, NC 27599; (919) 962-1328.

Edwards & Edwards get tickets to opera and classical music, theater, and other events in New York, London, Paris, Berlin, and some other European cities. Its computerized systems means that your seats are immediately confirmed. Tickets or confirmations are mailed or faxed in less than twenty-four hours. Hotel, sight-seeing, and packages (some with meals) can be arranged. For information call them at (800) 223-6108 or (914) 328-2150.

Sports

Playoffs, championships, finals, and series are all big business for operators of sports tours and packages. This business is so big that the Department of Transportation has declared that a package may not be advertised unless the travel company has tickets or a signed contract for them actually in hand. If you want to attend a popular sporting event that's likely to be full of "match madness," deal with a company that has been in this business for some time, and/or get guarantees about tickets in writing.

 You can get the names of a reputable agency through the sports department of your local college or university. Here are some we have found to be reliable.

- *Sports Empire* is the place to call if you want to see the Kentucky Derby, the Rose Bowl, the Olympics, and next year's World Series or any other special sporting event. They have numerous sports packages that include tickets, hotels, and transportation. For information call (800) 255-5258.

- *Sportsworld International* is the official tour operator for Wimbledon's Tennis Championship. It runs various packages including tickets to the matches and hotel accommodations with daily breakfast. Call (800) 278-6738 for information.

- *Sports Travel,* for tickets to major events, (800) 662-4424

Tickets

Getting tickets is seldom easy, especially when they're for foreign concerts or festivals, so plan ahead. Here are some little-known sources for tickets to well-known events.

• THE EDINBURGH FESTIVAL. This annual event, held every year in late August, is world-famous for its musical concerts, dramas, bands, etc. Contact: Edinburgh International Festival, 21 Market Street, Edinburgh, Scotland, EH 1 1BW, or call 031-226-4001.

• WIMBLEDON. Tickets for this world-famous tennis match are allocated primarily through a public ballot system. To get an application, send a self-addressed, stamped envelope to All England Lawn Tennis & Croquet Club, Box 98, Church Road, Wimbledon, SW 19 5AE, England. Your application must be returned to the club by December 31. A limited number of tickets are available on the day of the match. Or, contact these two official tour agents for tickets, as well as for packages that include hotel rooms and, sometimes, airfare: Sportsworld International (800) 278-6738, or Keith Prowse, (800) 669-8687.

• MUSICAL FESTIVALS & CONCERTS. This tour operator specializes in music tours and festivals around the world, including Russia, Finland, and Poland. Contact Allegro Enterprises, (800) 666-3553.

• LONDON THEATER. A number of U.S. companies sell tickets for London shows; they add on various service charges. Check prices with these reliable companies. Some also have packaged tours with airfare and hotel rooms included.

  • *Keith Prowse Ticket Agency,* (800) 669-8687; in England 44-81-795- 1111

  • *Edwards & Edwards,* (800) 223-6108

  • *Sterling Tours,* (800) 727-4359

 Keith Prowse has several London offices, including one in the basement of Harrods; the main office is at 156 Shaftesbury Avenue in London.

New York City

Here are ways to check on what's happening in the Big Apple.

1. The "New York City On Stage Hotline" (212-768-1818) tells what's playing and gives a plot synopsis, theater address, performance time, and information on ordering tickets.

2. Check *New York* magazine, the *New Yorker,* and the *New York Times,* and *Time Out New York.*

3. *WHERE New York,* a free monthly guide available in most Manhattan and area hotels, is the most complete listing of what's playing. Out-of-towners may subscribe by calling (212) 725-8100. *WHERE* also has editions in other

cities: Atlanta, Boston, Chicago, Los Angeles, Minneapolis/St. Paul, New Orleans, St. Louis, San Francisco, and Washington, D.C.

When you've decided what you want to see, you can order tickets by mail directly from the box office (be sure to enclose a check) or by telephone and charging the tickets to a major credit card. To order by phone, call Telecharge at (212) 239-6200, or Ticketmaster at (212) 307-7171 or (800) 736-2000.

Following are some resources for obtaining packages and discounts in the Big Apple.

- *THE MORE THE MERRIER.* Most theaters and concert halls in New York offer substantial discounts to groups of twenty or more. Group sales telephone numbers are listed in the show ads. Or check with Group Sales Box Office, 226 West 47th Street, Third floor, New York, NY 10036; (212) 398-8383. They place group orders for Broadway shows for a small handling fee.

- *THEATER PACKAGES.* From time to time, New York hotels will run theater weekends. They advertise in the Sunday *New York Times.*

- *THE NEW YORK GRAY LINE* also has packages that include theater tickets, dining, airport transfers, and sight-seeing, along with some hotel discounts. For a list, contact New York Gray Line, (800) 669-0051.

TENNIS CAMPS

Learn how to play tennis or fine-tune your game. There are a number of tennis camps and tennis resorts around the country that advertise heavily in travel publications and *Tennis Magazine.* Here are four, which you may not know about, that we like.

- *TENNIS CAMPS LTD,* Swathmore and Topnotch in Stowe, Vermont; (800) 223-2442

- *TENNIS & LIFE CAMPS,* Gustavus Adolphus College, St. Peter, Minnesota; (507) 931-1614

- *TOPNOTCH AT STOWE,* Stowe, Vermont; (800) 451-8686

- *VAN DER MEER SUMMER CAMP,* Sweet Briar College, Lynchburg, Virginia; West Town, Pennsylvania; Cornell University, New York; and Hilton Head, South Carolina; (800) 845-6138

VOLUNTEERING

Here are four ways to do some good and enjoy a change of scene at the same time.

1. *Guide to Volunteering for Older Americans* (publication #638Z) lists types of activities, needed experience, training, and organizations to contact. Write to Consumer Information Center, Dept. 638Z, Pueblo, CO 81009.

2. Volunteers for Peace, a UNESCO-affiliated organization, based in Belmont, Vermont, promotes work camps in forty countries, with community-service projects that run from two to three weeks at about $150 per work camp. You must pay your own transportation to and from the work camp. No foreign language proficiency is required. For information call (802) 259-2759.

3. Help restore the land with a Sierra Club Service Outing. You can rebuild trails, save exotic plants, etc. throughout the Appalachian Trail and in the Far West. Prices for week-long projects range from $250 to $380; airfare is extra. Call (415) 977-5653 for details.

4. Volunteer at a national park. You could wind up working as a campground host, curator, librarian, trail crew member, computer specialist, or something else. Every year the national parks, forests, and public lands need help. Some positions supply housing, academic credit, or reimbursement for food or travel expenses. For information, consult a copy of *Helping Out in the Outdoors* at your public library, or send $5.00 to American Hiking Society, Helping Out, Box 20160, Washington, DC 20041.

Here are three more organizations that provide various opportunities to volunteer.

- *Earthwatch* in Watertown, Massachusetts; (800) 776-0188 or (617) 926-8200

- *Global Volunteers* of St. Paul, Minnesota; (800) 487-1074 or (612) 482-1074

- *University Research Expeditions Program,* University of California at Berkeley; (510) 642-6586

12
Traveling in Good Health

*To eat what you don't want, drink what you don't like
and do what you'd rather not.*

—*Mark Twain*

These three things are often necessary in order to travel healthy. But they're worthwhile because there's nothing worse than getting sick while gallivanting about the globe. Sometimes it simply can't be helped, yet safe and sound travel is far more likely if you prepare ahead of time. Although there's no one repository for information about staying healthy while traveling, these sources and ideas will be useful. Of course, always check with your own doctor about your particular needs prior to leaving home. (For specifics on children's health needs while traveling, see pages 135–37.)

MEDICAL COVERAGE AWAY FROM HOME

Begin by reviewing your current health insurance policy: Many policies are not valid abroad.

 The Medicare program does not cover hospital and medical services outside the United States, except when a hospital in Canada or Mexico is more accessible than one in the United States. Eight of the ten standardized medigap plans, however, include overseas care on a temporary basis, including the AARP/Prudential Medigap Plan. If you live abroad permanently you will not be covered. Most Blue Cross/Blue Shield policies cover some emergency care outside the United States. Medigap plans typically reimburse you for your expenses, so you have to pay the bill when you're treated and then file a claim when you get home. Most of these supplemental plans have a maximum coverage per trip.

If your current health policy does not provide coverage, then a one-time travel insurance policy is adequate, as long as you travel infrequently. It generally picks up hospital and physician fees and the cost of emergency medical transportation to an appropriate facility or even back to the United States. Also typically included are on-the-spot assistance in finding a doctor, contacting your doctor at home, and filling prescriptions. Two policies that concentrate on medical care rather than trip cancellation and baggage insurance are Health Care Abroad (800-237-6615), and Travmed (800-732-5309). Both pay up to $250,000 in medical expenses such as hospital and doctor bills, ambulances, and emergency transportation. They also have free 800 lines for help in finding medical care and arranging emergency transportation. Coverage is excluded, however, for preexisting conditions, so read the fine print carefully if you've been ill.

A policy that is less restrictive regarding preexisting conditions, but offers less medical coverage, is Travel Guard International (800-826-1300). Other companies to check are Access America International (800-284-8300), International SOS Assistance (800-523-8930), and Travel Assistance International (800-821-2828). When calling any of these companies, ask about any deductible; preexisting condition clauses; copayments; the cost for various lengths of time; whether hospital, doctor bills, medication, and emergency transportation are covered; and how long any preexisting condition exclusion can reach back prior to your trip—for instance, it could be 60, 90, or 120 days.

A Freebie For a free copy of *Medical Information for Americans Traveling Abroad,* call The Bureau of Counsular Affairs, (202) 647–3000 or log on to travel.state.gov/yourtripabroad.html.

These medical-coverage plans may also cover baggage loss and trip interruption and cancellation insurance for an additional fee. A typical price range: from $5.00 per $100 of baggage, up to a maximum of $2,000; and $5.50 per $100, up to a maximum of $10,000, for trip cancellation.

Many credit cards, especially gold cards, offer some travel insurance and will replace lost tickets (if you used the card to purchase them) as well as lost baggage. Some credit-card companies will help you fill a prescription and arrange for an air ambulance. In order to avoid duplicating coverage, call your card issuer for details on what you can expect in terms of an emergency.

DOCTORS AWAY FROM HOME

American embassies and consulates can usually give you the names of hospitals, doctors, and dentists who speak English. Your credit card may also offer emergency traveler's assistance that includes names of English-speaking medical people and facilities. Some have phone consultation from a U.S. doctor who can help monitor your treatment in a foreign country.

What should you do if you're suddenly taken ill or if you have an accident while traveling? We recommend using one of the following medical services. For a fairly modest membership (or for free), you get access to a physician and/or medical information by phone, twenty-four hours a day. But before signing on, check your current credit-card coverage, your health insurance policy, or, if you're enrolled, the Medicare program. You want to avoid duplication of coverage.

- *HOTEL/DOCS.* Membership: free. Fee: $150 per visit. Has 1,500 AMA-approved doctors and specialists in more than 130 U.S. cities who will come to your hotel or any other location twenty-four hours a day upon call. (800) Hotel-DR or www.hoteldocs.com.

- *INN CARE OF AMERICA.* Membership: $39.95 per year. Fee: regular doctor's fees. Network of family doctors in 2,200 U.S. cities for nonemergency-type care. One hour after you phone a toll-free number, a doctor's office will contact you to set up an office visit. (800) 489-6277.

Medical Preparedness List

Take time to draw up your personal medical history. Keep one copy in your wallet, one in your suitcase, and one back home with a relative or close friend. Include:

- Your name, address, home and office numbers

- Blood type

- Doctor's name, address, office and emergency numbers

- Health plan: name of insurance company or HMO, your policy number, and contact phone numbers

- List of chronic health problems, such as diabetes, AIDS, high blood pressure

- Allergies—to medications, animals, insects, food

- Prescriptions for eye glasses and/or contact lenses

- Passport number

- Driver's license number

- Location of your will and name and address of lawyer

 Carry prescription medications in their original containers with labels; this helps you get refills and also to pass through customs.

- *INTERNATIONAL ASSOCIATION FOR MEDICAL ASSISTANCE TO TRAVELERS.* Membership: free. Fee: $55 for an office visit; $75 for a house or hotel call; $95 at night or on holidays. A nonprofit organization publishes a directory listing more than 850 English-speaking doctors in 130 countries who have agreed to treat travelers for a set price. Doctors are U.S., Canadian, or British trained. (716) 754–4883.

- *MEDIC ALERT.* Fee: $35 for a bracelet or pendant and $15 per year after the first year. Provides medical information by phone, twenty-four hours a day, for emergency situations. The phone number and your ID number appear on the bracelet or pendant, which, as a member, you should wear at all times. (800) 825–3785.

- *MEDJET ASSITANCE.* Annual fee: $150 ($225 per family). Guaranteed medically supervised transport (on a Lear jet, if required) from any airport-accessible hospital in the world to any other. Membership covers up to two evacuations per year; if you're age seventy-five to eighty-one, it's $225 per year. If you travel abroad more than ninety consecutive days, rates are higher. You can elect to return to your hometown hospital or any other hospital of your choice, although you must be in a hospital at least 150 miles from home and require extended hospital treatment. If you are presently hospitalized, on an organ transplant list, or have an infection at the time of enrollment, you are not eligible for air transport for those particular conditions. And, countries with U.S. State Department restrictions are not covered. (800) 963–3538 or www. medjetassistance.com.

A COMPENDIUM OF TIPS

The following directory of health-related issues is listed in alphabetical order. Refer to it *before* traveling, especially to exotic destinations.

Airplanes

Air on most planes, some trains, and older buses can be extremely dry, making you quite uncomfortable. Self-defense: Try not to use decongestants, antihistamines, and other drying agents unless you really need to. Drink lots of nonalcoholic beverages. Spray your nostrils with a water solution. Remove soft contact lenses and/or lubricate eyes. After you arrive immediately take a steamy shower or use a hot steam vaporizer.

The American Medical Association says if you've had a cold or other sickness or had recent surgery, it's a good idea to use an oral decongestant an hour before descent and/or a decongestant nasal spray or drops before and during descent. The AMA says you should not fly at all if you've had:

- A heart attack within the past month

- A stroke within the past two weeks

- Severe high blood pressure

- Severe heart disease

- Pneumothorax (air outside the lungs)

- Cysts of the lung or lung disease

- Acute sinusitis or middle ear infections

- Abdominal surgery within the past two weeks

- Intestinal viruses

- Recent eye surgery

- Wiring of the jaw

- Pregnancy beyond 240 days or threatened by miscarriage

According to experts, the rate of change in air pressure in an airplane during ascent and descent is about 550 feet per minute—too fast for blocked or swollen eustacian tubes to adjust. You've probably tried chewing gum and yawning—both of which help some people. But here's a new product for real sufferers: "EarPlanes." These inserts have two parts, a silicone earplug that provides an airtight seal between your ear canal and the surrounding atmosphere, and a ceramic pressure regulator. EarPlanes are recommended for flyers with allergies, colds, or sinus conditions. Drugstores sell them or you can order them for $19.95 by calling Harrington at (800) 622-5221. Check with your doctor first.

Allergies

If you have serious reactions or unique medical problems, wear a medical-alert tag or always carry a card that explains your condition. Tags are available from your doctor or Medic Alert Foundation, Box 1009, Turlock, CA 95381 (800-825-3785). Identification cards are available from American Medical Association, 535 North Dearborn Street, Chicago, IL 60610. Ask your doctor if you should carry adrenalin for reaction to wasp or bee stings.

The American Academy of Allergy and Immunology (800-822-2762) can provide information on how to get the right shots when traveling in a foreign country, what to do if your allergy acts up, and so on

Bites and Stings

If you've been bitten by an animal or stung by an insect, call the Rocky Mountain Poison Center at (303) 629-1123.

Blood

Needing a transfusion when overseas is a scary business. Although blood is carefully screened for AIDS and other infections in Canada, Australia, Japan, Singapore, Hong Kong, and Western Europe, in all other countries it is not. The poorer the country, the greater the risk that the blood supply could be contaminated.

If you're at all uncertain about the blood supply, you should leave the country, an expensive prospect but one that may be covered by insurance. International SOS (800-523-8930), for example, has a package that includes pretrip medical planning, on-site English-speaking doctors, and emergency medication and medical evacuation. The fee is about $55 for a fourteen-day trip (for couples traveling together, about $100; and for a family, $155). Similar plans are also available from USAssist (800-756-5900) and Worldwide Services Assistance (800-821-2828). In addition the American Express Gold Card and Visa and MasterCard gold cards offer evacuation-assistance numbers; although they won't cover your expenses, they will help you arrange for evacuation and see to it that the fees are billed to your card.

Further protection: If you're going to a poorer country, carry your own disposable medical items. Contact International SOS at (800) 523-8930 for information on its portable Steri-Safe Medical Kit, which sells for about $40 and includes latex gloves, sutures and needles, syringes, swabs, etc.

British Water Alert

Flakes of lead from old pipes have been discovered in many water systems and may appear periodically in tap water. About 20 percent of British homes have been found to have water-lead levels over and above those recommended by the World Health Organization. Lead retards the mental development of small children and is also dangerous for adults because it's a cumulative poison. If you're renting or living in an old house, use bottled water.

Cruise Ships

A sanitation program is run jointly by the Centers for Disease Control and the cruise-ship industry. All ships carrying more than fifteen passengers and stopping at foreign ports of call must be inspected twice a year. For a free copy of the most recent sanitation report, *The Summary of Sanitation Inspections of Cruise Ships,* write to Vessel Sanitation Program, National Center for Environmental Health, 1015 North American Way, Suite 107, Miami, FL 33132.

Diarrhea

This condition can be most unpleasant, with continually runny bowels, cramps, bloating, fever, etc. It is contracted through fecally contaminated food or water that contains organisms that your system cannot handle—food, either cooked or uncooked, tap water, ice, unpasteurized milk, ice cream, food from street vendors, etc. Imodium, which can be purchased over the counter in tablets or liquid form, is helpful. So is Pepto Bismol.

Avoiding Traveler's Diarrhea

SAFE	UNSAFE
Fresh dishes served very hot	Tap water, even for brushing teeth
Meats cooked well done and to order	Uncooked or reheated meats
Fruits that you can peel	The peel itself
Breads, baked goods	Ice, even in alcoholic drinks
Hot tea and coffee	Cold salads
Bottled or boiled water	Fruits that you can't peel
Bottled or canned soft drinks	Street-vendor food
Bottled or canned juices	Anything reheated
Imported wine or beer	Beverage from already-opened bottles
Evaporated milk	Fresh milk

Exercise

Walk rather than jog or run if the temperature, humidity, and altitude are different from those at home.

First-aid Kits

If you're headed for a remote area, your first-aid kit should contain broad-based antibiotics and steroids, gauze dressings, athletic tape, saline eye irrigator, bandages, sunblock, pain reliever, cold and diarrhea medicines, antacid, and water-purification equipment

Food

In areas where sanitation is below standard, avoid salads, uncooked vegetables, milk, cheese, ice cream, raw meat, fish, and shellfish; eat only food that has been cooked and is still warm and fruits that you have peeled. Canned evaporated milk and condensed milk are usually safe. Bottled water and soda are extremely safe, but insist on having bottles or cans opened in your presence.

Foreign Travel

Before going abroad, contact the Centers for Disease Control & Prevention for information about necessary vaccinations and local medical situations. You can reach the CDC voice line at (404) 332-4559.

Warnings from the State Department advise travelers about those countries currently considered dangerous for Americans to visit. These warnings mean that conditions are potentially threatening to American travelers and that the U.S. government cannot help them in emergencies. Warnings are updated every six months, but more often, of course, if events so warrant it. For copies of *Consular Information Sheets* or *Travel Warnings,* send a self-addressed, stamped, business-size envelope, stating the countries you want information on, to Office of Overseas Citizens Services, Room 4800, Department of State, Washington, DC 20520. To check on a specific country by phone, call (202) 647-5225 from a touch-tone phone. If you have a fax, call (202) 647-3000 for directions on receiving automated fax material.

Glasses

Take along an extra pair of glasses and/or contact lenses, as well as your prescription and an ample supply of appropriate solutions.

Health Records for the Chronically Ill

If you have a major chronic medical problem, you must take your vital records with you wherever you go. If your problems are relatively minor, a simple card listing important information for use overseas will do. For information contact:

- *Life-Fax Emergency Response Card,* IDR Technology, Inc., 200 Market Place, Roswell, GA 30075; (770) 552-4140 or (800) 487-0329

Hearing Aids

Bring along some spare batteries.

Hotels and Motels

Bring a portable smoke detector when you travel to protect against any hotel—in violation of state laws—that does not have detectors in its rooms, or has ones with dead batteries. Also pack a portable burglar alarm that trips when someone tries to enter your room or a wedge that fits under the door to keep it closed.

Immunizations

The only vaccination required, as of press time, is for yellow fever if you're going to French Guiana, Benin, Burkina Faso, Cameroon, Central African Republic, Congo, Ivory Coast, Gabon, Liberia, Mali, Mauritania, Niger, Rwanda, Senegal, São Tomé and Principe, Togo, and Zaire. Carry your "yellow card" as proof of inoculation and keep it with your passport. You must get your shot ten days prior to departure from a vaccination center approved by a state health department.

Other vaccinations depend on current situations in specific areas. Your physician can check the regularly updated *Summary of Health Information for International Travel,* published by the Public Health Service, or you can contact the Public Health Service's Centers for Disease Control, which has an automated hotline, twenty-four hours a day, at (404) 332-4559.

Insects

Mosquitoes carry malaria, yellow fever, and encephalitis; the plague is carried by fleas, Lyme disease by ticks. The U.S. Public Health Service recommends insect repellents containing permethrin for use on clothing, camping gear, and shoes, but not on your skin or hair. For the latter two, use a repellent containing a DEET concentration no higher than 30 percent.

Malaria

About 1,000 Americans contract malaria annually. It is transmitted by mosquito bites and is found in Africa, Central America, China, Haiti, India, Indonesia, Mexico, the Middle East, South America, Southeast Asia, and Turkey. The symptoms: fever, ongoing headaches, shaking, vomiting, aches, sweating, and a feeling of weakness. Check with your physician about anti-malarial pills, such as chloroquine. You may need to take medication as far as two weeks in advance of your trip. For information call the CDC Hotline at (404) 332-4559.

Medicines

Keep your prescription medicines in their original containers when going to foreign countries; otherwise they might be confiscated as illegal drugs. If liquid, put the containers in plastic, resealable bags. If you take exotic or narcotic prescription drugs, ask your doctor to write a statement describing your condition. In all cases pack a written prescription in case you need a refill or lose your medicine while traveling. Have your doctor use generic names on your prescriptions because brand names vary. Keep your prescriptions separate from your drugs.

Mountain Travel

Dehydration at heights is very common and can seriously interfere with your trip or vacation. Your lungs exhale more water in dry, oxygen-scarce air. In addition high altitudes suppress your thirst mechanism. Prevention technique: Drink at least twelve cups of water a day even if you don't feel thirsty.

Mystery Disease

In the spring of 1994, a "mystery" disease struck people in the Four Corners Region of Arizona, Colorado, New Mexico, and Utah. Beginning with a fever, muscle aches, headache, and cough, it progressed rapidly into lung disease and death. Called hantavirus pulmonary syndrome or Muerto Canyon virus, it is carried by rodents, particularly deer mice, and has killed mostly healthy adult American Indians. The virus is spreading and has been associated with about fifty deaths in western states. The Centers for Disease Control offers hikers and campers the following cautions:

- *Avoid* coming into contact with rodents and their dens.

- *Don't* use cabins or other enclosed shelters that are rodent infested.

- *Don't* pitch tents or put sleeping bags in areas near rodent activity, including garbage dumps and woodpiles.

- *Don't* sleep on bare ground. Cots should be at least 12 inches above ground; use tents with floors.

- *Keep* all food in rodent-proof containers.

- *Bury* or burn all garbage and trash or discard it in covered trash containers.

- *Use* only bottled water or boiled water for drinking, cooking, washing dishes, and brushing teeth.

Needles

If you require sterile needles for medical reasons and are traveling to a Third World country where they might not be available, take your own.

Oxygen

If you or someone in your family must be on oxygen, travel is still possible. The American Association for Respiratory Care has written a brochure, *Requirements for Traveling with Oxygen,* which outlines the policies of the major cruise lines, airlines, bus companies, and Amtrak. You can obtain a free copy from the American Lung Association (800-586-4872). Another useful publication, *Airline Travel with Oxygen,* is also available from the American Lung Association.

Skin Cancer

Send a self-addressed, stamped envelope to Skin Cancer Foundation, Box 561, New York, NY 10156, for a copy of *Simple Steps to Sun Safety* and *Simple Guidelines on Sun Protection.* Follow the guidelines outlined, especially when traveling to the tropics or spending time at the beach or any place where you're outdoors much of the time.

TB Risk

The odds of catching tuberculosis from contagious fellow airline passengers are very low. TB patients actually breathe out only a little bacteria, and contracting TB usually requires prolonged exposure to a contagious person. The dry airplane air, however, can cause itchy skin, headaches, and sinus troubles. So drink plenty of fluids while in the air, take a shower when you land, and move away from a coughing, sneezing seatmate.

Water

Water and many beverages contain viruses and bacteria that transmit hepatitis A, cholera, typhoid fever, dysentery, etc. In areas where sanitation is poor or chlorinated water is not available, drink beverages made with boiled water (tea, coffee, etc.), canned or bottled water (especially those with recognized brand names), beer, and wine. Avoid ice cubes and use bottled water for brushing your teeth. *Note:* Boiling water for twenty minutes kills most infectious agents.

Useful Publications   *Traveling Healthy Newsletter:* 108–48 Seventieth Road, Forest Hills, NY 11375; $29 for six issues

13
Shopping—Chic and Cheap

I will buy with you, sell with you, talk with you.
—*William Shakespeare,* The Merchant of Venice

Some people like to shop until they drop, while others are content to return home with an inexpensive souvenir or two. Regardless of the type of shopper you are, almost everyone enjoys buying something that is a reminder of a trip. It's even better when you land a bargain. Shopping is also an easy and interesting way to meet the local people. In fact, you learn a lot about a city or country by rummaging through its shops and bookstores, spending a day at the outdoor fairs and antiques markets, or walking through the art galleries and department stores.

This book does not attempt to be a definitive shopping guide—there are a number of good ones already in print—but we would like to share some insider and not-so-insider tips that will help make your shopping easier and perhaps less costly.

THINGS TO AVOID BUYING

First of all, don't get in trouble with the law. Some items that you can purchase overseas will not be allowed into the United States. You may think they are harmless, or a "clever" foreign salesperson may say so, but if you try to import them, they may be confiscated and/or you may be fined. For example, unlicensed firearms, illegal drugs, and pornographic materials are considered contraband.

Endangered wildlife and articles made from them are also prohibited, either for importation by the U.S. government or for exportation by the foreign country. Don't bring back the following items or products.

- Coral from most countries (chunks or jewelry)
- Chinese alligator
- Crocodile and caiman leather
- Feathers and feather products from wild birds
- Furs from spotted cats (jaguar, tiger, etc.)

- Furs from marine mammals

- Ivory from Asia or Africa

- Lizard-skin products from most countries

- Live or stuffed birds from Austria, Brazil, Colombia, Costa Rica, Ecuador, Guatemala, Mexico, Paraguay, Venezuela

- Mounted birds and skins

- Sea turtles, turtle-leather boots, sea-turtle oil, tortoise-shell jewelry and combs

- Snakeskin products from most countries

You should also avoid bringing home fresh fruits or vegetables or live animals. Monkeys, for instance, may not be brought into the United States except for scientific or educational purposes or for an approved exhibition. Endangered species of plants, too, can be confiscated. If you insist on bringing in a live animal, it will be kept in quarantine at your expense.

 Mexican markets and stores are filled with endangered wildlife products and souvenirs. Merchants love to sell unsuspecting Canadian and American tourists wildlife curios, parrots, parakeets, etc. Don't buy them. If you're stopped and inspected for livestock when you come back into the United States, you'll be fined and your purchase will be confiscated.

In a few countries antiques are considered the property of the state, and unauthorized export of such objects is considered theft. Check first with the U.S. Customs Department. For example, if you wish to leave Mexico with any pre-Columbian sculpture and murals, you must present proof that they are being exported legally.

Many of the ceramic pieces made in Mexico contain dangerously high levels of lead. Unless you have written proof of their safety, use such pieces for decorative purposes only; never eat or drink from them.

Finally, fakes ("knock-offs"), such as fake Rolex watches and perfumes, are considered illegal. They'll be confiscated if the customs inspector finds them.

GETTING THROUGH PASSPORT CONTROLS

When you arrive in the United States, you and your luggage may be checked by inspectors from one of these federal agencies: Immigration, Customs, Agriculture, or Public Health. Have your passport ready. (Although you may not need to when going to and from Mexico or Canada, be prepared to prove your identity with a valid driver's license, birth certificate, certificate of citizenship, or voter registration card.) And have the receipts for all items purchased abroad in an envelope, ready to show if you're asked for them.

Inspectors are entitled to check your luggage for purchases or contraband, so be certain you carry only your own luggage through customs. To make things quicker and easier, put all things acquired overseas in one bag or at the top of several bags.

Making a Declaration

When you return to the United States by air or sea, you'll be asked to fill out a Declaration Form. (Declarations are generally made orally if you're reentering the United States by land.) You must declare for U.S. Customs all items from abroad that you're carrying back to the United States. This includes things purchased abroad, gifts you received while abroad, things purchased in duty-free shops, and things you're bringing home for someone else.

You'll need to enter a price for every item on the Declaration form; use your receipts to guide you. If you received a gift, estimate its value. If you fail to declare an item and the customs inspector finds it, it could be seized and you could be slapped with a penalty or even prosecuted.

 If you are not sure whether an article should be declared, declare it and let the inspector tell you that you didn't need to.

DUTY—TO PAY OR NOT TO PAY

Duty is a tax that countries impose on various imported items. Our government gives each U.S. resident an exemption on items obtained abroad. All members of your family who are traveling together can make a joint declaration and combine their personal exemptions into one large one, even if only one member of the family purchased things. Children get the same exemption as adults, with one exception—the exemptions on alcoholic beverages.

The different kinds of duty exemptions are as follows. *Note:* You cannot save an unused exemption from one trip to the next. Also, you must wait thirty days before receiving another exemption.

The $400 Exemption

Generally you're allowed to bring back up to $400 worth of goods duty-free. This $400 is based on the fair market value of the item(s) in the country where they were purchased. Different rules apply to liquor, cigarettes, and cigars.

In order to get the $400 exemption you must have purchased the articles for your personal or household use; you must carry them with you, you must remain in the United States at least forty-eight hours, you must not have used the exemption during the previous thirty days, you must declare the articles, and the articles must not be on a restricted or prohibited list.

Within this exemption you can include up to 100 cigars and one carton of cigarettes (even kids get this exemption). In addition, one liter (33.8 ounces) of alcohol can be included, as long as you're twenty-one or older.

The $600 Exemption

You're allowed a $600 exemption when you return from certain countries in the Caribbean and Central America. All the other rules apply. At this time the countries listed below fall into this category.

Antigua and Barbuda	*Haiti*
Aruba	*Honduras*
Bahamas	*Jamaica*
Barbados	*Montserrat*
Belize	*Netherlands Antilles*
Costa Rica	*Nicaragua*
Dominica	*Panama*
Dominican Republic	*St. Kitts and Nevis*
El Salvador	*St. Lucia*
Grenada	*St. Vincent and the Grenadines*
Guatemala	*Trinidad and Tobago*
Guyana	*Virgin Islands, British*

The $1,200 Exemption

If you're returning from American Samoa, Guam, or the U.S. Virgin Islands, you'll be granted an exemption from duty on $1,200 worth of items.

How Much Duty?

What if you come home with suitcases, trunks, and duffle bags filled with goodies? If it's worth more than your customs exemption, then it's subject to the duty tax. A flat rate is applied to the first $1,000 worth of merchandise over your allotted duty exemption. That flat rate is 10 percent for items purchased in most countries, but only 5 percent for things brought back from the U.S. Virgin Islands, American Samoa, and Guam. Above the $1,000 level, the duty level varies according to the items and where they come from. Most countries have what is known as the "most favored nation status," and merchandise from these countries comes into the United States at a lower duty rate than items from nations without this special status.

The following duty rates apply to purchases in excess of your personal exemption plus $1,000. (The first $1,000 of merchandise over your personal exemption is charged at 10 percent.)

ITEM	DUTY RATE
Antiques	Duty-free if over 100 years old
Bone china dishes	8 percent
Cameras	4.5 to 6.6 percent

ITEM	DUTY RATE
Chess sets	4.6 percent
China figurines	9 percent
Clothes	3 to 21 percent
Crystal	6 to 20 percent
Diamonds (not set)	None
Jade (cut)	2.1 percent
Jade (set)	21 percent
Jewelry (silver)	27.5 percent
Jewelry (all other)	6.5 percent
Leather bags	5.3 to 10 percent
Perfume	5 percent
Shoes	2.5 to 20 percent
Toys	7 percent
Wooden carvings	5.1 percent

Exemption for Developing Countries

In an attempt to help the economies of developing nations, the U.S. government has exempted from duty tax some things that Americans buy in these countries. Called the Generalized System of Preferences, it applies to about 125 countries, including some Caribbean nations and Israel.

Money Taken Across Borders

There is no limit on the amount of money or negotiable instruments that can be brought into or taken out of the United States. Any amount over $10,000, however, must be reported on U.S. Customs Form 4790 when you leave or enter the United States.

Among the 4,000 items that you can bring in duty-free from developing countries are baskets, cameras, chinaware, furniture, golf equipment, jade, jewelry, music boxes, musical instruments, pearls, perfume, gems, records, shell products, silverware, skis, tape recorders, toys, and wooden carvings. If you're going to one of these countries, check with U.S. Customs beforehand or with the

American consulate or embassy in that country. Some of the countries to which
the Generalized System of Preferences applies are:

Albania	*Estonia*	*Papua New Guinea*
Angola	*Ethiopia*	*Paraguay*
Antigua and Barbuda	*Fiji*	*Peru*
Aruba	*French Polynesia*	*Philippines*
Argentina	*Gambia*	*Poland*
Bahamas	*Ghana*	*St. Kitts and Nevis*
Bahrain	*Grenada*	*St. Lucia*
Bangladesh	*Guatemala*	*St. Vincent and the*
Barbados	*Guyana*	*Grenadines*
Belize	*Haiti*	*Senegal*
Benin	*Honduras*	*Seychelles*
Bhutan	*Hungary*	*Sierra Leone*
Bolivia	*India*	*Slovakia*
Bosnia-Herzegovina	*Indonesia*	*Slovenia*
Botswana	*Israel*	*Solomon Islands*
Burundi	*Ivory Coast*	*Somalia*
Brazil	*Jamaica*	*Sri Lanka*
Bulgaria	*Jordan*	*Sudan*
Burkina Faso	*Kenya*	*Surinam*
Cameroon	*Latvia*	*Tanzania*
Cape Verdi	*Lebanon*	*Thailand*
Cayman Islands	*Lithuania*	*Togo*
Central African	*Macau*	*Tongo*
Republic	*Madagascar*	*Trinidad and Tobago*
Chad	*Malawi*	*Tunisia*
Chile	*Malaysia*	*Turkey*
Colombia	*Mali*	*Turks and Caicos*
Comoro Islands	*Malta*	*Islands*
Congo	*Mauritius*	*Uganda*
Costa Rica	*Montserrat*	*Uruguay*
Croatia	*Mexico*	*Venezuela*
Cyprus	*Morocco*	*Virgin Islands*
Czech Republic	*Mozambique*	*Western Samoa*
Dominica	*Namibia*	*Yemen*
Dominican Republic	*Nepal*	*Zaire*
Ecuador	*Netherlands Antilles*	*Zambia*
Egypt	*Niger*	*Zimbabwe*
El Salvador	*Oman*	
Equatorial Guinea	*Pakistan*	

If you think you'll go shopping in any of these countries, get a free copy of *Know Before You Go* from your local customs office or from U.S. Customs Service, Box 7407, Washington, DC 20044, (202) 927-6724.

Duty-Free Shops

Items from duty-free shops are duty-free and tax-free only for the country where the shop is located. They are sold for export, and the price does not include the tax you would have to pay if you purchased the same item within the country. These purchases are subject to duty when you bring them into the United States. In other words, duty-free does not mean free from U.S. duty tax.

Limit duty-free shopping to really high-taxed items. Also, know U.S. prices if you plan to do some serious duty-free shopping. Before leaving home, write down U.S. prices for items such as jewelry, perfume, liquor, china, watches, handbags, scarfs, and salmon. This will protect you from being swept away by others involved in a wild spending spree.

Gift Giving

You do not have to declare gifts purchased abroad and sent to friends and relatives in the United States. You declare only merchandise that you're carrying with you.

Any gift worth up to $50 that you send to someone in the United States is duty-free to that person. A person can receive only $50 worth of gifts per day, or $100 per day if it's from the U.S. Virgin Islands, American Samoa, or Guam. The receiver of your largesse must pay duty on gifts valued at more than these dollar amounts.

You're not supposed to send a gift to yourself.

Mark the package "unsolicited gift" and include your name, the name of the recipient, and the type of gift and its retail value. Most foreign post offices have a form for this.

Check the duty-free catalog on board your plane for prices.

Items that you purchase abroad and mail to yourself in the United States cannot be included in your duty exemption when you return to the United States. All shipped purchases are subject to duty when they arrive in the United States, with the sole exception of gifts valued at less than $50 that you ship to someone else.

For Further Information

If you want to bring something into the United States that you're not certain about, you can check it in advance with these sources:

- Animal & Plant Inspection Service, U.S. Department of Agriculture, Hyattsville, MD 20782

- Bureau of Alcohol, Tobacco, and Firearms, Department of the Treasury, Washington, DC 20226

- Division of Law Enforcement, U.S. Fish & Wildlife Service, 4401 North Fairfax Drive, Arlington, VA 22203

- Traffic USA, World Wildlife Fund, 1250 24th Street, NW, Washington, DC 20037

Money Matters:
BARGAINING AND PAYING

We seldom bargain in this country, at least not at retail stores. The price on the tag is what we unquestioningly pay. We do enter into price debates when purchasing automobiles, houses, and items at flea markets, at antiques fairs, and from antiques dealers, but it is not our everyday practice. In many foreign countries—particularly those in the Middle and Far East—bargaining is an accepted way of life. In Israel, as in many countries, even taxi cab rides are fully negotiable. In some countries, in fact, bargaining is a lively indoor and outdoor sport.

You'll have to use your own judgment in each situation, but if bargaining is the accepted custom, then you certainly should participate. Begin by offering about half of the asked-for price and go from there. If you're not really satisfied, then walk away; in many cases, the owner will call you back to seal the deal. But do be polite when haggling, respectful of the owner of the shop. It's perfectly acceptable to compliment him while you're telling him that the price is too high. Keep in mind that all merchants make their living by selling their wares, so whether you make a purchase or not, always say thank you as you leave.

It's a good idea to pay for anything costing more than $50 or $100 with a credit card. Then if there's any problem with the item, you may have some recourse. (See page 207 for how to get help.) This also gives you an accurate, official proof of your purchase, showing the name and address of the vendor and the amount you paid. In addition, ask for a receipt with a full description of what you purchased, particularly if it's expensive or of artistic or historic value.

- U.S. Public Health Service, Centers for Disease Control, Division of Quarantine for Pets, Atlanta, GA 30333

Two free pamphlets—*Know Before You Go; Custom Hints for Returning Residents* and *Pets, Wildlife, U.S. Customs*—are available from U.S. Customs Service, Washington, DC 20044.

Phony Customs Agents

Clever con artists impersonate Canadian and U.S. customs officials. They call you on the phone, saying they have valuable merchandise, being held at the border. All you have to do is mail them the tax or custom duty (or both) and it will be released.

The U.S. Customs Service never asks anyone for money over the phone. If you have a shipment coming to you from overseas on which you owe duty, the money will be collected at your post office when you pick up the package.

Sometimes, the criminals say they represent a Canadian law firm, a bonding company, or a delivery service.

Bottom Line: Just say "no."

Info: These free brochures will help you recognize fraudulent telephone orders. To order one copy, send a postcard to AARP Fulfillment, EE 01196, 601 "E" Street, NW, Washington, D.C. 20049

Consumer Fraud Sticker, #C1230

Telemarketing Fraud Sheet, #D15385

Telemarketing Fraud Special Report, #D16604

IF YOU'RE IN PARIS

Paris, known as the fashion capital of the world, is also home to some wonderful but little-known discount shops. Here's how to be a sharp dresser on a shoestring. Pack an empty folding suitcase for bringing home all your bargains.

The rue d'Alesia, which is lined with discount shops, is the place to be. To get there, take the Metro in the direction of Porte d'Orleans. In the 14th arondissement, a few stops before the Montparnasse station, you'll come to the rue d'Alesia stop. The trip takes about twelve to fifteen minutes from the famous Le Drugstore on St. Germain. Turn right when you exit from the station, and you'll be on rue d'Alesia. Here you'll find designer clothes by Lacoste, Capezio, Bally, Hechter, Cacharel, and others at nondesigner prices.

Note: Shops that display the word "stock" in their name have a special relationship with the designers and have agreed to sell their clothes for three months or more after they've been shown in regular retail stores for 20 to 50 percent off. Other phrases you'll need to understand: "solde" means sale; "degriffes" means the label is cut out; "depot vente" means resale, and "retro" means period clothing, usually from the 1950s or 1960s.

201

Shops are open from 10:00 A.M. to 7:00 P.M., Tuesday through Saturday, and they generally accept Visa and MasterCard but not always American Express or traveler's checks.

Our Best Picks

STORE	ADDRESS	DESIGNER LABELS
Cacharel Stock	114 rue d"Alesia	Cacharel
Evolutif	72 rue d"Alesia	Cerruit, Kenzo, St. Laurent
Pierre Klimo	74 rue d"Alesia	Capezio
Rostain	78 rue d"Alesia	Swatches
Carre d'As	62 rue d"Alesia	Lacoste
Daniel Hetcher	92 rue d"Alesia	Hechter

WHERE TO FIND GEMS AND PRECIOUS STONES

Many people look for a bargain in gems when traveling in foreign countries. It's often a great way to get a good deal; however, protect your wallet by doing a little homework first. Study the gems you're interested in at reliable stores in the United States and read about them at your library. You should also know American prices: Talk to dealers as well as retail sales people and jot down prices. Take your list with you. This way you'll know a bargain when you see one. Here's a general guide for what to look for where.

COUNTRY	LOCAL GEMS
Australia and New Zealand	Opal, emerald, sapphire, jade
Belgium	Diamonds
Brazil	Amethyst, emerald, garnet, topaz, tourmaline, citrine, uncut diamonds
Colombia	Emerald
Egypt	Turquoise, camelian
Hong Kong	Jade and pearl
India	Kashmir sapphire, ruby
Israel	Diamond
Japan	Pearl, coral, jade
Mexico	Opal, agate, turquoise
South Africa	Diamond, emerald, malachite, green garnet

COUNTRY	LOCAL GEMS
Sri Lanka	Sapphire, alexandrite, moonstone
Tahiti	Black pearl
Thailand	Ruby, sapphire, zircon stone

Holiday Shopping

An increasing number of big city hotels offer special holiday-shopping packages that make Christmas shopping fun and almost hassle-free. In many cases they arrange for in-room shopping by catalog or phone, free transportation to nearby shops, free delivery of packages to your hotel room, discounts at local stores, and free mailing of packages back home. In all cases, room rates are reduced. Check the ads in the Sunday travel section of the *New York Times* or other large city newspapers. If you have a favorite hotel, call around Thanksgiving to see if it will be offering a holiday package.

A COUNTRY-BY-COUNTRY GUIDE

Every country has its own special products—things they make better or more beautifully than any one else. Here's a thumbnail sketch of what some places are best known for.

 The country's tourist office will send you a list as well. Check the appendix for addresses and phone numbers.

COUNTRY	PRODUCTS
Algeria	Handicrafts, embroidered clothing, jewelry
Argentina	Wool and alpaca items, leather products (especially men's shoes)
Austria	Crystal, chinaware, chocolates
Belgium	Chocolates; diamonds (a famous world center but you must be knowledgable)
Chile	Wool coats, scarves, and 18-karat gold items
China	Silk, terra-cotta items, ivory (if allowed), paper items
Czech Republic	Embroidered clothing, glassware, hand-painted trays

203

COUNTRY	PRODUCTS
Denmark	Modern-design textiles, dishes, furniture
England	Antiques, crystal, old silver, woolen items, made-to-order men's suits, chinaware
Finland	Textiles, modern-design furniture and tableware, items handmade by the Lapps
France	Elegant clothes, perfume, wine
Germany	Automobiles (You can buy a BMW, Mercedes, or VW, drive it on your travels, and ship it home.)
Hong Kong	Electronic goods, custom-tailored clothing
India	Silk saris, carved jewelry, rugs
Ireland	Tableware, linens, books, wool items, old silver, crystal
Italy	Men's clothing, marble (but heavy to ship), handbags, and shoes
Japan	Automobiles, cameras, VCRs, camcorders, electronic equipment (Make certain your purchase will work in the United States)
Mexico	Silverware, ceramics
Norway	Woolens, glassware
Peru	Garments, scarves, blankets of alpaca or wool
Philippines	Mahogany furniture
Portugal	Ceramic items, wine
Russia	Icons, antiques, religious articles, caviar, jewelry
Singapore	Electronic items, made-to-order men's clothing
South Africa	Diamonds, malachite, wine
Spain	Leather shoes, handbags, attaché cases, and coats; Lladro ceramics
Sweden	Autombiles, textiles, glassware, modern furniture
Switzerland	Jewelry, watches
Taiwan	Electronic goods, custom-tailored clothing
Turkey	Rugs, antiques
U.S. Virgin Islands & Bermuda	Liquor, perfume, tobacco (duty-free)

14
Travel Potpourri

Travel: a childish delight in being somewhere else.

—Sigmund Freud

And to make your travels even more delightful, we've assembled a hodge-podge of travel tips that don't fit in any of the other chapters but are too valuable to be overlooked.

PACKING JUST RIGHT

These days it's difficult to find a porter, so use soft-sided luggage with a strap (or wheels attached to your bag) to ease the way and enable you to be an independent traveler. You can also try a carrying cart that slips into your luggage. There are also carry-on bags that you can wheel aboard the aircraft and fit under the seat or in the overhead compartments (crew members use them).

Lots of people, particularly those who travel infrequently, find packing a major deal, but it need not be if you follow this step system. Whether you use soft-sided luggage or the old-fashioned hard type, these tips will help you avoid overpacking. If possible, it's always best to take only what you can carry yourself; you may find it easier to carry two small bags rather than one large one.

1. *Never pack valuables* (financial, medical, jewelry, work documents) in anything but your carry-on bag.

2. *List all items you need to take* before you start packing. Then cut your list by at least one-quarter. Include specialty items such as resort wear, formal attire, and foul-weather gear. The basics include toiletries, hose and underwear (one set for each day plus one more for good luck), several outfits, a bathrobe, pajamas, and slippers. Leave really good jewelry at home.

3. *Pick a color theme* and select clothing that can be layered.

4. *Focus on clothes* that can be hand-washed and drip-dried.

5. *Lay out all clothes* on your bed or table at least one day ahead of time; then put about half of them back in the closet.

6. *Pack bags with the heaviest items on the bottom* and lightest on the top. Stuff underwear and socks inside shoes. On a long trip, however, pack according to your itinerary, with clothing for the last place at the bottom.

7. *Minimize wrinkling* by wrapping garments in tissue paper. Or skip worrying about wrinkles and pack an iron or steamer or use valet service upon arrival. An old trick for taking wrinkles out of clothes is to hang them in the bathroom, close the door, and turn on the hot water for about ten to twenty minutes. But don't forget about them; otherwise the bathroom wallpaper or paint will suffer.

8. *Take the following:* a plastic bag for dirty clothes, a small umbrella, a travel clock, and a foldable tote bag for purchases.

9. *Include a copy of your travel documents* and your name, address, and telephone on the inside of all your baggage.

10. *Write only your name* and business address and telephone number on luggage tags. A home address alerts a potential thief of a possibly empty house or apartment.

11. *Take a sweater or shawl in your carry-on luggage* as well as a change of underwear, pajamas, a toothbrush, a razor, and anything else you must have in case your luggage is lost.

Remember not to bend yourself out of shape with anxiety. After all, you can buy just about anything you need anywhere in the world with the exception of prescription medicines, prescription glasses, or contact lenses.

A Freebie For a free copy of *Global Outfitting Guide,* which spells out packing for six different types of trips, call TravelSmith Outfitters, (800) 950–1600.

Weather Wake-up Call

Dial the Weather Channel's service at 900–WEATHER. Pick a time within a twenty-four-hour period and you'll be called at that exact time with the day's weather. Away from home? Dial 800–WEATHER from any touchtone phone and charge the wake-up call to a credit card. In both cases, there is a 95 cents per minute charge.

PETS

If you're going to be bringing your dog or cat with you on your travels, make certain that your pet has a physical checkup beforehand and gets needed shots. If you're taking Fido outside the United States, call the appropriate consulate to find out that country's policy about animals. Many countries, plus Hawaii, require quarantine. Regardless of where you and your animal are going, travel with your pet's certificate of good health, medical history, and record of rabies inoculation. Keep in mind, too, that airlines allow only very small pets to fly in the passenger cabin. All others are placed in the cargo hold. It's always best to call the airline first for specific guidelines.

For a list of pet-friendly hotels and motels, get a copy of *Vacationing with Your Pet!* at (800) 496-2665. For a copy of *Air Travel for Your Dog and Cat*, contact Air Transport Association, Publications, 1301 Pennsylvania Avenue, NW, Washington, DC 20004; (202) 626-4172. For a free brochure with hints on traveling with your dog by train, plane, or car, call the American Kennel Club, (919) 233-9767.

A Freebie For a free copy of *What You Should Know About Traveling with Your Pet,* which covers airplanes, cars, buses, and trains, send a stamped, self-addressed, business-size envelope to American Veterinary Medical Association, 1931 North Meacham Road, Suite #100, Schaumburg, IL 60173.

Pet Sitting

The next time you go on a trip and need someone to watch Fido or Kitty, the nonprofit National Association of Professional Pet Sitters will help you locate an approved service. The twenty-four-hour hotline is (800) 296-PETS.

PROBLEMS WITH CREDIT-CARD PURCHASES

Purchased a camera abroad that doesn't work? The rug you bought arrives with a defect? Billed for an extra hotel night? If you've charged items to your credit card, you have some recourse. Credit-card companies are not legally obligated to investigate disputes involving goods purchased overseas, but many will try to help you. Also keep in mind that the merchant wants to maintain good relations with the credit-card company. Here's what to do.

1. *Examine carefully* any items you purchase in a foreign country before signing the charge slip.

2. *Insist that the merchant* write a detailed description of the item on the invoice, including model number.

3. *If an error appears* on your monthly bill, notify your credit-card company in writing within sixty days. The card company must acknowledge your letter within thirty days. Then your account must be credited within ninety days, or you must be told why your bill was correct. Note: Visa has extend-

ed coverage to 120 days from date of travel and MasterCard to 120 days from the date of purchase. American Express allows up to a year, and sometimes even longer, to contest payment if the tour operator accepts the AmEx card.

4. *If you're dissatisfied,* contact the appropriate source. With American Express it's the Federal Trade Commission (202-326-2222). With Visa and MasterCard call the bank that issued your card and ask which agency regulates that specific bank.

 If the problem occurred in the United States, notify the Better Business Bureau in the city where the retailer is based. The bureau gets full or partial settlements for well over 80 percent of the complaints it receives.

A Freebie For a free copy of *Telemarketing Travel Fraud: Facts for Consumers,* which spells out ways to protect yourself and identify scams, call the Federal Trade Commission, (202) 326–3128.

SCAMS

Be aware of mailings that promise you a free trip or terrific discounts if you call a 900 telephone number for additional details. Often you'll be told that you must pay a fee to join a travel club or simply to get access to the deal, or you may be told to call yet another 900 number—all of which quickly adds up on your phone bill.

Watch those postcards you fill out at your shopping mall or convenience store saying you'll get a free trip after receiving a phone call—don't get involved. Also, guard against schemes that go something like this: "Free airfare to Alaska or Hawaii" (but that are part of the purchase of an overpriced tour).

Insider Tip Keep your receipts for airline tickets, hotel stays, car rentals, and restaurants; most have your credit-card number on them.

To determine if a telemarketing or other deal is legitimate, ask these five questions, drawn up by the National Fraud Information Center. Call them for additional information at (800) 876-7060.

1. Does the telemarketer say that you were "awarded" the trip?

2. Does the telemarketer ask for your credit-card number? (If you have any doubts, don't give it out over the phone.)

3. Does the caller ask for a deposit? (Never give one.)

4. Does the caller press you to make an immediate decision and/or refuse to send you written material?

5. Will you have to wait a long time before taking the trip?

If the answer to any of the above questions is yes, don't get involved. *Rule of thumb:* If the deal sounds too good to be true, it probably is.

Terrorism

Because of the ongoing concern about terrorism, you may want to contact these groups for information.

- *U.S. Department of State* provides information on safety and related issues at (202) 647–5225 or travel.state.gov/travel_warnings.html. Additional warnings on global terrorism at www.state.gov/www/global terrorism.

- *The Association for Safe International Road Travel* provides road safety data for over ninety-five countries in its *Road Travel Reports* at (301) 983–5252 or www.asirt.org. There's no specific fee, but the group asks for a donation, which can be mailed to them at 11769 Gainsborough Road, Potomac, MD 20854.

- *The National Business Travel Association.* (703) 684–0836 or www.nbta.org, has a free brochure, *General International Travel Advice*, which includes hard-to-get information on how to avoid threats in foreign countries.

- *Pinkerton Global Intelligence Service,* (703) 525–6111 or www.pinkertons.com/pgis, has a World Status Map on which it rates countries in terms of risk levels. It also provides reports for each country, including information on immunization and document requirements. An annual subscription is $36.00; a single issue, $6.95.

- *Kroll Associates,* (800) 824–7502 or www.krollassociates.com/KTS, publishes *Kroll Travel Watch City Updates* for nearly 300 cities in the United States and abroad. Each report covers data on trouble spots, exchange rates, airport information, key phone numbers. A report is $19.95.

TAXI TIPS

Riding in a taxi can be an enjoyable, daunting, or unpleasant experience, depending on the driver, the city, and you. Here are our tried-and-true tips for making it a smooth ride.

1. Don't take an unmetered cab unless you have no other choice. They are rarely regulated by the city or municipality.

2. If you must, settle on the fare *before* getting in. If you have no idea of how much it should be, ask the hotel concierge, the staff at the tourist desk, or a local whom you know.

3. In a metered cab, if the meter is not running, point it out to the driver. If he or she says it's broken, get out.

4. Let the driver think you know the city. Don't announce that you're from somewhere else and have a good idea of where you're going.

5. Hail a cab in a well-traveled safe area, where others are waiting, in front of a hotel, station, or airport.

6. In a country where you don't know the language and/or the drivers don't speak English, take your hotel's stationery or matches for getting home and have the concierge write out where you're going in the local language.

7. Always take taxi receipts; write down the cab number and driver's name and ID number as well . . . they will come in handy if you leave something in the cab, need to file a complaint, or wish to write a letter of praise.

TOURS

Years ago people traveled independently, making the so-called grand tour of Europe and hiring local guides when necessary. Tours then were regarded as being for the old, infirm, or, at best, people who were stodgy or xenophobic. But times have changed, and tours are now interesting, flexible, and often the least-expensive way to see the world.

You can buy a *fly/drive* tour that includes round-trip airfare, a car, and a book of coupons that allow you to stay at lodgings en route. At the other extreme, you can get an *escorted packaged tour*, in which everything is taken care of—transportation, lodging, meals, and sight-seeing.

In between these independent tours and escorted ones are many variations on the theme. Our recommendation: If it's your first time in a country, and especially if you don't know the language, you should swallow your pride and take some type of escorted tour, or at least a *hosted tour*, which gives you airfare, lodgings, and sight-seeing in each place you visit. The next time you can go independently and more knowledgeably.

When booking a tour, it's important to understand who is responsible for what. Travel agents, who are the retailers, generally don't get involved with anything other than booking the tour and advising you on which operators are the most reliable, deluxe, economical, etc. The tour operator, or wholesaler, on the other hand, is *totally responsible* for the tour. He or she is often the Marco Polo of the travel business—finding exotic destinations and bringing people there.

Travel Trivia: Questions Tourists Have Actually Asked

- When do they turn on the Northern Lights and where should I stand to get the best view? (Anchorage C&V Bureau)

- Who mows the tundra? (Juneau C&V Bureau)

- My wife lost her purse while traveling through Iowa; did you find it? (Des Moines C&V Bureau)

- When does the Grand Canyon open? (Tucson C&V Bureau)

- I'll be in San Diego next month. What time will the whales be swimming by? (San Diego C&V Bureau)

You can also help make your selection the right one by knowing just what tour operators do. Once they decide on a place, exotic or popular, they make a deal for lodgings, another one for local transportation and sight-seeing, and yet another one with the airlines (or train or motorcoach) to get you there. After this is costed out, marketing expenses—including a commission for the travel agent, plus a profit percentage—determine the tour price.

When you read the tour brochure from the wholesaler or packager, there are six items (listed below) that you should be particularly concerned about. If these items are not mentioned in the brochure, then they're not included in the price. You should always call if there's something you don't understand or something that seems to be missing.

1. *TIME INTERVAL.* When the brochure reads "seven days/six nights," it means a six-day tour because the last day is usually spent getting ready to leave, going to the airport, and returning home. If you're going overseas, the first night of the tour is often spent on the plane.

2. *TRANSPORTATION TO THE DESTINATION.* The airline is important. If it's a scheduled line, you'll go pretty much on time and in relative comfort. If it's a nonscheduled or charter airline, however, departure may not be so prompt, and seats are likely to be closer together. If you require an aisle seat, request it early on.

3. *INTERNAL TRANSPORTATION.* Travel from the airport to the hotel and everywhere else while you're on the tour is generally included in the price, but if you're flying from one place to another within the tour, it may or may not be included. Find out.

4. *LODGINGS.* The category of accommodation, which may be brushed over lightly in the brochure, is important. The category—deluxe or one-, two-, three- or four-star—will give you some idea of the luxury level. Terms like "tourist

hotel" or "family lodging" cloud the issue (they're usually two-star). Ask your travel agent to find out exactly what type of hotel you'll be sleeping in.

5. *MEALS.* "Full" breakfast means just that. "English," "Israeli," and "Irish" breakfasts are particularly lavish. "Buffet" breakfast is generally a full breakfast, but you serve yourself. "Continental" breakfast consists of juice, tea or coffee, and rolls, pastry, or toast with jam. Some brochures indicate how many meals are included, whereas others merely say "some" or "welcome dinner." The cost of meals on your own can add up, so you'll want to know.

 A good breakfast provides enough bread and cheese or jam for a picnic lunch. Take along some foil or plastic baggies in anticipation.

6. *SIGHT-SEEING.* Find out if sight-seeing is "on your own" or with a guide. A good package will include, at a minimum, an escorted, half-day to full-day tour of each major city visited.

Count Carefully
Tours and cruise lengths are not always as advertised. A seven-day tour is really only six nights. Always count the number of nights the trip lasts so you'll know exactly what you're paying for.

Comparing Prices

"All-inclusive" tours include just about everything in one price—airfare, accommodations, meals, beverages, and activities—but tips and taxes are often extra.

If you're into number crunching, you can figure out the price per night of the tour and use it as a way to compare tours. Be certain to take off the night you spend on the plane, if you do.

- Subtract from the total price the approximate round-trip airfare.

- Divide the remaining figure by the net number of nights.

Currently $125 or less per day is economy, $150–$250 is average, and $250 and up is luxury.

Defensive Moves to Protect Your Packaged Tour

Because some tour operators are fly-by-night operations, and others, who have had fine programs, have failed, you must know with whom you are booking a tour. Here are nine ways to protect yourself.

1. *Talk with your travel agent* about the packager's reputation.

2. *Pay by credit card.* When you pay by credit card, if a problem arises, you may be able to cancel and/or you'll have documented proof of payment.

Also, very often the credit-card company will go to bat for you. Needless to say, keep all charge receipts.

 Using a credit card isn't totally bulletproof protection, however. The Fair Credit Billing Act allows only sixty days from the date of your bill, not the date of travel, to contest a charge. In other words, complain quickly.

3. *Check that the company is a member* of the National Tour Association or U.S. Tour Operators Association. These are organizations that guarantee the performance of their members. (Note: There are many fine operators that are not members, however.)

4. *Before booking,* call one of the hotels offered in the tour brochure and ask if rooms for the group have, indeed, been reserved.

5. *Ask the tour operator for names of people* who have taken one of their trips. Call to get their opinions.

6. *Steer clear of one-time-only tours;* tours that offer a series of trips, or several during the year, are likely to be better financed.

7. *Insist upon receiving a brochure.* Does the company appear to be successful?

8. *Never sign up* with someone who has called you on the phone and has not followed up with written material.

9. *Note the cost,* then check the airline for the actual fare. If the fare alone is more than the entire package, you may have a good deal, but proceed with caution.

Travel Trivia: What's the Weather
USA Today has excellent weather coverage. Or for a fee you can check out conditions in any destination by calling (900) WEATHER.

The United States Tour Operators Association (USTOA), which is the professional organization representing many tour operators, recommends that you buy tours only from their members. It's a good idea because the association underwrites their members' responsibility. Active members must have eighteen references from industry sources and financial institutions and meet minimums in terms of tour passengers and/or dollar volume. Companies must also have been in business at least three years under the same ownership and carry a minimum of $1 million professional-liability insurance and furnish USTOA with a $250,000 indemnity bond to protect consumers against losses of tour payment or deposits as a result of bankruptcy or insolvency.

In addition, all active members must participate in the $5 million Consumer Protection Plan, which will reimburse consumers for tour payments or deposits lost because an active member became insolvent, declared bankruptcy, or failed to refund consumer deposits/payments within 120 days after cancellation or nonperformance of a tour. The Consumer Protection Plan does not cover airfares, car rentals, and rail tickets when sold separately and not as part of the tour package or if you cancel a tour. Claim forms may be obtained from USTOA, 342 Madison Ave., New York, NY 10173; (212) 599-6599.

During the past several years, four USTOA members have failed as a result of the recession, wars, and terrorist activity around the world, yet those who booked with them got their money back because of USTOA's consumer protection plan. It paid $1.7 million in consumer refunds after just one of the companies, Olson-Travelworld, declared bankruptcy in 1992.

Helpful Information

The Convention & Visitors Bureau Telephone Directory, a worldwide list with 400 telephone numbers (almost all are toll-free), is available from the International Association of Convention & Visitors Bureau, on-line at www.iacvb.org.

For a list of state travel offices, send a self-addressed, stamped envelope to Travel Industry Association of America, 1100 New York Avenue, NW, Washington, DC 20005, and ask for a copy of *Discover America*.

TRAVEL AGENT PROBLEMS

Contact the American Society of Travel Agents, 1101 King Street, Alexandria, VA 22314; (703) 739-ASTA. At the same time ask for a copy of the free pamphlet *Avoiding Travel Problems*.

You should also read *The Standard for Confident Travel*, which explains the U.S. Tour Operators Association's $1-millionconsumer-protection plan; and *How to Select a Tour or Vacation Package*, which tells you what to do if things go wrong. Both are available from USTOA, 342 Madison Avenue, New York, NY 10173; (212) 599-6599.

Used Goods

The Unclaimed Baggage Center in Scottsboro, Alabama, sells luggage, backpacks, rollerblades, sports equipment, and other items airlines wind up with. Get 50 percent to 80 percent off retail. Log on to www.unclaimedbaggage.com.

15
Using the Internet

Bargains abound now on the Internet, with approximately three-quarters of all hotels, airlines, and car rental companies now operating Web sites. Yet, not all Internet deals are good deals, and scams and problems are not uncommon. There are times, in fact, when using a travel agent is still the best way to go.

ADVANTAGES OF USING A TRAVEL AGENT

1. *If your agent regularly travels,* then he or she will have the first-hand knowledge to pick out the best resort, hotel, cruise, or tour for you and your family. To find out how up-to-date your agent is, ask what "fam" (familiarization) trips he or she has taken within the last year.

2. *A large or busy travel agency* is able to use its leverage with hotels, resorts, and cruise lines to upgrade your accommodations and/or to get lower rates.

3. *A good agent can find* the most convenient flights and connections. Airline Web sites show only their flights as primary ones and do not explore databases to see if connecting flights or cities could be cheaper. It's also difficult to find lower fares based on time of day, day of the week, or airport.

4. *If you have to make a last-minute change,* an agent is often able to re-ticket you without a whopping penalty.

5. *If you get bumped* from your flight or the hotel says it doesn't have your reservation, your agent will come to the rescue.

 Always carry your agent's phone and fax numbers with you; ask if there's a special emergency number for late-night problems.

8. *If you're pressed for time,* an agent is "the" solution. Finding deals on the Internet is time consuming and sometimes very frustrating.

ADVANTAGES OF USING THE INTERNET FOR AIRLINE SEATS

It used to be a sure thing: Book twenty-one days in advance and stay over on a Saturday night and you were guaranteed to get the very best fare. But that's no longer the case. The internet has changed forever what for years was a given. Now the lowest fare may come to you in an e-mail offer or in a bidding situation. Here's what we feel you need to know. Then it's up to you to spend a lot of time moving your browser around.

- *AIRLINE WEB SITES.* Airlines obviously want you to book your fare directly from their site. The worst thing you can do as far as they're concerned is use a site that lets you compare one airline against another. On the other hand, if you book with the airline, that saves them the agent commission and the expense of paying reservation clerks. To tempt you to book with the airlines, they offer bonus frequent-flier miles and other specials that are not available elsewhere. Some carriers, such as American, post one-day specials on the Web. Don't dillydally. You must book the special during the short time that it's posted.

- *INTERNET AUCTIONS.* The most popular and successful of these as of press time was/is Priceline.com. Here you name the price you're willing to pay for the particular flight, guaranteeing your offer with a major credit card. Priceline.com then tries to find a seller who can fulfill your request. Within an hour, Priceline either accepts or rejects your bid via e-mail. If your bid is accepted, you are booked and the ticket is nonrefundable. Log on to www.priceline.com.

 Priceline.com also operates similar services for booking hotel rooms.

- *E-MAIL SPECIALS.* Just about every airline's Web site allows you to sign up for free weekly electronic lists of special fares. These fares are not available through travel agents or by calling the airline directly. E-mail specials are almost always last-minute deals, typically for short stays, with three days notice. With some carriers, if there are too many unsold seats seven days before the flight, the airline will hold an e-mail fire sale. It's a lot cheaper than advertising. Discounts can be as much as 70 percent off the twenty-one day fare.

FOUR STEPS TO FINDING THE BEST FARES ON-LINE

STEP 1. Type your criteria and itinerary into at least two of the larger general travel booking sites such as:

www.expedia.com

www.travelocity.com

www.thetrip.com

www.travelpreview.com

Each of these sites is connected to one of the four largest airline computer systems—Amadeus, Apollo, Sabre, or Worldspan. You can also use the four sites for planning trips to practically anywhere as well as for booking hotels, resorts, and car rentals.

STEP 2. After you've checked out the possibilities for your destination (don't forget to look into nearby alternative airports), then go to that airline's Web site. Note the fare(s).

STEP 3. Next, check with your travel agent to see if a better fare is available.

STEP 4. Then submit a lower bid to www.priceline.com.

HOW TO AVOID GETTING RIPPED OFF

When shopping on-line, whether for travel or other items, follow these protective tips:

1. *USE A SECURE SERVER.* Use a Web site that offers the option of going into an SSL mode (secure server). A secure server scrambles credit-card numbers and other personal information before it travels over the internet.

2. *KNOW THE PRIVACY POLICY.* The site should post a policy about what happens to your personal information.

3. *GET A GUARANTEE.* A Web site should offer a safe-shopping guarantee so that if your credit-card information is stolen and then used to make a fraudulent charge, you will be reimbursed for the $50 liability you incur as the credit-card holder.

 Travelocity and Expedia say they will reimburse the liability charge up to $50 per transaction for any unauthorized credit-card use—as long as the original purchase was made using the sites' secure servers.

4. *LOOK FOR AN ENDORSEMENT.* The site should post third-party endorsements from industry leaders and/or well-known publications.

5. *GO WITH KNOWN NAMES.* If you're uncertain about dealing with a particular company, check with the Better Business Bureau (www.bbb.online.org). Members can post a BBB logo on their Web site, documenting that they have been in business at least one year and that they will agree to binding arbi-

Thirteen Key Web Sites

Keep in mind that finding value on-line takes time—more than you may want to give to the process. And, no single Web site routinely has better prices than any other. Even sites that say they cover all bases, really don't. You still have to do multiple searches. Here are our thirteen favorites, in alphabetical order.

- *Airwise* (www.airwise.com) covers various types of transportation to/from airports and downtown and suburban areas—for taxis, trains, buses, and subways. It also gives directions, key telephone numbers, parking rates, and more for the larger U.S. and overseas airports.

- *Best Fares Online* (www.bestfares.com) has daily postings of special and limited-time airfares. They must be booked almost immediately, as they disappear very quickly.

- *Cheap Fares* (www.cheapfares.com) enables you to bid on cruises, tours, and airline fares being auctioned off for trips with just a few days —two to sixteen—in advance.

- *Gomez Advisors* (www.gomez.com) regularly rates the top twenty sites that let you book air, hotel, and car rentals on-line. If you like what you read, you can then link to the individual sites.

- *Expedia* (expedia.msn.com) lets you look for the lowest published fare between any two airports—for nonstop flights only. It also has a wide variety of hotels and the usual car rentals.

- *Priceline.com* (www.priceline.com) is the place to bid for an airline tick-et. If your price is met you'll find out by e-mail within an hour during the business day. You cannot specify either departure time or the airline. Offers a similar service for hotel rooms.

- *Preview Travel* (www.previewtravel.com) has a "best fare finder" site where you can specify three departure airports. You can request as many as thirty flights per query. After you pick your itinerary, it tries to find a similar flight for an even lower fare. It also has rental cars and hotels.

- *Real-Time Flight Tracking* (www.flight.the.trip.com/flightstatus) has a minute-by-minute update on where a flight is and its estimated arrival time for flights between major U.S. cities. You need to know the airline and flight number.

- *Rules of the Air* (www.rulesoftheair.com) covers various airline procedures and policies pertaining to overbooked flights, if you're bumped, what the small print on your ticket means.

- *Smarter Living* (www.smarterliving.com) rounds up special deals on a regular basis, making it easier to track weekly bargains than going to each airline's individual Web site. Pick your departure and destination cities, hotel, and car rental. Once you find an airfare you like, you can then link to that airline's own site for comparison purposes.

- *Top Ten Links* (www.toptenlinks.org) is a good place to look for a variety of travel Web sites.

- *Travelocity* (www.travelocity.com) asks that you enter criteria by level of importance: price, time, nonstop, airline. Then, it does extensive fare searches. It provides only three round-trip itineraries per search.

- *Webflyer* (www.webflyer.com) is a good source for frequent flier information and advice on how to manage mileage plans. It surveys airline Web sites and e-mail lists and then organizes the best bargains from them in one place. You tell Webflyer the city you want to travel to and it will give you the best fares available, along with discount prices for hotels and car rentals.

tration if there's a dispute.

6. *GET WRITTEN INFORMATION.* Ask the site to send you material on the company. Read it carefully. (If literature never arrives, make one more request and then forget it.)

 Be very leery of sites that do not give a physical address and phone number, and when they do, check them out.

Bottom Line: If you do get burned, report your situation to the National Fraud Information Center (www.fraud.org/ifw.htm). The Center will then refer your case to the appropriate government agencies. While on-line, read what the Center advises on how to avoid Internet fraud.

Other Useful Sites

- *DISNEY* (www.disney.com). This family-friendly site has information on all the Disney resorts, plus a reservation form.

- *FAMILY TRAVEL FORUM* (www.familytravelforum.com) has chat rooms, links to related wholesalers, and articles about traveling with children.

- *GREAT OUTDOORS RECREATION PAGES* (www.gorp.com) has information about national parks, forest, wildlife refuges, and wilderness areas.

- *HEALTH WARNINGS* (www.cdc.gov). The Centers for Disease Control and Prevention site, which is maintained by the Department of Health and Human Services, has up-to-date health cautions and recommendations for areas around the world.

- *OANDA'S CHEAT SHEET FOR TRAVELERS* (www.oanda.com/converter/travel) will figure out exchange rates for over 160 currencies. It also has the history of any currency for any day, going as far back as January 1, 1990.

- *PARKNET* (www.nps.gov). Information, maps, and campground reservations for our national parks are available on this still evolving site.

- *TOURISM OFFICES WORLDWIDE DIRECTORY* (www.towd.com) is a guide to official tourism in the United States and foreign countries—from Afghanistan to Zimbabwe. It does not list travel agents, hotels, or tour operators. You can locate state tourist offices, government offices, and convention & visitors bureaus with addresses, telephone numbers, and e-mail addresses for each.

- TRAVEL BARGAINS (www.unclaimedbaggage.com). Here's where you can buy unclaimed luggage and other items left behind by airline passengers. You'll find more than 200 items listed for sale at any one time, with up to 80 percent off retail.

Appendices

Seven Bargain Destinations

C an't make up your mind where to go? Been put off by the high cost of many destinations? Here are our picks of popular places that won't break your bank.

BAHAMAS AND THE CARIBBEAN

Resorts on these islands are dramatically lower in cost, year after year, from spring and summer and into mid–December. Contact each of the following organizations for off-season literature and resort prices.

Anguilla Tourist Board	(800) 553-4939
Aruba Tourist Board	(800) TO–ARUBA
Bahama Tourist Office	(800) 422-4262
Barbados Tourism Authority	(800) 221-9831
Caribbean Tourist Organization	(212) 682-0435
Jamaica Tourist Board	(800) 233-4582
Puerto Rican Tourism Company	(800) 223-6530
Puerto Rico Visitors Bureau	(800) 866-7827
St. Barts/French Tourist Office	(900) 900-0040
St. Croix Hotel Association	(800) 524-2026
St. Kitts & Nevis Tourism Assn	(800) 582-6208
St. Thomas/St. John Hotel Assn	(800) 77-HOTEL
U.S. Virgin Islands Dept. Tourism	(800) 372-USVI

BERMUDA

Every January, February, and March, a number of hotels drop their rates and offer a "temperature guarantee" program. Here's how it works:

You get at least 10% off your daily room rate on any day that the temperature fails to reach sixty-eight degrees. (This is on top of the already lower, off-season rates that run through March.)

You also get free admission to various tourist spots plus shopping discounts at certain stores for the day after the temperature fails to hit sixty-eight.

Among the twenty hotels participating are some of the island's best: The Belmont, Elbow Beach, Fourways Inn, Harmony Club, Marriott's Castle Harbour, Princess, Reefs, Sonesta Beach, and the Southampton Princess.

For information call the Bermuda Department of Tourism, (800) BERMUDA.

A Freebie For a free copy of *Bermuda For Two*, a guide to the island's most romantic places plus information on where to get married, call (800) BERMUDA.

BRANSON, MISSOURI

Called by many the "Music Show Capital of the World," Branson is a family-oriented, country-music kind of place in the Ozarks. It's Las Vegas without the rough edges and gambling. You can go on your own, but if you take a tour you'll see a lot more for a lot less.

Trieloff Tours is one of many tour companies specializing in Branson with regular departures year-round. It has a seven-day tour with round-trip airfare from Los Angeles, San Diego, San Francisco, or Phoenix for about $1,300 per person, double occupancy. And the company can get low airfares from other major cities. You fly into St. Louis and spend a night and then move on to Eureka Springs and Branson. Price includes most meals, sight-seeing, and about seven different shows.

For information call Trieloff Tours, (800) 248–6877 or (714) 855–2126.

BULGARIA

This little-explored country, which supplies 75 percent of the rose oil for the world's perfume industries, is delightful—both in terms of its history and scenery and also because of its prices. Highlights include the ancient city of Sofia, a center of art and the theater; and Plovdiv, Bulgaria's second largest city, a thousand years older than Sofia; the Valley of the Roses; the Black Sea coast; and the country's numerous medieval monasteries.

For information on visiting Bulgaria, call Balkan USA, (800) 822–1106 or (212) 822–5900.

CANADA

Go where the dollar stretches far. Every time you exchange a U.S. dollar for a Canadian one, you'll get about 30 cents extra because of the favorable exchange rate.

If you don't live within an easy drive of our northern neighbor, check with Air Canada. Because of the U.S.-Canadian Open Skies agreement, Air Canada now has more than thirty gateway cities within the U.S. It runs a number of reasonably priced packaged tours in a series called "Air Canada's Canada." They include round-trip airfare, hotel rooms, and sight-seeing. For information call (800) 774-8993.

Two Toronto hotels that often offer packages, alone or in conjunction with Air Canada, are

* *Royal York Hotel,* (800) 441-1414 or (416) 368-2511

* *Delta Chelsea Inn,* (800) CHELSEA or (416) 595-1975

Prince of Wales Hotel, Alberta Just over the border from Montana's Glacier National Park, this hotel has many rooms overlooking Waterton Lake; (602) 207-6000.

JAPAN

With the yen at historic lows, you can finally visit Japan without losing your entire savings account. The easiest way to get there and see the most, of course, is with a tour.

TBI Tours has a number of options in its "PriceBuster" series . . . for example, eight days with two meals a day, five to eight days in a first-class hotel, and airfare from Los Angeles runs about $1,800 per person double occupancy. Fifteen-day tours combining China and Japan run around $1,750 to $2,850 per person.

For information call (800) 223-0266.

MAURITIUS

Located in the Indian Ocean, 500 miles east of Madagascar, this unique island is largely undiscovered and not too pricey. It has colonial plantations, Hindu temples, game fishing, diving, golf, and beautiful beaches.

The local carrier, Air Mauritius, runs excellent packaged tours at various times throughout the year. For example, one week with round-trip air from New York or Boston starts at $1,750 per person, and the second week is just $350. This rate includes seven nights at an elegant resort, two meals a day, a one-hour golf lesson, most water sports, and unlimited golf. Ask for rates from Washington, D.C., Los Angeles, San Francisco, Miami, and Orlando. For information call Air Mauritius, (800) 537-1182.

Getting Airline Tickets in Peak Season If cheap

airline seats are sold out, call a tour operator and request "air-only" reservations. If the tour hasn't sold out, you may get a last-minute discounted ticket from the operator.

GROUPS

And ... wherever you're headed, see if Go Ahead Vacations has a packaged tour for that spot. If you bring seven friends along, the eighth person often goes for free. A consultant will help you coordinate your group's plans.

To enroll in the "Travel Together Program," call (800) 438-7672.

The "Top Seven" Charts

You often see "top ten" lists—travel writers do them all the time. Very often they reflect the largest businesses or those that advertise the most, which is of little practical use to the individual traveler. Instead, we draw up our annual Top Seven list in consultation with *Travel Smart's* travel agent, Jim Maggio of Hastings Travel in Hastings, New York. The three of us have not only traveled the world over and sent people on trips to the far corners of the earth, we have also been privy to honest feedback from readers and clients.

The list for each "favorite" category is alphabetical, because when you're in the top seven there's very little difference between one and seven.

TRAVEL SMART'S FAVORITE SEVEN HOTEL GROUPS

Luxury Category

Concord Hotels

Four Seasons

Grand Heritage Hotels

Leading Hotels of the World

Relais & Chateaux

Ritz-Carlton

Wyndam Hotels

Best Value

Best Western International

Courtyard

Days Inn

Doubletree
Embassy Suites
Radisson Hotels
Residence Inns

TRAVEL SMART'S FAVORITE SEVEN TOUR PACKAGES

Luxury Category

Abercrombie & Kent
Caravan Tours
Maupintours
New Society Expeditions
Olson Tours
Tauck Tour
Traveco

First Class/Value

Delta Tours
Escapade Holidays
Gate 1 Tours
Globus Tours
Insight Tours
Pacific Delight Tours
Trafalgar Tours

TRAVEL SMART'S FAVORITE SEVEN U.S. SPAS

Canyon Ranch, Lenox, Massachusetts
Canyon Ranch, Tucson, Arizona
Deerfield Manor Spa, E. Stroudsburg, Pennsylvania
Greenhouse Spa, Dallas, Texas
New Age Health Spa, Neversink, New York
Rancho La Puera, Baja, California
Sanibel Harbour Resort & Spa, Sanibel, Florida

TRAVEL SMART'S FAVORITE SEVEN NEW ENGLAND INNS

Admiral Fitzroy Inn, Newport, Rhode Island

Boulders, Lake Waramaug, Connecticut

Inn at Saw Mill Farm, Dover, Vermont

Inn at Strawbery Banke, Portsmouth, New Hampshire

Middlebury Inn, Middlebury, Vermont

Old Tavern, Grafton, Vermont

Salem Inn, Salem, Massachusetts

TRAVEL SMART'S FAVORITE SEVEN INNS OUTSIDE NEW ENGLAND

Bernards Inn, Barnardsville, New Jersey

Inn at Cooperstown, Cooperstown, New York

Little Inn at Washington, Virginia

Maison de Ville, New Orleans, Louisiana

Morrison-Clark Inn, Washington, D.C.

The Priory, Pittsburgh, Pennsylvania

Seven Gables Inn, St. Louis, Missouri

Getting Tickets
TO GAME SHOWS AND TALK SHOWS

I f you live or plan to spend time in any of these cities, here's how to get tickets to live shows or tapings. Be sure to call or write at least six weeks in advance; if writing, mark the outside of your envelope: "Tickets."

Chicago

- *The Oprah Winfrey Show,* Box 909715, Chicago, IL 60690; (312) 591-9595

- *Jenny Jones Show,* 454 North Columbus, Chicago, IL 60611; (312) 836-9400

Los Angeles

- *Jeopardy!* 10292 West Washington Boulevard, Culver City, CA 90232; (800) 482-9840

- *The Price is Right,* CBS TV, 7800 Beverly Boulevard, Los Angeles, CA 90036

- *Wheel of Fortune,* Box 3763, Hollywood, CA 90028; (800) 482-9840

- *The Tonight Show,* 3000 West Alameda Avenue, Burbank, CA 91523; (818) 840-4444

New York City

- *Ricki Lake,* 401 5th Avenue, 7th floor, New York, NY 10016; (212) 889-7091

- *Montel Williams;* call only: (212) 830-0300

- *Live with Regis and Kathie Lee,* Box 777, Ansonia Station, New York, NY 10023; (212) 456-3054

- *Late Show with David Letterman,* Ed Sullivan Theater, 1697 Broadway, New York, NY 10019; (212) 975-1003

- *CBS This Morning,* 524 West 57th Street, New York, NY 10019; (212) 975-7000

- *Today Show:* no tickets. Stand outside window at 10 Rockefeller Plaza in Manhattan; show up before 7:00 A.M.

Orlando

- *Nickelodeon* tapes a number of kids' game shows. Call (407) 363-8500 two to three weeks before visiting to get list of which shows will be taping while you're there.

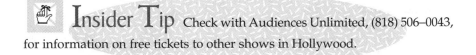

Insider Tip Check with Audiences Unlimited, (818) 506–0043, for information on free tickets to other shows in Hollywood.

Travel Talk:
WHAT THE INSIDERS REALLY MEAN

Add-on fare: A dollar amount added to a gateway fare to produce a through fare that's usually cheaper. For example, a tour with a regular New York–London route might have a special add-on fare for a Los Angeles–New York–London booking. Always ask if there will be an add-on fare if the tour is not departing from your home city.

Airport code: Three-letter codes used to identify airports; LAX for Los Angeles, JFK for John F. Kennedy.

 Look to see that your luggage has been checked to the right place; make sure the airport code is to your final destination.

Air taxi: An aircraft that carries about twenty passengers and flies unscheduled service within a 250-mile radius. Use only if you're in a great rush. Small planes do not have a good safety record.

American plan: Hotel rate that includes three meals a day in the price.

 Best bet if you don't want to make restaurant decisions every night and/or if there aren't many good eateries in the area. (See also Modified American Plan.)

APEX fare: Stands for "advance purchase excursion fare" and is one of the lowest but most restricted round-trip airfares on a given route. Use this as a basis of comparison with all other fares to the same destination.

ATB: Stands for "automated ticket boarding pass." Has a magnetic stripe on the back that includes the ticket, boarding pass, and baggage check. Don't lose it!

Back-to-back ticketing: Booking two or more overlapping round-trips to get a discount fare (avoiding a Saturday-night stayover) and then using one segment from each round-trip for each direction of a single trip in order to reduce the cost of the trip. If you fly regularly between two points, your travel agent can do this for you (but airlines don't like it).

Bait and switch: Advertising a sale item for which there is little availability in order to get people to pay a higher price for an alternative item. This is regarded as unethical.

 Beware. A number of airlines do this all the time.

Blackout periods: Times of high demand, such as holidays, when hotel, airline, or cruise discount rates are not in effect. Go before and stay later; for example, for Christmas, leave December 15 and come home January 3, if you can.

Boarding pass: A card given to airline passengers indicating their seat assignment. You sometimes get this in exchange for your ticket, so don't lose it.

Boutique hotel: A small hotel with an intimate atmosphere that caters to the well-to-do; it often has fewer services than larger business-style hotels.

 Usually safe, especially for women traveling alone; you're known by your name, not by your room number.

Bulk fare: The net per ticket price paid by a travel agency to an airline when buying a large number of seats.

Bulkhead: A wall that separates areas within an airline cabin.

 Seats in facing the bulkhead have more legroom and are ideal for tall people and those traveling with children. Request them—there's no extra charge

Bumping: Practice of removing confirmed passengers from overbooked airline flights. If you're bumped, the airline as a rule will get you on the next flight and give you a free ticket or an equivalent amount of cash.

Cabana: A hotel room that is separated from the main building, usually near or on the beach or at a pool. Before accepting, ask if the rate is higher than in the main buidling.

Cancellation penalty: The amount (or percentage) of a prepaid, "non-cancelable" fare that an airline subtracts from refunds if you cancel your reservation.

 You might be able to reduce the penalty if you change your ticket rather than cancel it.

Charter: An aircraft or motor coach reserved for use by a particular group at a particular time; not scheduled service. Charter flights are usually cheaper; those that are "public chartered airlines" fly regularly between two points and always cost less than scheduled service. Charterers often have unused seats that they sell to the public at a cheap price.

City pair: The origin and destination of a flight segment.

City terminal: An airline office located outside the airport where you can check in, get seat assignments, and sometimes get free or inexpensive transportation to the airport. Easy way to get to the airport if you don't have a car.

Club floor: A section of a hotel offering private breakfast, lounges, business services, and other amenities for an additional fee or as incentive to frequent guests. Worth the extra cost if you like being coddled.

Coach: The least expensive cabin or seating section on an airline or train. Also called economy or tourist class.

 If you're paying "full fare" coach, ask for an upgrade to "business class." There's often space.

Code-sharing: A marketing arrangement under which two carriers use the same computerized reservation system booking codes on certain routes. For example, Airline A flies from Chicago to New York; Airline B from New York to London. The travel agent finds the entire route listed under the code for just one of the airlines. Always ask your agent if you'll have to change planes; if you don't, you can check more luggage through and reduce the number of carry-on pieces.

Collision-damage waiver (CDW): A per day fee paid by a car renter in order to avoid liability for accidental damages to the car.

Your credit card or personal insurance may already cover this. Check before leaving home.

Commuter carrier: Regional airline operating from small localities to larger cities, generally under an affiliate relation with a major carrier. They have a variation of the major carrier's name on the tail. For example, United Express commuter line is affiliated with United Airlines. Avoid commuters if you can get to your destination by other means; they do not have good safety records.

Concierge: An individual in a hotel who attends to guests' special needs and services, such as getting theater tickets, limo service, and out-of-town newspapers. Don't be shy about requesting assistance; very helpful, but be sure to tip.

Concorde: The supersonic commercial aircraft operated by British Airways and Air France. Also called SST for supersonic transport. Although noisy, cramped, and expensive, the Concorde is fast and a way to avoid jet lag.

Configuration: The pattern in which seats are arranged on an airplane.

It's to your advantage to know the configuration beforehand if you're tall, plump, or traveling with children, or if you like an aisle seat.

Connecting flight: A flight on which you must change airplanes at some point. Know in advance so you can reduce the amount of carry-on luggage you have.

Consolidator: A business that buys international airline tickets at a big discount from airlines that anticipate that the seats will remain unsold. The consolidator then resells the tickets at a discount price to travel agencies or to the public.

Be cautious in dealing with them; not all are totally scrupulous. Use your credit card so you can stop payment if there's a problem.

Consulate: Your government's office in a foreign country can provide service and help you. Take the address and phone number with you.

Continental breakfast: A light morning meal, usually consisting of coffee, tea, hot chocolate, juice, toast and/or rolls, butter, and jam. Always ask if it's included in the room rate.

Continental plan: A hotel rate that includes continental breakfast in the price.

Cross-border ticketing: Writing an international airline ticket in such a way as to make it seem that the trip starts outside the country where in reality it begins. Done to take advantage of a lower fare or better currency exchange rate. Your travel agent can handle this for you.

CRS: Computerized reservation system; an interactive electronic system linking travel agencies to a central computer.

 Use only an agent who is part of such a system because he or she can give you up-to-the-minute fare quotes and discounts.

CTS: Certified travel counselor; indicates completion of a study program administered by the Institute of Certified Travel Agents. Use one.

Customs: Governmental agency inspection of goods brought into a country, as well as imposing of taxes (or customs duties) on these goods.

 Get a free copy of the booklet *Know Before You Go* from the U.S. Custom Service, Room 246, 1301 Constitution Avenue, Washington, DC 20029; (202) 927–6724.

Day tripper: A traveler who takes one-day trips.

Deregulation: The 1978 federal law that phased out the Civil Aeronautics Board and began eliminating government regulation of airline routes and fares.

Direct flight: A flight that does not require you to change planes, although it may make stops.

 This is not "non-stop," and it takes longer. Avoid: The more take-offs and landings, the greater the risk of an accident.

Double booking: Two or more reservations for the same person for the same date; done to make certain that a space on a flight or train will be available. Considered unethical.

Double-occupancy rate: The per person rate if two people share the same room or cabin.

 If you are traveling alone, the tour operator or cruise line may be able to arrange a "share" or roommate to save you money; ask in advance.

Drop-off fee: Amount charged when a rental car is picked up at one location and dropped off at another. You can avoid this fee if you return your car to the same location.

Duty: The import tax on certain goods brought into a country.

 Pool the individual exemptions allowed for each member in your family or party.

ETDN: Electronic ticket delivery network; a network of airline ticket printers in public spots, such as hotels and airports, which enables travel agencies to send travel documents to customers at these locations and receive a commission.

European Community: Group of countries that have formally ended many economic boundaries in an effort to create a single commercial market. Went into effect in 1992-93. Makes border crossings and customs processing faster and easier.

European plan: Hotel rate that does not include meals. This leaves you free to dine out but may cost more than the American plan; also requires continual restaurant decision making.

Eurotunnel: The tunnel under the English Channel connecting England and France that opened in 1994; also called the Chunnel.

 Use it to get from London to Paris or Brussels quickly and cheaply— the cost is usually less than flying.

Excursion fare: Round-trip fare with restrictions, typically minimum and maximum stays and advance-purchase requirements.

 Protect yourself by reading the fine print carefully.

Extended stay: Refers to a hotel stay of seven nights or more.

 Negotiate a lower rate if you plan to stay this long.

Fam trip: Means "familiarization trip" and is one offered to travel agents, meeting planners, and press to promote a destination.

Feeder carrier: A small, local airline that "feeds" business to larger carriers at airports. See Commuter carrier.

FIT: Stands for "foreign independent tour"; also used for domestic travel. In both cases it refers to an itinerary put together for a client as opposed to a prepackaged tour. Usually more expensive than an off-the-rack package, but it's custom-made just for you.

Folio: The written or computerized record of a guest's account with the hotel.

Franchise: Arrangement under which an independently owned business (car rental or hotel, typically) buys the rights to distribute or sell the products and services of another (typically larger) company known as the franchisor. The franchise generally receives marketing and advertising help and the right to use the franchisor's name and 800 number. Examples: Holiday Inn, McDonald's.

 Franchises are expected to meet certain common standards for that franchise.

Freedom rights: A series of international bilateral air rights between two countries. These are:

First freedom: the right for an airline to fly over another country

Second freedom: the right to land in another country

Third freedom: the right to carry revenue traffic from one's own country to another country

Fourth freedom: the right of an airline to carry revenue traffic from a foreign country into its own country

Frequent-flyer program: An airline club in which members build up points (or miles) for trips taken. These are then turned in for free travel or upgrades.

 Don't hold on to frequent-flyer miles too long; rules may change, making them less valuable.

Frequent-guest program: A hotel's version of the frequent-flyer program. Guests get points for nights stayed and can turn them in for free stays, upgrades, and other goodies.

Fuel charge: The amount charged if a car renter does not fill up the car's gas tank to the agreed-upon level when returning it.

Return the car with a tank full of the least expensive gas you can find.

Full-service hotel: One that has a restaurant, bar, room service, porter, etc.

Gateway city: The city that serves as an airline's point of entry to or departure from a country. Example: Denver is a gateway for Continental Airlines.

Ground operator: A company that provides on-the-ground services, such as sightseeing tours, taxis, vans; hired by a tour operator.

Group rate: A rate charged for a group (usually ten or more); typically lower than the regular or rack rate. It applies to hotels, tours, cruise cabins, and many forms of travel.

 Gather together ten family members and friends in order to save money.

Head tax: The amount charged each arriving and departing passenger by some countries and cities. Read the brochure/ticket fine print to determine amount.

Hidden-city ticketing: Used to get a lower airline fare, assuming that the fare for a flight from city A to city C stops in city B and is less than the fare for flying directly from city A to city B. The ticket shows the destination as city C, but the passenger gets off in city B. Considered unethical.

 Some travel agents will do this for you, but remember, you can't check your luggage.

High season: The time of the year when rates in an area increase, such as winter in the Caribbean or at ski resorts. Plan to vacation in the off-season, if convenient. The Caribbean, Florida, and the ski resorts, for example, are much cheaper in summer than during the winter months.

Hub: An airport where an airline bases its major operations; the central point for connections with flights to smaller cities.

Hub-and-spoke: System set up by major airlines that designates individual cities as central points to which many flights are scheduled; a city is the hub, the collecting point, and the flights to other places are the spokes.

Hush kit: Equipment that's been retrofitted on existing airplane engines to make them less noisy.

Incentive travel: A vacation or trip offered as a prize or bonus for superior work or performance; used to motivate employees.

Interline connection: When you change planes and airlines in the middle of a trip.

International date line: The imaginary 180-degree line of longitude that passes through the Pacific Ocean. When you cross the line going east, you gain a day; going west you lose a day.

Jet stream: A high-velocity wind that moves around the globe from west to east at high altitudes. *Result:* longer flight times for east-to-west flights.

Junket: A trip that is said to be for business but that really is for fun.

Leg: A segment of an airline itinerary, such as the Boston-to-Chicago part of a Boston-to-Los Angeles flight that makes a stop in Chicago.

Liability coverage: Insurance protection against injury or damage claims by a third party; available when renting a car.

 Check with your credit-card company and your insurance broker before you leave home; you already may be covered.

Lift: The maximum number of airline seats scheduled for service to a given destination during a time period.

Load factor: The number of airline seats sold as a percentage of the number available. For example, if the flight has one hundred seats and seventy-five are sold, the load factor is 75 percent.

Manifest: The official list of all passengers and cargo aboard a plane, train, or ship.

Meeting rate: Airline discount, typically for ten or more travelers going to the same meeting or event. Airlines assign a special number for booking a discounted fare to those attending the meeting; unscrupulous travelers use the number to buy a ticket at a reduced rate without attending the meeting.

Mileage cap: The number of miles you can drive a rental car at no additional cost beyond the daily rate. Also called a mileage allowance.

Most rentals give unlimited mileage; don't book without it.

Mileage charge: The cost assessed for each mile that one drives a rental car over a stated threshold.

Modified American plan: The hotel rate that includes two meals a day, usually breakfast and dinner.

 If you take rolls, fruit, and cheese from breakfast, you'll have enough food for a picnic lunch. (Remember, the hotel cannot offer the bread to anyone else once it's on the table.)

Narrow body: An airplane with one center aisle and no others.

Nautical mile: Measurement used in both sea and air travel; equal to one minute of latitude, or 6,076 feet. The land mile is 5,280 feet.

Net fare: The price for a travel service minus the agent's commission. Corporations are constantly looking for net-fare arrangements with airlines, and getting them.

Nonstop: A flight that goes directly to your destination with one takeoff and one landing.

 Always try to get a nonstop—they are less demanding and safer.

Occupancy rate: The percentage of the total hotel rooms actually occupied at a particular time.

 When occupancy is low, hotels are more anxious to talk about discounts. Always ask if there is a corporate rate or a senior citizens' discount, or if kids sleep free.

Open ticket: One that is good for transportation between certain points but with no specific reservation. You can book your reservation at a later date when you know when you want to travel.

Overbooking: The practice of confirming more seats or hotel rooms than are really available; hotels and airlines do this to protect themselves against people not showing up.

If you have confirmed reservations and are "bumped" because of overbooking, demand compensation.

Passport: Government document indicating your identity and citizenship; required for most foreign travel. If you forget yours or lose it en route, contact the nearest consulate immediately for a temporary replacement.

Peak fare: The highest fare; charged when traffic is heaviest.

 Obviously, to be avoided.

Rack rate: The posted rate for a hotel room or car rental. Because there are so many discounts, weekend packages, and special rates, this is usually a fictitious rate. Always ask for the lowest rate; never settle for rack rate.

Rebating: *See* Revenue sharing.

Red eye: A late-night or overnight flight.

Retrofit: Making a technical modification on an older piece of equipment. This is the main reason it's difficult to pinpoint a plane's age; most are constantly being retrofitted.

Revenue passenger mile (RPM): The number of airline seats sold multiplied by the distance flown. For example, an airline that carries 1,000 passengers a combined total of 10,000 miles has 10 million RPMs.

Revenue sharing: When a travel agency gives a certain percentage of the commission revenue it receives on a client's bookings to the client (almost always a corporate client); also called rebating.

 If you do a substantial amount of business with one agency, they may give you a rebate. Ask.

Shoulder season: The time just before and just following the high season. Rates are not as high as during the peak time but not as low as during the low season.

 Ideal time to get high season goodies without paying high season rates.

Soft opening: That time when a new hotel is open but not all facilities are operational.

 You should be able to get a lower, "introductory" room rate in this situation.

Spa: A health- and exercise-oriented resort; also the health club facility of a hotel. Ask if use of the spa is included in your room rate.

Split ticketing: Issuing two one-way tickets instead of one round-trip ticket. Done to get a lower fare, especially with overseas trips where one can benefit from different currency exchange rates. Check both one-way and round-trip rates before booking.

Standby: An air-travel arrangement in which you do not have confirmed reservations and are willing to be on a waiting list for space.

 Check with your travel agent or airline regarding the standby and reduced standby fares.

Surcharge: An assessment put on top of a published price. Must be included in the fine print on a ticket or in a brochure.

Through service: Air service from one city to another that allows you to remain on the same plane even if it stops along the way. Also known as direct service.

Tour operator: Also known as a wholesaler. A company that contracts with hotels, transportation companies, sightseeing specialists, ground operators, and others to offer a planned tour package.

 Usually cheaper than independent travel. A tour operator or wholesaler sells tours and packages to a travel agent who, in turn, sells them to you.

Transfer: Transportation between a hotel and an airport, railroad station, or other terminal.

 Ask if transfers are included in the tour or package. If so, you can save quite a bit, especially in major cities or on islands.

Travel agent: A retailer who sells travel tickets and accommodations to you and receives 8 to 20 percent commission from airlines, hotels, car-rental companies, and tour operators. Use one agent for all your travel needs; he or she will earn enough commission to give you excellent service and sometimes a discount.

Turndown service: An evening amenity that includes turning down the bedspread, setting out fresh towels, leaving candy on your pillow.

Unlimited mileage: A car rental agreement in which you can drive an unlimited number of miles and pay no additional per-mile charge. Always get this as part of your written contract.

VAT: Value-added tax. A government-imposed tax on goods and services in many countries.

 Be sure to get receipts, as VAT is refundable if you fill out the proper forms before leaving the country.

Visa: Stamp or endorsement, generally placed in a passport by a foreign consulate that permits you to enter their country for a certain time period. Most countries do not require a visa, but ask your travel agent before leaving home.

Waitlist: A list of people without confirmed reservations who are waiting for cancellations so they can board. Stay close to the check-in counter so you can hear the announcements.

Walked: Industry talk for when a person with a reservation arrives at a hotel and finds no room available, and so the hotel pays for accommodations at another hotel (which they are not legally required to do). If you have a confirmed reservation, expect the hotel to do something for you.

Walk-in: Someone who arrives at a hotel without a reservation. If this is you, ask about discounts and try not to pay rack rate.

Walk-up: A person who purchases his or her air ticket just before a trip rather than making an advance reservation.

Wet bar: A small drink area, usually with a mini-refrigerator in a hotel room.

 If the refrigerator is stocked, check the price list before eating or drinking anything; outrageously high prices are typical. Instead, bring in drinks and munchies.

Wide body: A plane that carries large numbers of people, such as a Boeing 747 or a DC-10.

Wind shear: A sudden downward draft of air; this has been said to be the cause of some airline accidents.

Yield: The average revenue per unit; an airline's yield, for example, is the average revenue per mile flown by a paying passenger.

Yield management: A computerized system used by airlines, cruise companies, and hotels to adjust their prices either up or down based upon the anticipated demand for their space, often a year in advance.

Index

A

AARP. *See* American Association of Retired Persons
Academic Arrangements Abroad, 172-73
Accommodations Express, 95
adventure tours, 148
Aerolitoral Airlines, 25
Aeromexico, 25, 141
Air Canada, 25, 141, 223
Air France, 25, 141
Air New Zealand, 141
AirTran, 22
air travel
    airline charge cards, 30-31
    airline clubs, 44
    airline toll-free numbers, 24, 25
    bereavement fares, 22
    bucket shops, 27
    bumped, 31, 34
    charter flights, 36-37
    children and student fares, 26
    consolidators, 26-28
    convention fares, 22
    courier discounts, 35
    dry air on board, 184
    frequent-flyer plans, 28-29
    jet lag, 42-43
    meals on board, 44
    military fares, 26
    no-frills carriers, 22
    resolving complaints and problems, 40-42
    safety, 43
    senior discounts, 22, 23, 139-40
    small carriers, 39
    standby fares, 37
Alabama, golfing in, 169
Alamo Rent A Car, 63, 65, 71
Alaska
    Alaska Wildland Adventure tours, 148
    cruises in, 85
Alaska Airlines, 24, 31, 141
All Cruise Travel, Inc., 77
Allegro Enterprises, Inc., 175, 177
allergies and travel, 185
Alitalia, 25, 141
Allstate Motor Club, 60, 62
America At 50% Discount, 97
America West Airlines, 22, 24
American Airlines, 24, 25, 140
American Association of Retired Persons
    hotel and motel discounts, 92, 144-47
    member discounts, 66, 139
American Automobile Association, 60-62, 66
American Bar Association, member discounts, 66
American Canadian Caribbean Line, 84, 85
American Express, 6, 7, 9, 10, 14, 30, 65
American Hawaii Cruises, 120
American Hiking Society, 179

American Indian territory, 173
American-International
    Homestays, 102
American Odyssey Voyages, 84
American Small Business Association,
    member discounts, 66
American Society of Travel Agents, 214
American Trans Air, 39
American Travel Network discount
    calling card, 16, 17
Amoco Motor Club, 60, 62, 66
Amtrak, 45–51
    ski packages, 51
Anderson Ranch Arts Center, 165
animals, See pets
Appalachian Mountain Club, 171
Archaeological Conservancy, 168
Archaeological Institute of America,
    168
Argonne National Laboratories, 43
Arizona, golfing in, 170
artistic retreats, 165–66
Aston Hotels & Resorts, 144
ATN or AT&T card, 11, 16, 17, 18
Auto Driveway Company, 74
Auto Europe, 71
ATMs or automatic teller machines, 8
Automobile travel
    car rental, 61–68
    clubs, 60–61, 62
    insurance, 63–64, 66
    renting abroad, 70–72
    safety, 67–68
Avis, 65
Award Guard Insurance, 29

B

Bahamas, 221
Balair, Inc., 37
ballroom dancers, 154–55
Barefoot Windjammer Cruises, Inc., 87
barges, 85
baseball camps, 166

bed & breakfasts, 97
Bergen Cruise Line, 86
Bermuda, 222
Best Inns, 144
Best Western International, 144
bicycling, 167
    American Youth Hostels, 167
    Backroads Bike Trips, 148, 157
    Bon Voyage Specialty Tours, 167
    Elderhostel's Bicycle Tours, 148
    International Bicycle Tours, 148
    Vermont Bicycle Touring, 157
bird-watching, 157
Bishops Lodge, 117
blood transfusions, 86
Branson, Missouri, 222
Branson Nights Reservations, 95
British Airways, 25, 141
British West Indies, 24
BritRail Travel International,
    55–56
bucket shops, 27
budgeting, 3, 76–80
Budget, 71
Bulgaria, 222
bus travel, 57–58

C

California
    California Reservation, 95
    Djerassi Resident Artists Program,
        165
    Montecito-Sequoia Family Camp,
        117
    Northstar-at-Tahoe Resort, 119
    Robert Mondavi Winery/Great
        Chefs School, 167
    skiing in, 118–19
    Tante Marie's Cooking School, 167
    The Oaks Spa at Ojai, 175
    Western Railway Museum, 135
    Yosemite National Park, 127
Calinda Inns, 144

camps & camping
in national parks, 125–28
in state parks, 128
Ludlow's Island Lodge, 118
Montecito-Sequoia Family
Camp, 117
Canada, 223
Canadian Airlines, 31, 141
Canadian Pacific Inns, 144
Canyon Ranch, 149
Carnival Cruise Lines, 120
car rentals, 61–68, 70–72
in foreign countries, 70–72
car travel. *See* Automobile travel
cash
carrying when traveling, 6–7
currency conversion, 6
Catalyst Cruise Line, 85
Cellular phones, 68–69
Centers for Disease Control, 135
charter flights, 36–37
charter operators, 37
Chautauqua Institution, 147
Chevron Motor Club, 62
children and travel
car trips, 111–13
cruises, 115–16, 120–21
Disney World and theme parks,
113–16
family resorts, 116–18
with grandparents, 133–35
illness when traveling, 135–37
living-history museums, 122–24
national parks, 124–28
packing, 113
skiing, 118–20
state parks, 128
train travel, 122
Chimo Hotels, 144
Choice Hotels, 144
Citibank credit card, 11
Clipper Cruises, Inc., 83
Club Med, 134, 150, 155
college stays, 96

Colonial Williamsburg, 123
Colony Hotels and Resorts, 144
Colorado
Anderson Ranch Arts Center, 165
Durango, 124
skiing in, 118–20
Comfort Inns, 144
concierges, 107–9
Conner Prairie, 123
consolidators, 26
Continental Airlines, 23, 24, 141
*Convention & Visitor Bureau
Telephone Directory,* 214
cooking schools, 167
Cornell's Adult University, 173
courier air travel, 35
Courtyard by Marriott, 144
credit cards, 8–11
for air travel, 30–31
problems with, 207–8
Cross Country Motor Club, 60
cruises
bargains and discounts, 77
budget and costs, 76, 78–80
cruise specialists, 76, 77
dance cruises, 142
dining, 82–83
family cruises, 20–21, 89
for seniors, 141–42
free passage, 81, 141–42
freighter travel, 88
gentlemen hosts, 141
Great Lakes, 84
Hudson River, 84
insurance, 89
Mississippi River, 84
physically handicapped, 89
sanitation reports, 186
theme cruises, 83
tipping, 89–90
U.S. cruises, 84–85
windjammer cruises, 86–87
cruise specialists, 77
Cunard Cruise Line, 120, 142

currency conversions, 6
customs, 194–201

D

Days Inns, 144
Delta Airlines, 23, 24, 141
Delta Queen Steamboat Co., 84, 142
DER Tours, 71
diarrhea, 186–87
Diners Club card, 30
Dirigo Cruises, 86
Discover card, 10
Disney Institute, 115
Disney World, 113–16
Djerassi Resident Artists Program, 165
doctors in foreign countries, 182–84
Doral Hotels, 144
Doubletree Inns, 145
duty
    paying, 195–201
    duty-free shops, 199

E

Earthwatch, 168
Edinburgh Festival, 177
El Al Israel Airlines, 25, 141
Elderhostel, 102, 133–34, 147
Embassy Suites, 145
Enterprise Rent A Car, 65
Europe
    bus travel, 58
    car rental, 70–72
    RV travel, 72
    train travel, 52–53
Evergreen Club, 150
Express Reservations, Inc., 95
Exxon Travel Club, 62

F

factory tours, 131–33
Fairfield Inns by Marriott, 145
fall foliage trips, 49–50

family resorts, 116–20
Fantasy Holidays, 37
field research programs,167–68
Finnair, 25, 141
Florida
    cruises, 84
    Disney World, 113–16
    Kennedy Space Center, 124
fly-fishing schools, 168
foreign-language schools, 168–69
fox hunting, 172
France
    cooking schools, 167
    shopping, 201–2, 204
freighter travel, 88
Frequent-flyer plans, 28–29
Friendship Force, Inc., 102
Frontier Airlines, 39

G

gems and precious stones, 202–3
gentlemen dancers, 141–42, 156
gifts and souvenirs, 199
Go Ahead Vacations, 147
Golden Companions, 150, 155
golf vacations, 169–71
Grand Circle Travel, 151
grandparents. *See* Children
Grandtravel, 134
Gray Line of Alaska, 85
Great Britain
    railpass, 142
    theater tickets and packages, 177
    university dorm rooms, 96
    university study programs, 173
    Wimbledon, 177
Great Lakes, cruises, 84
Greenfield Village, 122–23
Greyhound Bus, 57

H

Hampton Inns, 145
Hawaiian Airlines, 24, 141

Hawaiian Hotels & Resorts, 145
health. See Illness and travel
Hertz Corporation, 65, 66, 71
Hideaways International, 104
hiking, 171
  for seniors, 148
  for singles, 157
Hilton Hotels, 145
History America Tours, 173
Hobson's Bluffdale Farm, 117
Holiday Autos, 68
Holiday Inns, 145
Holland America, 121
home exchange programs, 102-3
  agents, 104
homeowners insurance, 5
Homeric Tours, 37
homestay programs, 101-3
horseback riding, 172
hostels and retreats, 97
hotel concierge, 107-9
Hotel Reservations Network, 95
hotels and motels
  brokers, 94-95
  discount rates, 91-93
  half-price, 95-96
  late checkouts, 100
  major chains, 105
  New York City hotels, 99-100
  senior citizen discounts, 143-47
  small, safe hotels, 93
  valuables in, 106
  See also: Bed & Breakfasts
Hudson River cruises, 84
Hyatt Hotels & Resorts, 145

I

Iberia Airlines of Spain, 25, 141
ice fishing, 172
Idaho, skiing in, 120
Illinois
  Fox River Trolley Museum, 135

Hobson's Bluffdale Farm, 117
Illinois Railway Museum, 135
illness and travel
  allergies, 185
  blood transfusions, 186
  diarrhea, 186-87
  finding a doctor, 182-84
  general tips, 181-82
  getting medical records, 188
  health insurance, 5, 181-82
  immunizations, 188, 189
  malaria, 189
  medicines, 190
  mystery disease, 190
  oxygen, 190
  ship sanitation, 186
  tuberculosis risk, 191
  water contamination, 191
  with children, 136-37
immunizations, 136, 188, 189
Indiana, Conner Prairie museum, 123
insurance
  cruise insurance, 89
  frequent-flyer, 28-29
  health, 5, 181-82
  luggage and personal property, 5
  rental car, 63-64, 66
  trip cancellation, 5
Interhostel, 133, 147
Iowa
  Living History Farms, 123
  University of Iowa Writers
    Workshop, 166
ITS Car Rental, 71
Ivaran Cruise Line, 88

J

Japan, 223
jet lag, 42-43
Journeys into American Indian
  Territory, 173

K

Kansas, Boot Hill Museum, 124
KD River Cruises of Europe, 121
Keith Prowse ticket agency, 177
Kemwel Car Rental, 71
Kentucky
    Cumberland Gap Historical Park,
        174
    Hensley Settlement, 124
Kiwi Air, 22, 24, 39
KLM Royal Dutch Airlines, 25, 141

L

Lake Upsata Guest Ranch, 117-18
Language Study Abroad, Inc., 69-69,
    173
learning vacations, 172-73
    cooking, 167
    field research, 167-68
    fly-fishing, 168
    foreign languages, 168-69, 173
    golf, 169-71
    Great Britain, 173
    history, 173
    horseback riding, 129, 172
    ice fishing, 172
    painting and music, 165-66
    sailing, 129, 157, 174
    writing, 166
Le Boat, Inc., 85
lighthouses
    staying in, 101
    tours to, 173
    U.S. Lighthouse Society, 173
living-history museums
    Amish and Mennonite Farms, 124
    Boot Hill Museum, 124
    Broken Boot Gold Mine, 124
    C&O Canal, 124
    Colonial Williamsburg, 123
    Conner Prairie, 123
    Durango & Silverton Narrow
        Gauge Railroad, 124
    Greenfield Village, 122-23
    Hale Farm and Western Reserve,
        124
    Hensley Settlement, 124
    Kennedy Space Center, 124
    Living History Farms, 123
    Mystic Seaport, 123
    Old Sturbridge Village, 123
    Plimoth Plantation, 123
    Roanoke Island, 124
    Ranching Heritage Center, 124
    Tsa-La Gi, 124
lodging, affordable, 94-100
Loners on Wheels, 157
Ludlow's Island Lodge, 118
Lufthansa German Airlines, 25, 141

M

MacDowell Colony, The, 165
Maine
    L.L. Bean Fly-Fishing School, 168
    Seashore Trolley Museum, 135
    Windjammer Association, 87
malaria, 189
Marriott, 145
Martinair Holland, 37
Maryland
    Baltimore Streetcar Museum, 135
    National Capital Trolley Museum,
        135
Massachusetts
    Old Sturbridge Village, 123
    Plimoth Plantation, 123
MasterCard, 10, 30
matchmakers, 154-56
Mauritius, 223-24
MCI, 11, 17
Medic Alert Foundation, 136
medical records, in an emergency,
    188, 189
men, travel groups for, 141-42
Merry Widows, 142, 154
Mexicana Airlines, 25, 141

Michigan
    Greenfield Village, 122–23
    ice fishing in, 172
    Ox-Bow Writer's Retreat, 166
Midway Air, 22, 39
Midwest Express Airlines, 22, 24, 141
Minnesota
    Fair Hills Resort, 117
    ice fishing in, 172
    Ludlow's Island Lodge, 118
    Tennis & Life Camps, 178
Mississippi River cruises, 84
money
    automatic teller machine cards, 8
    car rental insurance, 63–64, 66
    cash, 6–7
    children and travel budget, 112
    credit cards, 8–11
    cruise insurance, 89
    currency calculations, 6
    duty-free shops, 199
    paying duty, 195–201
    sending, 13–14
    tax deductions, 20
    tipping on cruises, 89–90
    travel scams, 208–9
    traveler's checks, 6–7
    vacation budgets, 3
    VAT, 11–13, 15
Montana
    Bighorn Canyon, 174
    Glacier National Park, 125–26, 223
    Lake Upsata Guest Ranch, 117–18
Montecito-Sequoia Camp, 117
Montgomery Ward Motor Club, 62
Moorings Preferred Yacht Holidays, 86
motorhomes. *See* recreational
    vehicles
musical travel
    events and tickets, 176–78
    tours, 175
Mutual of Omaha, 89
Mystic Seaport, 123

N

Naggar Tours, 134
National Association for the Self-
    Employed, 66
National Association of Retired
    Federal Employees, 66
National Audubon Society, 157, 168
National Car Rental, 65, 68
national parks
    Bighorn Canyon, 174
    Cape Lookout National Seashore,
        174
    Cumberland Gap, 174
    Glacier National Park, 125–26
    North Cascades, 174
    Wind Cave National Park, 174
    Yellowstone National Park, 126–27
    Yosemite National Park, 127
National Tour Association, 213
Nature Conservancy, 168
nature tours, 173–74
New Frontiers, 37
New Hampshire
    MacDowell Colony, 165
    skiing in, 120
    Taste of the Mountains
        Cooking School, 167
New Mexico
    Bishop's Lodge, 117
New York Botanical Gardens Tours,
    174
New York City
    bed & breakfasts, 100
    hotels, 99–100
    theater packages, 177
New York State
    Chautauqua Institution, 147
    Joan and Lee Wulff Fishing School,
        168
    New Age Health Spa, 175
    Rocking Horse Ranch, 117
    Yaddo Writers Retreat, 166

North Carolina
    Cape Lookout National Seashore,
        174
    Roanoke Island, 124
Northwest Airlines, 25, 141
Norwegian Cruise Line, 121
Novotel, 145

O

Ohio
    Hale Farm & Western Reserve, 124
    Mario's Aurora House Spa, 175
Oklahoma, Tsa-La Gi, 124
Old Sturbridge Village, 123
Omni Hotels, 145
Oregon, North Cascades National
    Park, 174
Orient Express train, 53-54
Orient Flexi Pax Tours, 155
Outrigger Hotels, 145
Outward Bound, 171
Overseas Motorhome Tours, Inc., 72
Oxbow, 166

P

packing
    for children, 113
    general tips, 205-6
parks. See Camping; State parks;
    National parks
Passport Travel, Inc., 155
Passports, 2, 4
Payless Car Rental, 71
Pennsylvania
    Amish and Mennonite Farms, 124
    Deerfield Manor Spa, 175
    farm vacations, 129
    Rockhill Trolley Museum, 135
pets
    traveling with, 206-7
physically handicapped travelers
    cruises, 89

    etiquette tips, 162
    in London, 163
    in New York City, 161, 163
    organizations for, 160-61
Plimouth Plantation, 123
Premier Cruise Line, 121
Puget Sound Cruises, 85

Q

Quikbook Reservations, Inc., 95

R

Radisson Seven Seas, 81
Radisson Hotels, 145
Rail Canada, 49
Rail Europe, 52-53, 55
rail passes, where to buy, 55-56
Rainbow Adventures, 154
Ramada Inns, 145
recreational vehicles (RVs). See also
    National parks; State parks
    in Alaska, 85
    overseas, 72
    travel clubs, 157
Red Carpet Inns, 145
Red Lion Inns, 146
Red Roof Inns, 146
Regency Cruises, 121
Renaissance Cruises, 120
Renaissance Hotels & Resorts, 146
Reno Air, 22, 39
Rent-A-Wreck, 65
renting abroad
    apartments, villas, etc., 103-4
    cars, 70-72
Residence Inns, 146
retreats, 98, 165-66
River Valley Tours, 84
Rocking Horse Ranch, 117
Royal Caribbean Cruise Line, 121
Royal Cruise Line, 81, 83
Ruesch International, 7, 13

S

Sabena Airlines, 25, 141
safety and travel
    airline, 43
    before leaving home, 1-2, 6-7
    car travel, 67-68
    general tips, 106
    hotel, 106
    protecting cash and belongings,
        9-11
Saga Holidays, 151, 155
sailing, 129, 157, 174
San Francisco Reservations, 95
Sandals Resorts, 150
Sandman Motels, 146
SAS (Scandinavian Airlines), 25, 141
SAS International Hotels, 146
schools. *See* learning vacations
senior citizens
    airline discounts, 140
    biking and hiking tours, 148
    companion-finding services, 150
    cruise discounts, 141-42
    hotel and motel discounts, 143-47
    learning vacations 147-48
    sightseeing discounts, 143
    single travel, 155
    sports vacations, 149-50
    train discounts, 142-43
    travel with grandchildren, 133-35
    volunteer vacations, 151
senior citizen travel groups and clubs
    Elderhostel, 134, 147
    Evergreen Club, 150
    Go Ahead Vacations, 147
    Golden Age Travellers, 151, 155
    Grand Circle Travel, 151, 155
    Grandtravel, 134
    Interhostel, 133, 147
    Over the Hill Gang, 149-50
    Saga Holidays, 151, 155
    Seniors Abroad, 151

Servas, 102, 151
    TraveLearn, 148
Servas, Inc., 102, 151
Shell Motorist Club, 62
Sheraton Inns, 146
shopping
    bringing back gifts, 199
    duty-free shops, 199
    gems and precious stones, 202-3
    going through customs, 194-95
    in Paris, 201-2
    paying duty, 195-97
    tax-free, 12
Sierra Club, 168, 171
single travelers
    dance partners for, 154, 155
    male escorts, 155, 156
    roommate matching, 154-55
    spas, 157
    tour operators, 150-51
    travel companions for seniors, 150
skiing
    and children, 118-20
    by train, 50-51
    for singles, 157
    in California, 119
    in Canada, 119
    in Colorado, 119, 120
    in New Hampshire, 119
    in Pacific Northwest, 119
    in Utah, 119
    in Virginia, 119
    in Vermont, 120
Small Hotel Directory, 93
Smithsonian Institution, 168
Snappy Car Rental, 65
softball vacations, 149
Solo Flights, Inc., 155
Sonesta International Hotels, 146
South Carolina, golfing in, 170
South Dakota
    Broken Boot Gold Mine, 124
    Wind Cave National Park, 174

Southwest Airlines, 22, 23, 24
souvenirs, 199, 203–4
spas
  for singles, 157
  less well known, 175
Spirit Airlines, 39
sports
  baseball camps, 166
  softball vacations, 149
  tickets and tours, 176
Sprint, 16, 17, 18
state parks, 128
Stouffer Inns, 146
Sun Jet International, 22, 39
Sun Trips, 37
Super 8 Motels, 146
Swissair, 25, 141

T

Tall Ship Adventures, 86–87
TAP Air Portugal, 25, 141
tax deductions, 20
taxis, 209–10
telephone calls, 11, 14–18
television shows, 228–29
tennis vacations, 178
  Wimbledon tickets, 177
terrorism, 209
Texas, Ranching Heritage Center, 124
theater tours and tickets, 176
Thomas Cook and Sons, 6
Thrifty Car Rental, 65
tickets
  theater, 176–77
  concerts, 176–77
  sports events, 176
timesharing, 104–6
tipping on cruises, 89–90
tours
  picking the best, 210–14
  protecting your money, 9–10, 217
Tower Air, 22, 39

trains
  Amtrak specials, 45–51
  and children, 122
  Chunnel, 55
  fall-foliage tours, 49–50
  in Europe, 52–53
  Orient Express, 53–54
  senior discounts, 142–43
  ski packages, 50–51
  trolley cars, 135
  U.S. train trips, 48–52
travel agents, 214, 215
Travel Charter, 37
Travel Discounters, Inc., 27
TraveLearn, 147
traveler's checks, 6–7
Travel Guard Insurance, 89
Travel Industry Association of
  America, 214
Travelodge, 146
TravLtips, Inc., 88
trekking, 171
trolleys, 135
TWA, 24, 141

U

USAirways, 24, 141
U Save Car Rental, 65
U.S. Department of Transportation, 40,
  42
U.S. Postal Service, 13–14
U.S. Tour Operators Association,
  213–14
Ugly Duckling Car Rental, 65
United Airlines, 31, 141
University Vacations, 173
Utah
  Green Valley Health Spa, 175
  Inn at Prospector Square, 118
  skiing in, 119

V

Vagabond Inns, 146
VAT (Value-Added Tax), 11-13
VAT refunds, 11-13, 15
Vermont
    Bennington College Writer's
        Workshop, 166
    Middlebury College Language
        School, 168
    New Life Spa, 175
    Orvis Fly-Fishing School, 168
    skiing in, 119, 120
    Topnotch at Stowe (tennis), 178
Virgin Atlantic Airways, 24, 141
Virginia
    Center for the Creative Arts, 166
    Colonial Williamsburg, 123
    skiing in, 120
    Van Der Meer Summer Tennis
        Camp, 178
    Wintergreen Resort, 117
Visa card, 10, 30, 63
Visiting Friends, Inc., 122
volunteer vacations
    in national parks, 179
    for seniors, 179
    organizations for, 179

W

Walk About the West, 148
Walking the World, 148
Washington, D.C.
    The C&O Canal, 124
Wayfarers, Inc., 171
Welcome Inns, 146
Western Union, 14
Westin Hotels & Resorts, 146
white-water rafting trips, 157
Wimbledon, 177
windjammer cruises, 86-87
Wintergreen Resort, 117
Wisconsin, Aveda Spa, 175
women
    and safety, 106
    special tour groups, 142, 154
Woodfin Suites, 146
World Explorer Cruises, 81, 83
World Wide Cruises, Inc., 77
World Wildlife Fund, 168
writer's retreats and schools, 166
Wyndham Hotels & Resorts, 146
Wyoming, Yellowstone National Park,
    126-27

Y

Yaddo Writer's Colony, 166
Yankee Schooner Cruises, 87

About the Authors

HERBERT TEISON is editor, publisher, and founder of *Travel Smart*, a newsletter that for twenty years has brought expert travel advice for a readership of 50,000. Previously he was an executive with *The Saturday Review* and lectured at New York's New School. Mr. Teison has written numerous articles for leading magazines and has traveled in many countries by plane, train, boat, car, balloon, camel, elephant, and mule.

NANCY DUNNAN, managing editor of *Travel Smart*, is the author of more than twenty books on a variety of subjects. Just released was her annual, *The 2000 Dun & Bradstreet Guide to Your Investments* (HarperCollins), and *The Amy Vanderbilt Complete Book of Etiquette* (Doubleday), written with Nancy Tuckerman. She also writes monthly columns for top magazines and is a regular commentator on WNYC Public Radio and CNN-TV.